Peter Krauthausen

Learning Dynamic Systems for Intention Recognition in Human-Robot-Cooperation

Karlsruhe Series on Intelligent Sensor-Actuator-Systems

Volume 11

ISAS | Karlsruhe Institute of Technology
Intelligent Sensor-Actuator-Systems Laboratory

Edited by Prof. Dr.-Ing. Uwe D. Hanebeck

Learning Dynamic Systems for Intention Recognition in Human-Robot-Cooperation

by
Peter Krauthausen

Dissertation, Karlsruher Institut für Technologie (KIT)
Fakultät für Informatik
Tag der mündlichen Prüfung: 3. Februar 2012

Impressum

Karlsruher Institut für Technologie (KIT)
KIT Scientific Publishing
Straße am Forum 2
D-76131 Karlsruhe
www.ksp.kit.edu

KIT – Universität des Landes Baden-Württemberg und
nationales Forschungszentrum in der Helmholtz-Gemeinschaft

KIT Scientific Publishing 2013
Print on Demand

ISSN 1867-3813
ISBN 978-3-86644-952-7

Learning Dynamic Systems For Intention Recognition in Human-Robot-Cooperation

zur Erlangung des akademischen Grades eines

Doktors der Ingenieurwissenschaften

von der Fakultät für Informatik
des Karlsruher Instituts für Technologie (KIT)

genehmigte

Dissertation

von

Peter Krauthausen

aus Mönchengladbach/Niederrhein

Tag der mündlichen Prüfung: 3. Februar 2012

Erster Gutachter: Prof. Dr.-Ing. Uwe D. Hanebeck

Zweiter Gutachter: Prof. Dr.-Ing. Rainer Stiefelhagen

Acknowledgement

The thesis you hold in your hands is the product of several years of work. During this time it benefited from the support of many people. At this point I would like to express my gratitude especially to those named below.

This thesis was conducted at the Intelligent Sensor-Actuator-Systems Laboratory of the Karlsruhe Institute of Technology (KIT) as part of the Collaborative Research Center 588 "Humanoid Robots - Learning and Cooperating Multimodal Robots" (CRC588). I would like to thank Prof. Dr.-Ing. Uwe D. Hanebeck for the supervision of this thesis, his support over the years, and the possibility to work in his laboratory while conducting this thesis. I am very grateful to Prof. Dr.-Ing. Rainer Stiefelhagen for co-supervising this thesis, his helpful comments, and the cooperation in the CRC588.

I am grateful to everybody at the ISAS and CRC588 as well as the staff members of the KIT each for contributing his part to an inspiring and constructive research environment. In particular, I would like to thank my co-authors and collaborators Marco F. Huber, Frederik Beutler, Dirk Gehrig, Lukas Rybok, Henning Eberhardt, Masoud Roschani and Patrick Ruoff for their cooperation and the numerous inspiring evenings of discussion.

I would also like to thank Werner Bleier, Hannes Merkle, Anita Oberle, Alexander Riffel, and Wolfgang Rihm for their technical support in uncountable ways as well as Dagmar Gambichler and Birgit Meindl for their administrative support. Additionally, I am grateful to all students cooperating with me in student research projects and assisting me, especially, Dominik Perpeet, Johannes Rittter, Mathias Ziebarth, and Florian Pfaff.

Finally, I would like to thank my family for their firm support throughout the years, without which this thesis would not have come into existence.

Karlsruhe, 2012   Peter Krauthausen

Contents

Notation

Conventions

x	Scalar
$\underline{x}$	Column vector
$\underline{1}$	Vector of ones
$\boldsymbol{x}/\underline{\boldsymbol{x}}$	Random variables/vectors are printed in bold face
$\hat{x}/\underline{\hat{x}}$	Mean or fixed value/vector of $\boldsymbol{x}/\underline{\boldsymbol{x}}$
$x^*/\underline{x}^*$	Optimal value/vector
$\underline{x} \preceq \underline{y}$	Component-wise inequality between the vectors $\underline{x}$ and $\underline{y}$
$\underline{x} \prec \underline{y}$	Component-wise strict inequality between the vectors $\underline{x}$ and $\underline{y}$
$\underline{x} \odot \underline{y}$	Component-wise multiplication
$1 : L$	Indices $1, \ldots, L$
$\mathbf{M}$	Matrices are printed in bold uppercase letters
$\underline{m}^{\mathrm{T}}/\mathbf{M}^{\mathrm{T}}$	Vector/matrix transpose
$\mathbf{M}^{-1}$	Matrix inverse
$\lvert\mathbf{M}\rvert$	Determinant of matrix $\mathbf{M}$
$\mathbf{M}_{ij}$	Matrix element in row i and column j
$\mathrm{diag}\,(\underline{x})$	Matrix with main diagonal entries identical to $\underline{x}$
$\mathbf{I}$	Identity matrix
$\mathcal{S}$	Sets are printed in uppercase calligraphic letters
$\lvert\mathcal{S}\rvert$	Set cardinality
$\mathrm{vol}\,(\cdot)$	Volume of a space or interval width
■	End of example
□	End of proof

Probability Density Functions

$f(\cdot)/f(\cdot\vert\cdot)$	Generic (conditional) probability density function
$F(\cdot)$	Generic cumulative distribution function
$\widetilde{f}(\cdot)$	True probability density function
$\widetilde{F}(\cdot)$	True cumulative distribution function
$\sim$	Distribution operator, as used with $\boldsymbol{x} \sim f(x)$, denoting $\boldsymbol{x}$ is distributed according to $f(x)$
$\mathrm{E}\{\,.\,\}$	Expectation operator
$\delta(\cdot)$	Dirac delta distribution
$\mathrm{H}(\cdot)$	Heaviside function
$\mathcal{N}(\underline{x}\,;\,\underline{\mu}\,,\,\mathbf{C})$	Multivariate normal density function
$\mathcal{K}_{\mathbf{S}}(\underline{x}\,,\,\underline{\mu})$	Multivariate kernel function

Abbreviations

BB	Branch-and-Bound
CPT	Conditional Probability Table
PBB	Probabilistic Branch-and-Bound
EM	Expectation Maximization
GM	Gaussian Mixture Density
GP(R)	Gaussian Process (Regression)
GP-ADF	GP-based Analytic Moment-based Filter
GP-UKF	GP-based Unscented Kalman Filter
ISD	Integral Squared Distance
KF	Kalman Filter
K(C)D(E)	Kernel (Conditional) Density (Estimation)
KLD	Kullback-Leibler-Divergence
LCD	Localized Cumulative Distribution
MC	Monte Carlo
MP	Model-Predictive
ML	Maximum Likelihood
MCvMD	Modified Cramér-von Mises Distance
(E)PDF	(Empirical) Probability density function
PF	Particle Filter
RKHS	Reproducing Kernel Hilbert space
SV(M/R)	Support Vector (Machine/Regression)
UKF	Unscented Kalman filter
i.i.d.	independent, but identically distributed
w.l.o.g.	without loss of generality
w.r.t.	with respect to
s.t.	subject to
p.(s.)d.	positive (semi-)definite

Other Symbols

$\mathbb{R}$	Real numbers
$\mathbb{N}$	Whole numbers
$\mathbb{S}^N$	Real symmetric matrix of size $N \times N$
$\mathbb{S}^N_{+(+)}$	Real symmetric (semi) positive definite matrix of size $N \times N$
$\mathcal{H}$	Hilbert space
$< ., . >_{\mathcal{S}}$	Scalar Product w.r.t. space $\mathcal{S}$
$D(.,.)$	Distance
$\mathcal{O}(g)$	Landau notation
$d \in \mathcal{D}$	Element of data set
$\mathcal{T}$	Training set
$\mathcal{V}$	Testing/Validation set

Zusammenfassung

Aufgrund der jüngsten Fortschritte in der Elektrotechnik, Mechatronik und Mikrosystemtechnik werden stetig mehr informationstechnische Geräte in der Umwelt des Menschen eingesetzt. Um den Menschen optimal zu unterstützen, ist es unabdingbar, dass diese Systeme die Intention des Menschen auf Basis multimodaler Beobachtungen seines Verhaltens erkennen. Der Intentionserkennung kommt insbesondere bei humanoiden Robotern eine wichtige Rolle zu, da der Mensch von einem mensch-ähnlichen Roboter mensch-ähnliches Verhalten erwartet. Gleichzeitig stellt die Intentionserkennung für einen humanoiden Roboter unter Alltagsbedingungen besonders hohe Anforderung an die Robustheit gegenüber unvollständigen und verrauschten Beobachtungen, an den Detailgrad der verwendeten Modelle und an die echtzeitfähige Inferenz, um eine natürliche Interaktion zu gewährleisten. In dieser Arbeit wird untersucht, wie diese Probleme durch eine durchgängige Unsicherheitsbeschreibung, automatische Modellidentifikation und situationsbedingte Inferenz gelöst werden können.

Um eine durchgängige Unsicherheitsbeschreibung und eine strukturierte Wissensmodellierung zu gewährleisten, wird in dieser Arbeit die Intentionserkennung als ein Problem der Modellierung der menschlichen Rationalität in Form von hybriden, dynamischen Bayesnetzen sowie der Inferenz mit diesem Modell betrachtet. Hervorzuheben ist, dass wertdiskrete und wertkontinuierliche Größen generisch modelliert werden können. Hierdurch werden Diskretisierungsfehler vermieden und eine einheitliche Inferenz unter durchgängiger Berücksichtigung der Unsicherheit erreicht. Weiterhin erlaubt die verwendete Modellierung eine exakte, analytische Inferenz auch bei nichtlinearen stochastischen Abhängigkeiten.

Ein Schwerpunkt der Arbeit liegt auf der automatischen Modellidentifikation der verwendeten nichtlinearen stochastischen Abhängigkeiten. Das Identifikationsproblem wird als Ausgleichsproblem betrachtet. Es werden mehrere Ansätze zur Optimierung des Verhältnisses zwischen der Distanz der vorhandenen Beobachtungen zur geschätzten nichtlinearen Funktion im Verteilungsraum und der Unebenheit der Oberfläche der Schätzfunktion vorgestellt. Es wird gezeigt, dass die Betrachtung der Unebenheit der Oberflächen ausreichend ist, um eine ansonsten nur durch die explizite Annahme eines unterlagerten, generativen Modells erreichbare Qualität der Modellidentifikation zu erhalten. Die erhaltenen Ergebnisse sind jedoch signifikant effizienter repräsentierbar und erlauben eine analytische Weiterverarbeitung, z.B. für die rekursive Zustandsschätzung.

Der zweite Schwerpunkt der Arbeit liegt auf der situationsbedingten Inferenz in großen dynamischen Bayesnetzen bei der eine Beschleunigung der Inferenz durch Ausnutzung der Situationsabhängigkeit des menschlichen Verhaltens demonstriert wird. Ausgehend von einer gegebenen Dekomposition des Gesamtmodells in eine Menge kleinerer Teilmodelle wird die schritthaltende Inferenz auf jeweils das Teilmodell beschränkt, welches die aktuell vorherrschende Situation am besten abbildet. Für die Auswahl wird das im Modell enthaltene Wissen über die zukünftige Zustandsentwicklung ausgenutzt. Für zwei Bewertungskriterien wird gezeigt, dass dieser modell-prädiktive Ansatz eine signifikante Beschleunigung der Inferenz bei vernachlässigbarem Approximationsfehler erlaubt.

Die durch die durchgängige Unsicherheitsbeschreibung, automatische Modellidentifikation und situationsbedingte Inferenz erzielte Robustheit, Qualität und Skalierbarkeit der Intentionserkennung wird in Simulationen, durch eine videobasierte kombinierte Bewegungs-, Aktivitäts- und Intentionserkennung sowie in Testszenarien in der weiträumigen Telepräsenz analysiert. Die verwendete durchgängige Unsicherheitsbeschreibung lässt sich ohne Einschränkungen für andere Anwendungen nutzbar machen. Die erzielten Ergebnisse für die Schätzung stochastischer nichtlinearer Abhängigkeiten in Form von bedingten Dichtefunktionen wurden auf die Dichteschätzung übertragen und sind für die Identifikation allgemeiner nichtlinearer stochastischer Abhängigkeiten verwendbar. Das Prinzip der situationsbedingten Inferenz läßt sich erfolgreich auf die Inferenz in generischen dynamischen Bayesnetze übertragen, wenn für diese situative Dekomposition möglich ist.

Abstract

Recent advances in electrical engineering, mechatronics, and microsystem technology promote the deployment of an increasing number of computing devices into the environment of the human. In order to support the human optimally, it is inevitable that these systems recognize the human's intention from multimodal observations of his behavior. The intention recognition is especially important for humanoid robots as the human user expects a human-like behavior from a humanoid robot. At the same time, it is challenging for the intention recognition of a humanoid robot in everyday's life to achieve robustness against uncertain and incomplete observations, to maintain a high degree of detail of the used models, and to perform inference in real-time to allow for natural interactive behavior. This thesis investigates how these challenges may be addressed by a consistent uncertainty processing, automatic model identification, and situation-specific inference.

In order to achieve a consistent uncertainty processing and allow for structured modeling of domain knowledge, the intention recognition problem is phrased as a problem of modeling the human rationale in the form of hybrid, dynamic Bayesian networks as well as inference with these models. Additionally, discrete- and continuous-valued quantities may be modeled uniformly. This approach avoids unnecessary discretization errors and allows for a uniform inference with consistent uncertainty treatment as well as for exact, analytic inference even with nonlinear stochastic dependencies.

The first focus of the present thesis is the automatic model identification of the employed nonlinear stochastic dependencies. The identification problem is considered as a trade-off problem: several approaches to balancing the distance between the given observations and the estimated nonlinear function as represented by their respective cumulative distribution function and the function estimates' surface roughness are presented. It is shown, that the consideration of the surface's roughness is sufficient to achieve a comparable quality of the model identification, which has so far only been shown by approaches making explicit assumptions about an underlying generative model. The obtained function estimates may be represented much more efficiently and allow for analytic processing, e.g., in recursive state estimation.

The second focus of this thesis is the situation-specific inference in large dynamic Bayesian networks for which a speed-up in inference by exploitation of the situation dependency of the human behavior is demonstrated. Given a decomposition of a large model into a fixed set of smaller models, the step-wise inference is limited to the model reflecting the prevailing situation best. The model selection exploits the information contained in the model. For two evaluation criteria, it is shown that these model-predictive approaches allow for significant speed-ups of the inference at negligible approximation error.

The robustness, quality, and scalability achieved by the consistent uncertainty processing, automatic model identification, and situation-specific inference is analyzed in simulations, a video-based combined motion, activity, and intention recognition setup, as well as experiments in an extended-range telepresence scenario. The employed consistent uncertainty processing may be easily generalized to other applications. The obtained results for the estimation of stochastic nonlinear dependencies in the form of conditional density functions have been successfully transferred to density estimation and may be used for the identification of general nonlinear stochastic dependencies. The principle underlying the situation-specific inference may be employed to generic dynamic Bayesian networks if these allow for a situation-specific decomposition.

If a man will begin with certainties,
he shall end in doubts;
but if he will be content to begin with doubts,
he shall end in certainties.
—FRANCIS BACON

1 Introduction

Recent scientific progress in microelectronics, telecommunications, and power supply led to the widespread deployment of technical devices into the human environment. The variety of these devices ranges from intelligent power steering and smart washing machines at home to control systems installed in industrial facilities or in air conditioning systems at work. The most apparent technical devices to humans are laptops and smart phones as personal companions, but also transparent state of the art infrastructure, e.g., smart gas grids, consist of many technical devices. Thus, technical devices influence every aspect of human life. Furthermore, from today's perspective, it appears certain that further technical devices, such as service robots, will find popular distribution in the near future and an end of this development is not foreseeable.

These technical devices are deployed to support the human either in tasks at their workplace or household in general. The distribution will be linked to the benefits offered, i.e., how much more efficient a task may be carried out with the assistance of the devices. In order to assist the human at its best, the devices need to cooperate closely with the human. For this reason, it is necessary for the devices to hypothesize about the human's intentions at any given time. The intention is estimated based on the observed behavior of the human and a model of his rationale. Depending on the task at hand, this model of the human's rationale reflects the relevant relations between the human's belief of the state of the world, his desires, and the derivable intentions. Based on noise-perturbed audio and visual signals, the human's long to short term intentions shall be automatically inferred to provide optimal support. This problem may be understood as an instantiation of a state estimation problem, where the hidden state needs to be estimated from noisy measurements. Fig. 1.1 shows how the intention recognition is incorporated in a simplified control loop of an assistive system, e.g., a humanoid robot. Given the noisy sensor readings of the human behavior and domain knowledge, e.g., in this case about the objects present in the scene, the intention recognition derives the intention estimate. This estimate serves as an input to the high-level planning system of the humanoid robot. The derived plan causes a change of the state

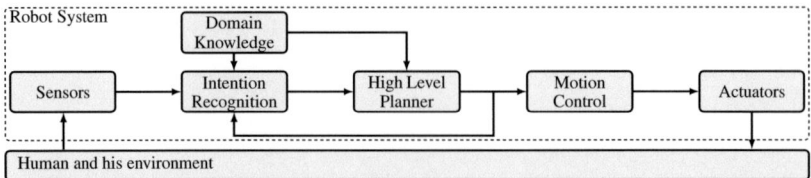

Figure 1.1: A simplified control architecture for the humanoid robot ARMAR [182, 45] as adapted from [160].

of the world by the application of its actuators, e.g., by moving the robot or manipulating objects. The quality of the state estimator is fundamental to the device's decision process.

Because the sensor readings are prone to error and noise, the described model of the human's rationale needs to account for the uncertainty inherent in the problem. This problem may be cast as a problem of representation, inference, and learning in a probabilistic graphical model. In this thesis, this view will be adopted and intention recognition using hybrid dynamic Bayesian Networks will be considered, i.e., a probabilistic graphical model captures the sequentiality of the rationale as well as the unified treatment of discrete and continuous variables. This thesis presents contributions to two topics central for the intention recognition problem: model identification and inference in large scale models.

- Model identification considers the problem of automatically determining the probabilistic models fundamental to the probabilistic graphical model and therefore is of extreme importance to the intention recognition application. The considered problem is restricted to the estimation of (conditional) density functions relating continuous random variables as used in the motion models of the example application. The main contributions of this thesis, are approaches towards conditional density estimation of sparse mixture conditional densities based on information-theoretic and superficial regularization.

- The quality of the learned models is irrelevant, if inference in these models is too slow. For realistic scenarios with hundreds of objects and actions related to these intentions, complex probabilistic graphical models arise. For these large-scale models, real-time inference as a basis of natural interactions is challenging. The main contribution of this thesis is an approach to restricting the inference to the relevant situational task structure. This exploitation of the situational dependency allows for real-time inference in larger models.

Both contributions complement each other, as the identification of the continuous conditional densities may be understood as obtaining the substrate for large scale models, and only if inference in larger models is efficient enough to allow for natural interaction, the identified models will be used. In the following, an outline of the thesis will be given by chapter. Disregarding the chapters on the problem definition, conclusion and future work as well as this chapter, this list reflects the two major problems addressed in this thesis. Each chapter concludes with a summary of the main contributions and limitations.

Problem Definition   In the problem definition, the relevant assessment criteria and the related work for both parts of the thesis are reviewed and discussed. The deficiencies in the state of the art will be pointed out and how these are addressed in this thesis. The key idea as well as the major assumptions will be given.

Non-Parametric Density and Conditional Density Estimation   With regard to system identification, the estimation of density and conditional density functions from data is considered. In this chapter, the specific difference in the estimation is discussed. The key idea common to density and conditional density estimation as a sparse extension to kernel density estimation is derived. This idea consists of phrasing the estimation as an optimization problem balancing data fit with roughness of the probability density function surface. Based on the different mathematical problem statements, the general challenges and key ideas are extended to optimization approaches for each problem. For the conditional density estimation, the specific problem structure is further discussed and exploited.

Full Parameter Conditional Density Estimation   The drawbacks of the sparse kernel conditional density estimation are the restriction to components' means coinciding with data points as well as fixed and identical kernel parameters for all components. In this chapter, these limitations are removed by the introduction of a novel roughness penalty and a covariance calculation relative to the local data density. The novel roughness penalty is based on the curvature of the probability density function allowing for an optimization of mean positions that regularize the mean function's curvature. Additionally, an efficient implementation of these key ideas and a comparison to the other presented approaches as well as the state of the art are proposed.

Hyperparameter Optimization All of the presented non-parametric and full parameter estimators perform density and/or conditional density estimation based on different sets of hyperparameters. In this chapter, a generic algorithm for determining hyperparameters is presented. The generic optimization may then be instantiated w.r.t. each estimator and its set of hyperparameters, e.g., the kernel parameters and/or the parameter determining the trade-off between fit and roughness or the loss-function's parameters. The properties of the presented cross-validation–based minimization of the error on held-out sets is discussed in simulations.

Conditional Density Estimation given Samples and Prior Knowledge Typically, not only a set of data points is given when estimating densities and conditional densities. There might be information from prior experiments, e.g., exploring other parts of the state space, or expert/domain knowledge. The challenge is to use this information if it is not given in form of data points, but in the form of generative or probabilistic models with the proposed optimization scheme. Note, that even if data from a previous measurement campaign might be given, depending on the size of the data set it might be prohibitive to merely join the data sets, but an abstraction is necessary. In this chapter, approaches using additional information in the form of a generative or probabilistic model and its benefits will be given.

Intention Recognition This chapter introduces the models and inference methods used for the intention recognition in the human-robot-cooperation scenario as introduced in the problem definition. In detail, an introduction to hybrid dynamic Bayesian Networks is provided and the entire design process and inference mechanism described using an exemplary case-study. On the basis of the model developed for this case study, more realistic models for human-robot-cooperation in the household setting will be presented, i.e., the number of entities will be increased. Inference in the hybrid dynamic Bayesian Networks is challenging for large scale models, e.g., if the household setting for the human-robot-cooperation scenario is modeled with a realistic number of objects and associated intentions. The key idea is to use the fact that even though the household setting entails a

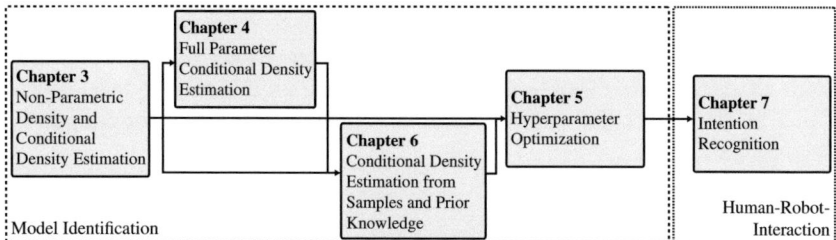

Figure 1.2: The chapters of this thesis and dependencies between different chapters.

lot of unstructured intention sequences it is possible to identify clusters of related intentions. As these clusters are describable using time and space constraints, the concept of situations is adopted and used for an online model selection of smaller models for each situation. In order to discuss the properties and limitations of the intention recognition as means of tacit human-robot-cooperation, the proposed models are adapted for a set of real and mixed-reality experiments. In the real scenario, the purely video-based recognition of everyday kitchen tasks is presented. The reported results are based on a large data set. The scalability of the inference for larger models is evaluated using an extended range telepresence scenario given a 1:1 scale layout of a given kitchen, providing reproducible experimental setups.

Conclusions and Future Work The thesis concludes with a summary of the contributions and a list of the limitations, which remain as future work. Given the results presented in this thesis promising approaches for addressing these remaining challenges are given.

Structure of the Thesis This thesis may be read sequentially and selectively. Fig. 1.2 shows the dependencies between the different chapters of the thesis. As the state of the art, the notation, and mathematical problem setup are discussed in the problem definition, it is recommended to read this chapter first. The other chapters may be read according to Fig. 1.2. Reading Ch. 3 about non-parametric density and conditional density estimation second, the remaining parameters may be determined by hyperparameter optimization, Ch. 5, or by hyperparameter optimization and the full-parameter optimization, described in Ch. 4. For all chapters, conditional density estimation may not only be performed given samples but also if prior knowledge is given in the form of generative or probabilistic models, as described in Ch. 6. This chapter may be considered as optional. The intention recognition considered in Ch. 7 may be read independently from the model identification chapters, even though some models used in Ch. 7 may be identified with the methods described in the prior chapters.

Essentially, all models are wrong,
but some are useful.
—GEORGE BOX

2 Problem Definition

This chapter precedes the main matter of the thesis and is meant to prepare the ground for an in-depth treatment of the contributions. Resembling the rest of this thesis, this problem definition is divided into a part dealing with model identification and a part considering the intention recognition. In each part, the respective scope will be given, i.e., the considered problem will be formalized and the employed assessment criteria will be introduced. The state of the art will be discussed and the deficiencies addressed in this thesis described. In detail, the used assumptions, the contributions, and their properties as well as restrictions as derived in the following chapters will be briefly outlined.

2.1 Density and Conditional Density Estimation

The estimation of density functions and conditional density functions[1] f lies at the heart of descriptive and inferential statistics. One of the earliest known scientific publications about density estimation [189] was concerned with determining the probability density function describing the forehead to body lengths of a population of crabs, dating back to the 1890s by Karl Pearson [144]. Pearson tried to estimate a heteroscedastic mixture density with two components describing the scalar data best. Using this model, he was able to describe all 1000 data points by only four numbers and used these statistics to infer the presence of two subspecies in the given sample set. From an abstract point of view, Pearson tried to estimate the inaccessible true density function $\tilde{f}$, describing the phenomena, based on the measurements. In general, density and conditional density function estimation are methods for determining the closest estimate f to the true density or conditional density function $\tilde{f}$. The estimation of

---

[1] For the sake of brevity, the nomenclature is imprecise: the term (conditional) density estimation is ambiguous as it may be understood as denoting the estimation of a single probability value for one set of events or it may refer to the estimation of the (conditional) density function, i.e., the entire function for all events and sets thereof.

density and conditional density functions relating continuous random variables is challenging, as the only information about $\widetilde{f}$ is the observed data $\mathcal{D} = \{\underline{d}_1, \ldots, \underline{d}_{|\mathcal{D}|}\}$, where $\underline{d}_i \in \mathbb{R}^N$ are specific measurements. Note, that other forms of data may be available too, e.g., uncertain data in the form of a distribution. For the further derivations, it is convenient to formalize the data as the derivative of the empirical cumulative distribution function, i.e., the empirical probability density function (EPDF) [174],

$$f_{\mathcal{D}}(\underline{x}) = \sum_{i=1}^{|\mathcal{D}|} w_i \, \delta(\underline{x} - \underline{d}_i), \qquad (2.1)$$

with $w_i = 1/|\mathcal{D}|$ for all $1 \leq i \leq |\mathcal{D}|$ and $\underline{x} \in \mathbb{R}^N$. As for large $|\mathcal{D}|$, the cumulative distribution of the EPDF $F_{\mathcal{D}}$ converges towards the true function $\widetilde{F}$ [190], $f_{\mathcal{D}}$ can be considered an approximation of $\widetilde{f}$—similar to a kernel density estimate [179, Ch. 3.7]. Therefore, in density and conditional density estimation the distance $\mathrm{D}(f_{\mathcal{D}}, f)$ between the estimate and the data shall be minimized. Note, that for both, density and conditional density function estimation, $f_{\mathcal{D}}$ is a probability density function. In the case of conditional density estimation, $f_{\mathcal{D}}$ is the joint density describing the observed combinations of input and output values.

Assessment Criteria Even though this setup might appear appropriate at a first glance, it is doomed to fail because in hardly any application an infinite amount or at least a sufficiently[2] large number of samples are either obtainable or may be obtained only at prohibitive costs. Therefore, $|\mathcal{D}|$ has to be assumed to be small. This assumption means that only a very small number of points in $\mathbb{R}^N$ conveys information as for most events the probability is zero. The problem is ill-posed in the sense that infinitely many functions f minimize $\mathrm{D}(f_{\mathcal{D}}, f)$ but potentially differ "between" the data points. In order to arrive at meaningful results, the quality of an estimate is assessed according to the following criteria:

Descriptive Validity The observed data $\mathcal{D}$ shall be described well by the estimate f in the sense that the elements of $\mathcal{D}$ are very likely to be generated from the model.

---

[2]In this context, sufficiently large shall be understood as a number of samples large enough to allow for the calculation of an estimate with a precision beyond the numerical precision of the given computing device.

Prescriptive Validity For unobserved data $\mathcal{U}$, $\mathcal{U} \cap \mathcal{D} = \varnothing$, generated according to $\tilde{f}$, the estimate f shall generalize well, i.e., the function shall assign high probability to $u \in \mathcal{U}$.

Besides these mandatory properties, an important property for the practitioner is:

Computational Efficiency Besides the quality of f, it may be necessary to optimize the representation of f with respect to its future use, i.e., space and time complexity of its processing. For some applications, only a low testing time, e.g., a sparse function representation, is needed, whereas others additionally require a efficient training.

The above defined criteria will be used to assess contributions of this thesis as well as the state of the art for density and conditional density estimation. These assessment criteria could be formalized even further, e.g., with respect to the consistency [174, 179] or capacity/structural risk minimization [190, 191], but this would exceed the scope of this thesis.

Difference between Density and Conditional Density Estimation Before giving the detailed problem definitions, it is imperative to discuss the difference between density and conditional density function estimation. In theory, conditional density function estimation is entailed in the density function estimation problem as the following relation

$$f(\underline{y}|\underline{x}) = \frac{f(\underline{y}, \underline{x})}{f(\underline{x})} \,, \tag{2.2}$$

holds for continuous random variables $\underline{x} \in \mathbb{R}^N, \underline{y} \in \mathbb{R}^M$. Determining the conditional density function $f(\underline{y}|\underline{x})$ requires the knowledge of $f(\underline{y}, \underline{x})$ only, as $f(\underline{x})$ can be obtained by marginalization. From a theoretical point of view, the obtained conditional density fulfills all necessary conditions, i.e., non-negativity and integration of the probability mass to one for each fixed input value. Ex. 2.1 demonstrates the main objection against subsuming conditional density estimation by density estimation by a counterexample based on a trigonometric functional dependency perturbed by additive Gaussian noise.

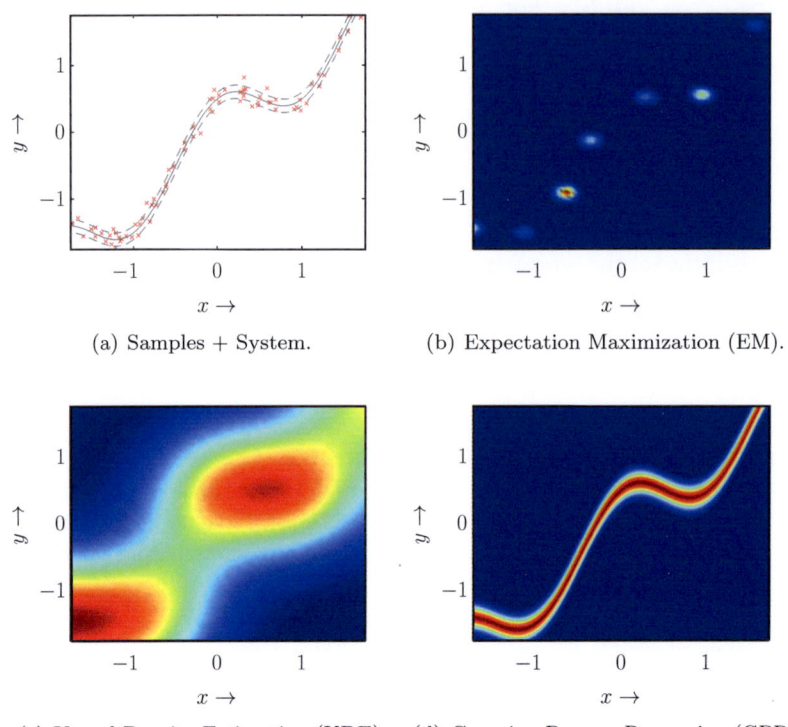

(a) Samples + System.

(b) Expectation Maximization (EM).

(c) Kernel Density Estimation (KDE).   (d) Gaussian Process Regression (GPR).

Figure 2.1: Conditional density function estimates obtained from EM, KDE, and GPR.

Example 2.1 A cubic function disturbed by additive noise, as shown in Fig. 2.1 (a) is given by

$$y = x + 0.5 \cos(\pi \cdot x) + w, \qquad w \sim \mathcal{N}(0, 0.1).$$

From this functional dependency, 100 pairs of input and output samples were obtained by randomly sampling x uniformly in $[-\pi/2, \pi/2]$ and y according to the distribution of the noise term w. Two common density estimators for mixture models of Normal densities were used: Expectation Maximization (EM) algorithm [43] and a kernel density estimator (KDE) [140, 179]. As additive noise is assumed, EM only trains models with axis-aligned components, i.e., covariance matrices with non-zero entries on the main diagonal only. For

KDE, the kernel bandwidths were chosen according to "rule-of-thumb" [179]. The conditional densities for EM and KDE are obtained by a point-wise numeric division of the obtained density function estimates $f(y, x)$ and $f(x)$ according to (2.2). Fig. 2.1 (b) and (c) show the conditional density functions resulting from this application of EM and KDE. The given results are robust to different ways of regularization for EM, i.e., homoscedastic or heteroscedastic mixtures model, automatic choice of component number by AIC, or addition of diagonal stabilization matrices to the components' covariance matrices. For KDE, the results are invariant w.r.t. different bandwidth selection algorithms discussed below in Ch. 2.1.2. In contrast, Fig. 2.1 (d) shows the result obtained from Gaussian Process Regression (GPR) [152], which avoids (2.2) and calculates $f(y|x)$ directly. ∎

In Ex. 2.1, two state of the art density estimators are used for obtaining the density functions $f(x, y)$ and $f(x)$. The conditional density function estimates obtained by using these $f(x, y)$ and $f(x)$ as input to (2.2) are shown in Fig. 2.1 (b) and (c). Clearly, one of the estimators overfits and the other underfits $\tilde{f}$. This effect is inherent when using (2.2) as the models are optimized to fit the data while ignoring the functional dependency. In contrast, the result of an estimator dedicated to conditional density function estimation is shown in Fig. 2.1 (d). This estimator exploits the problem structure, e.g., by distinguishing between input and output dimensions. This experiment shows that the problems of density and conditional density function estimation need to be differentiated. Additionally, this subsumption approach yields results which are computationally inefficient to use. This can be seen in the resulting expression in (2.2), as it consists of a conditional density function representation involving the division of two densities of potentially arbitrary type, for which in general no analytical calculation is possible.

2.1.1 Restriction to Mixtures of Normal Densities

The state of the art in density and conditional density estimation may be categorized according to the type of density function considered and the type of estimator used. There is a wide variety of density types, e.g., Normal, Exponential, Weibull, Ξ^2, Dirichlet or finite and infinite mixtures of component densities. We refer the interested reader to [174] for an extensive enumeration of density types and the book series [49, 113] for an in-depth review of the most frequently used state of the art density

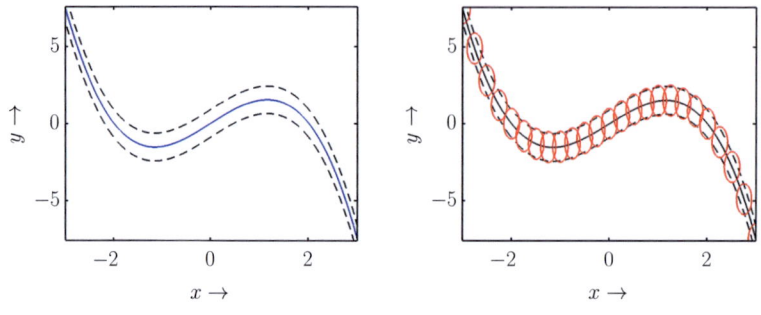

(a) True conditional density function described by $\mu \pm \sigma$.   (b) Gaussian mixture approximation.

Figure 2.2: Approximation of a probabilistic model (a) by a Gaussian mixture density with 25 components (b).

types and estimators. Each of the density representations offers a different trade-off between approximation capability and modeling/processing cost, e.g., when using them in Bayesian state estimation. For example, a Normal density is not a universal approximator, i.e., a Normal density cannot represent any density function. Yet, a normal density may be very efficiently represented and identified, as the moments μ and $\mathbf{C}$ suffice to define it. Additionally, the Normal density allows for efficient processing as marginalization, conditioning, and the product of two Normal densities may be calculated analytically [152]. In contrast to the Normal density, a mixture of Normal densities, i.e., a Gaussian mixture density (GM) is a universal approximator at least for an infinite number of components [128]. Even though the result of a product of Normal densities could still be described by two parameters, the representation size of a GM grows during multiplications, cf. Appendix A.1.2.

For the remaining part of this thesis, only Normal densities and Gaussian mixture densities will be used. Due to their reasonable trade-off between representation power and quality, estimators for GM with a finite number of components will be considered. An approximation of a conditional density function by means of a finite Gaussian mixture is depicted in Fig. 2.2.

2.1.2 Density Estimation

In this section, the state of the art in density estimation will be summarized w.r.t. GM density representations. As mentioned in the beginning of this chapter, the density estimation problem is central to statistics and has therefore gained a lot of attention for a long time. We refer the interested reader to the statistics literature for a more detailed treatment and omitted aspects, e.g., [174, 179, 189] or more recent treatments [49, 53, 129]. For a GM, density estimation corresponds to the determination of the number of components $L \in \mathbb{N}$ and the parameters of each component of the mixture density function

$$f(\underline{x}) = \sum_{i=1}^{L} \alpha_i \, \mathcal{N}(\underline{x}; \underline{\mu}_i, \mathbf{C}_i) \, . \tag{2.3}$$

The parameters for the i-th normal density are the weight $\alpha_i \in \mathbb{R}^+$, $\underline{\alpha} = [\alpha_1 \ldots \alpha_L]^{\mathrm{T}}$, $\underline{\alpha}^{\mathrm{T}} \underline{1} = 1$, the mean $\underline{\mu}_i \in \mathbb{R}^{\mathrm{N}}$, and the covariance matrix $\mathbf{C}_i \in \mathbb{R}^{\mathrm{N} \times \mathrm{N}}$ with matrix elements $\mathbf{C}_i^{(j,k)}$. The parameters may be summarized in vectors

$$\underline{\alpha} := [\alpha_1 \ldots \alpha_L]^{\mathrm{T}} \, , \tag{2.4}$$

$$\underline{\mu} := \left[\underline{\mu}_1^{(1)} \cdots \underline{\mu}_1^{(\mathrm{N})} \cdots \underline{\mu}_L^{(1)} \cdots \underline{\mu}_L^{(\mathrm{N})} \right]^{\mathrm{T}} \, , \tag{2.5}$$

$$\underline{\Sigma} := \left[\sigma_1^{(1,1)} \cdots \sigma_1^{(\mathrm{N},\mathrm{N})} \cdots \sigma_L^{(1)} \cdots \sigma_L^{(\mathrm{N},\mathrm{N})} \right]^{\mathrm{T}} \, , \tag{2.6}$$

and collected into one vector-valued parameter $\underline{\theta}$, i.e.,

$$\underline{\theta} = \left[\begin{array}{ccc} \underline{\alpha}^{\mathrm{T}} & \underline{\mu}^{\mathrm{T}} & \underline{\Sigma}^{\mathrm{T}} \end{array} \right]^{\mathrm{T}} \, . \tag{2.7}$$

The restriction to finite GM reduces the set of relevant estimators [53, 129, 189]. The remaining estimators may be categorized according to the minimized scoring function or measure: log-likelihood, mean integrated squared error, or a distance.

Maximum Likelihood Estimator This class of estimators is the most popular and reflects the aforementioned descriptive validity. The key idea is to maximize the likelihood by which the estimate f produced $\mathcal{D}$. This can be formalized by the data likelihood function

$$\mathcal{L}(\mathcal{D}) = f(d_1, \ldots, d_{|\mathcal{D}|}) = \prod_{i=1}^{|\mathcal{D}|} f(d_i) \, . \tag{2.8}$$

By a simple application of the logarithm to (2.8), the log-likelihood is derived

$$\bar{\mathcal{L}}(\mathcal{D}) = \sum_{i=1}^{|\mathcal{D}|} \log f(d_i).$$ (2.9)

The (log-)likelihood assumes $\mathcal{D}$ to be i.i.d. Because the factors of the likelihood decompose into a sum in $\bar{\mathcal{L}}$ and the maximizers are identical, $\bar{\mathcal{L}}$ is maximized typically. Using this score, the parameters θ are estimated for a fixed number of components L using the Expectation Maximization (EM) algorithm [43]. A maximum likelihood estimator (MLE) iteratively maximizes (2.9) or a lower bound thereof. Note that there exists a wealth of variants of this algorithm. The interested reader is referred to [49, 53, 129]. The log-likelihood captures only how well the data is described by the model. If a component coincides with a data point, the log-likelihood for a GM is trivially maximized by a singular covariance matrix. In order to avoid this effect and improve the prescriptive validity, e.g., a stabilizing matrix may be added to the covariance matrix or a penalized log-likelihood estimator [49] may be employed. The former regularization approach is popular but lacks an intuitive interpretation w.r.t. the densities' shape. The latter is a theoretically well-founded approach, but suffers from inefficient implementation and has not found widespread application.

Kernel Density Estimator The key idea of the so-called kernel density estimator (KDE) [87, 140, 153] is to allow the data "[...] to speak for themselves [...]" [179, p.1]. This estimator may be understood as an extension of data histograms obtained by replacing bins with kernels [49, 179]. The kernels are placed on each $\underline{d}_i \in \mathcal{D}$, e.g., for the M-dimensional case [179]

$$f(\underline{x}) = \frac{1}{|\mathcal{D}| \, h^{\mathrm{M}}} \sum_{i=1}^{|\mathcal{D}|} \mathcal{K}\left(\frac{\underline{x} - \underline{d}_i}{h}\right), \quad \mathcal{K}(\underline{x}, \underline{x}_i) := \mathcal{K}\left(\frac{\underline{x} - \underline{x}_i}{h}\right)$$ (2.10)

where the kernel satisfies certain conditions, cf. Appendix A.1.5. The most important is

$$\int_{\mathbb{R}^{\mathrm{N}}} \mathcal{K}(\underline{x}, \underline{x}_i) \, \mathrm{d}\underline{x} = 1,$$

asserting that the probability mass integrates to one for each component and any convex combinations of components subsequently. For the sake of simplicity, the rest of this section considers only the univariate case, where the only free parameter in (2.10) is the smoothing parameter h. Many methods for determining h exist. The interested reader is referred to [87, 140, 153] for an overview. Typically, the value of this parameter is calculated by minimizing an approximation to the mean integrated square error (MISE) [153, 179], e.g.,

$$
\begin{aligned}
\mathrm{MISE}(f) &= \mathrm{E} \int_{\mathbb{R}} \left(f(x) - \tilde{f}(x) \right)^2 \, \mathrm{d}x \\
&= \int_{\mathbb{R}} \mathrm{E} \left(f(x) - \tilde{f}(x) \right)^2 \, \mathrm{d}x \\
&= \int_{\mathbb{R}} \left(\underbrace{\mathrm{E}\, f(x) - \tilde{f}(x)}_{\text{bias}} \right)^2 \, \mathrm{d}x + \int_{\mathbb{R}} \mathrm{var}\left(f(x) \right) \, \mathrm{d}x \, .
\end{aligned}
\tag{2.11}
$$

By reordering the operators, the integral of the mean square error is obtained (2.11). Further calculations result in a sum of the integrated square bias of f and the integrated variance [179]. Both bias and variance may be further simplified and approximated [179][3], yielding

$$
\mathrm{MISE}(f) \approx \frac{1}{4} h^4 k_2^2 \int_{\mathbb{R}} \tilde{f}''(x)^2 \, \mathrm{d}x + \frac{1}{|\mathcal{D}|h} \int_{\mathbb{R}} \mathcal{K}(t)^2 \, \mathrm{d}t \, ,
\tag{2.12}
$$

and therefore the optimal bandwidth $h \in \mathbb{R}_+$ minimizing (2.12) is [179, Sec. 3.3.2]

$$
h^* = \arg\min_{h} k_2^{-\frac{2}{5}} |\mathcal{D}|^{-\frac{1}{5}} \left[\int_{\mathbb{R}} \tilde{f}''(x)^2 \, \mathrm{d}x \right]^{-\frac{1}{5}} \cdot \left[\int_{\mathbb{R}} \mathcal{K}(t)^2 \, \mathrm{d}t \right]^{\frac{1}{5}} \, ,
\tag{2.13}
$$

where k_2 is the constant variance of the density of the kernel function. Because $\tilde{f}$ is not accessible, a minimizer to (2.13) cannot be found without further assumptions. Several approximations have been used for this purpose. The most popular assumption is that $\tilde{f}$ is normally-distributed with a given standard deviation $\tilde{\sigma}$. Calculating the factor depending on $\tilde{f}$ and instantiating for a specific kernel gives an approximate result for h^* [179]. For a Gaussian kernel, the following estimate of the optimal bandwidth is obtained

$$
h^* \approx \left(\frac{4}{3} \right)^{\frac{1}{5}} \tilde{\sigma} \, |\mathcal{D}|^{-\frac{1}{5}} \, .
\tag{2.14}
$$

---

[3]The interested reader is referred [179], Ch. 3, for a more detailed derivation as only a brief review is given here.

The unknown $\tilde{\sigma}$ may be estimated from data, e.g., using the standard deviation of the empirical probability density function, a robust estimate thereof, or calculated by a more complicated spread calculation, which yields the most common variant of (2.14) known as Silverman's "rule-of-thumb" [179]. Note, that the choice of h w.r.t. an assumed density regularizes the results and therefore improves generalization properties of the estimate, i.e., the prescriptive validity.

Minimum Distance Estimator   The KDE minimizes the MISE error between the inaccessible true density and its estimate w.r.t. an assumed true density type and the data, in order to determine the smoothing parameter. The key idea of minimum distance estimators (MDE) [189] is the use of the EPDF as an approximation of the true density only and the minimization of a given distance measure w.r.t. $\underline{\theta}$

$$\mathrm{D}\left(f_{\mathcal{D}}(\underline{x}),\, f(\underline{x})\right).\tag{2.15}$$

Note that even though $\mathrm{D}\left(.,.\right)$ in (2.15) is commonly referred to as a distance, it only needs to satisfy the following properties [189], which are automatically satisfied by a distance,

$$\mathrm{D}\left(f_1(\underline{x}),\, f_2(\underline{x})\right) \geq \mathrm{D}\left(f_1(\underline{x}),\, f_1(\underline{x})\right),\quad \forall f_1, f_2 \in \mathcal{F},\tag{2.16}$$

and for the considered function space $\mathcal{F}$

$$\mathrm{D}\left(f_1(\underline{x}),\, f_2(\underline{x})\right) = 0 \quad \Rightarrow \quad f_1 = f_2.\tag{2.17}$$

The condition (2.17) may be relaxed in the sense that the equality holds if the two densities are identical only almost everywhere [189, Sec. 4.5.1]. The minimization of (2.15) may be performed by standard optimization algorithms. These conditions do not assume the triangle inequality or the symmetry of D to be fulfilled [189, p. 115]. Because the approach uses the EPDF, minimizing (2.15) asymptotically guarantees convergence to the true density, if the density is identifiable [189]. The minimum distance approach has been employed with many types of distances, e.g., the l_2 norm of the densities or distributions, the Kullback-Leibler divergence (KL) or the Hellinger metric. The interested reader is referred to [189, p. 115] for a more extensive overview. It is also interesting to see that the MLE may be obtained from the MDE as a special case, when using the KL divergence [189], cf. Appendix A.2.2. Even though the MDE approach exhibits mathematical simplicity, it did not gain much interest outside of the academic community. This remains unexplained, but might be attributed to the computational difficulties inherent in the minimization problem. In general, the MDE attempts to solve a non-convex nonlinear function minimization problem for arbitrary distances w.r.t. a high-dimensional parameter space. The size of the parameter space grows most often quadratically with the dimensionality of the data points and for the considered mixture densities at least linearly with the number of components, too. Additionally, the prescriptive validity is not explicitly addressed by the MDE as the distance does not regularize the solution.

Combinations of Estimators The presented types of estimators are prototypical. Some estimators aim at combining the advantages of each estimator type as presented below:

- In order to advance "from kernels to mixtures" [175], i.e., to increase the expressiveness of the density estimate, a KDE is used to construct an initial estimate of the density. Given this initial estimate, an MLE is employed to obtain a mixture density. The key idea is to capture the major characteristics of the density function by means of the KDE estimate and use the MLE as a post-processing in order to obtain a sparse mixture density.

- Another approach is to make a KDE estimate sparse by means of a weight optimization w.r.t. the integral squared distance (ISD). The advantage of this approach is a sparsification of the KDE estimate at a low computational cost. The sparsification is formulated as a weight optimization problem which can be solved in $\mathcal{O}\left(L^2\right)$ operations only. Again, the key idea is to capture the major characteristics of the density function by means of the KDE estimate, but in this approach a sparsification of the estimate is sought [63].

Comparison The presented approaches may be contrasted w.r.t. descriptive and prescriptive validity as well as its efficiency. Tab. 2.1 lists the major differences for the three prominent estimators MLE, KDE, and MDE. Additionally, the most important heuristics/assumptions necessary for implementing the considered estimator are described.

Table 2.1: Brief summary of the properties
of the MLE, KDE, and MDE.

	Descriptive Validity	Prescriptive Validity	Efficiency	Heuristics
MLE	Fits arbitrary mixtures	Augmentable Penalty	#Comp. selectable	Initial values
KDE	Mixtures $\{\underline{\mu}\} = \mathcal{D}$	Choice of kernel, smoothing parameter	#Comp. $= \|\mathcal{D}\|$	Smoothing parameter only
MDE	Fits arbitrary mixtures	Augmentable Penalty	Large optimization problem	Initial values

Descriptive Validity The respective MLE, KDE, and MDE estimators
for GMM inflict different limits to the functions estimated, i.e., the
descriptive validity. KDE restricts the set of GM estimates to all
GM with means identical to the data points. Additionally, KDE only
involves the determination of one common kernel and its smoothing
parameters, whereas MLE and MDE determine for all parameters
for each component.

Prescriptive Validity In order to assure prescriptive validity MLE needs
to be augmented by a penalty term, yielding the penalized log-
likelihood score [49, 179], KDE implicitly regularizes the optimization by referencing to a fixed distribution and the restriction of the
mean positions. The choice of the distance measure impacts the solution of MDE, e.g., penalize differences in the tails of the distributions
or at points of high probability. Yet, to obtain non-trivial results for
small $|\mathcal{D}|$ additional regularization is necessary.

Computational Efficiency Regarding the computational efficiency, KDE has lower training times than MLE and MDE due to the fewer number of parameters to optimize. In contrast, the resulting density of KDE–except for additional sparsification–will entail by default $|\mathcal{D}|$ components and the estimates for MLE and MDE may contain drastically less.

Heuristics This advantage for MLE and MDE is accompanied with the problem of selecting how many components to use, which is easily bypassed by the KDE as all means as well as the covariance matrix are fixed a priori. In addition, for the MLE a cautious initialization of the components is necessary to avoid trivial results, e.g., singularities. Start value selection is typically performed by employing heuristics [53, 129]. The kernel parameter selection of the KDE is similarly heuristic w.r.t. to a reference distribution.

Remaining Challenges Each of the three main approaches MLE, KDE, and MDE as presented and discussed above suffer from several drawbacks listed below. The following section describes how these challenges are addressed in this thesis.

- The maximum likelihood approach is theoretically not sound, as a point-wise evaluation of continuous densities is not well defined. MDE on the basis of cumulative distributions allows for a comparison w.r.t. the entire state space. Yet, the MDE approach is in general computationally inefficient, whereas the MLE is acceptable from a computational point of view. Additionally, it should be noted, that the standard cumulative distributions for univariate random variables are not well defined w.r.t. to density comparisons for multivariate random variables.

- The state of the art approaches lack an easy implementation of regularization mechanisms for improving the prescriptive validity of the obtained density function estimates. For MLE, regularization may be introduced by penalty terms. An implementation thereof is non-trivial. MDE allows for regularization by choosing the employed distance measure. KDE regularizes the estimates by the kernel choice and the assumptions used for determining the smoothing parameter.

- Regarding the computational efficiency, the trade-off between sparse representations as produced by MLE as well as MDE and efficient density estimation by KDE, i.e., a trade-off between training and testing time, may be improved.

Contributions of this Thesis   The contributions of this thesis w.r.t. density estimation may be summarized as an MDE approach allowing for optimization of all mixture parameters and an MDE approach to sparse KDE.

- A novel cumulative distribution function and the corresponding distance measure is introduced to MDE. The novel cumulative distribution function resolves the ambiguity induced by extending the univariate cumulative distribution to the multivariate case. This distance asserts symmetry and uniqueness of the estimates.

- A regularized MDE approach using the same novel distance measure for estimating sparse kernel densities is presented. This approach may be understood as a combination of the MDE approach with kernel density estimation, which is phrased as an optimization problem and produces sparse KDE estimates.

2.1.3   Conditional Density Estimation

In this section, the relevant state of the art in conditional density estimation (CDE) will be summarized. As shown in Ex. 2.1, the problem of estimating conditional density functions differs from density estimation. The DE cannot be subsumed by CDE, because the functional dependency manifesting in the different interpretation of the input and output dimensions is neglected. Nevertheless, both densities and conditional densities are estimated given only samples of a (joint) density. For two random variables $\underline{x} \in \mathbb{R}^N$ and $\underline{y} \in \mathbb{R}^M$, the conditional density $f(\underline{y}|\underline{x})$ is estimated using the empirical joint density

$$f_{\mathcal{D}}\left(\underline{y}, \underline{x}\right) = \sum_{i=1}^{|\mathcal{D}|} w_i\, \delta\left(\begin{bmatrix} x \\ y \end{bmatrix} - \underline{d}_i\right),\qquad(2.18)$$

with $w_i = 1/|\mathcal{D}|$ for all $1 \leq i \leq |\mathcal{D}|$ and $\underline{d}_i = [\underline{d}_{i,x}^{\mathrm{T}}\ \ \underline{d}_{i,y}^{\mathrm{T}}]^{\mathrm{T}} \in \mathbb{R}^{N+M}$, and the following identity

$$f(\underline{y}, \underline{x}) = f(\underline{y}|\underline{x})\, f(\underline{x}).\qquad(2.19)$$

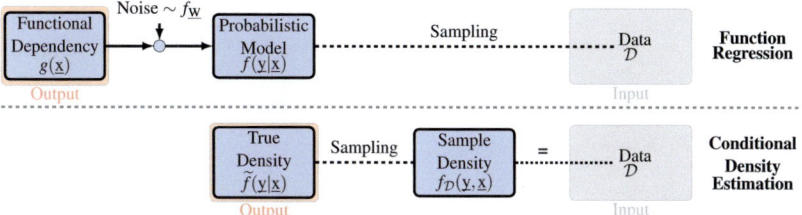

Figure 2.3: Different objectives and models used by function regression and conditional density estimation.

Since neither the true joint density over the input and output variables $f(y, x)$, nor the density about the input variable $f(x)$ are directly accessible, they may be substituted by an estimate, e.g., the respective EPDF (2.18), as in [107, 190], or a Gaussian mixture estimate of the EPDF [105]. The discrepancy between the estimates obtained in Ex. 2.1 results from the fact, that only the parameters of $f(y|x)$ in (2.19) should be learned, yet in the case of calculating the conditional density from density estimates the joint densities' parameters are optimized. The problem of finding a solution satisfying (2.19) is challenging if descriptive and prescriptive validity as well as computational efficiency shall be ensured for the same reasons as in DE. The true underlying conditional density function may be obtained only by observing sample output realizations for each input realization relative to its frequency. Due to different objectives, there are several approaches towards CDE. The major distinction is whether the problem is understood as a function regression problem, i.e., estimation of an underlying generative model and a superimposed noise term, or the identification of the probabilistic model only. Fig. 2.3 depicts the different objectives of function regression and conditional density estimation, which are discussed in the next sections.

Generative Model   The most restrictive approach to CDE assumes the existence of a functional dependency g relating input to output values according to

$$\underline{y} = g(\underline{x}, \underline{w}), \qquad (2.20)$$

where $g : \mathbb{R}^N \times \mathbb{R}^W \mapsto \mathbb{R}^M$ is a potentially nonlinear function and $\underline{w} \in \mathbb{R}^W$ is a noise term $\underline{w} \sim f_{\underline{w}}$ capturing the modeling deficiencies. In (2.20), the noise may effect the deterministic dependency arbitrarily. For additive

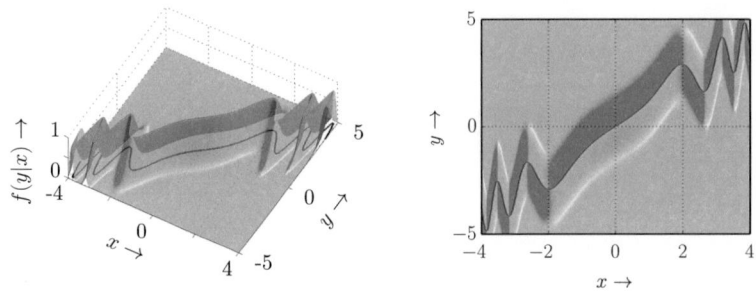

Figure 2.4: Top-down and perspective view of the probabilistic model $f(y|x)$ (translucent) derived from a generative model with mean function g (dark gray) and additive zero-mean Normal noise.

zero-mean noise, i.e.,

$$\underline{y} = g(\underline{x}) + \underline{w}\,,\tag{2.21}$$

the corresponding probabilistic model is obtained according to

$$f(\underline{y}|\underline{x}) = \int_{\mathbb{R}^N} \delta(\underline{y} - g(\underline{x}) - \underline{w})\, f_{\underline{w}}(\underline{w})\, \mathrm{d}\underline{w}\tag{2.22}$$

$$= f_{\underline{w}}\left(\underline{y} - g(\underline{x})\right)\,.\tag{2.23}$$

Fig. 2.4 is an illustration of an exemplary probabilistic model corresponding to a univariate input/output dependency, $g : \mathbb{R} \mapsto \mathbb{R}$, and obtained according to (2.22). CDE in this setting corresponds to estimating g and $f_{\underline{w}}$ simultaneously based on $\mathcal{D}$. In general, every algorithm for function regression, e.g., linear/kernel smoothing [73] or smoothing splines [194], might be used to estimate g. The estimated generative model might be augmented with a noise term perturbing the function value for each input value subsequently. Alternatively a function approximator may be used to estimate the generative model and noise parameters jointly. For example in Mixture Density Networks (MDN) [17, 18] a neural network is used to determine the parameters of a GMM noise model. In contrast, a Gaussian Process Regression (GPR) [152] calculates a distribution over mean functions $f(g)$ or colloquially, a mean function with error bars. A Gaussian process ($\mathcal{GP}$) is defined by a multivariate Normal density for $\mathcal{D} = \{(y,x)\}_{i=1}^{|\mathcal{D}|}$, consisting of input and output tuples, e.g., in the scalar-valued case

$$\{y\}_{i=1}^{|\mathcal{D}|} \sim \mathcal{N}\left(\mu(\{x\}_{i=1}^{|\mathcal{D}|}); \mathbf{K}_{\mathcal{D}}\right)\,,\tag{2.24}$$

with a covariance matrix $\mathbf{K}_\mathcal{D} \in \mathbb{R}^{|\mathcal{D}| \times |\mathcal{D}|}$ composed of the pairwise similarities of the data points

$$
\mathbf{K} = \begin{bmatrix}
K(x_1, x_1) & K(x_1, x_2) & \cdots & K(x_1, x_{|\mathcal{D}|}) \\
K(x_2, x_1) & K(x_2, x_2) & & \vdots \\
\vdots & & \ddots & \\
K(x_{|\mathcal{D}|}, x_1) & \cdots & & K(x_{|\mathcal{D}|}, x_{|\mathcal{D}|})
\end{bmatrix}, \tag{2.25}
$$

where K a kernel function, cf. Appendix A.1.5. Note that for every finite subset of the input values in $\mathcal{D}$, the distribution of output values needs to be a multivariate Normal density to define a $\mathcal{GP}$. The probabilistic model reflecting $f(g)$ is calculated by conditioning and marginalizing over all mean functions $\mathcal{G}$, i.e.,

$$
f(y|x, \mathcal{D}) = \int_\mathcal{G} f(y|x, g, \mathcal{D}) \, f(g|\mathcal{D}) \, \mathrm{d}g \, .
$$

Dropping the explicit dependency on $\mathcal{D}$ and following [152], one obtains

$$
f_{\mathcal{GP}}(y|x) = \mathcal{N}(y; \mu(x), \sigma(x)), \tag{2.26}
$$

which corresponds to a Normal density. Using the pairwise similarity between a fixed input value x and the observations $\mathcal{D}$, i.e., $\underline{k} = \left[K(x, x_1) \ldots K(x, x_{|\mathcal{D}|}) \right]^\mathrm{T}$, the vector of all output values in $\mathcal{D}$, i.e., $\underline{y} = \left[y_1 \ldots y_{|\mathcal{D}|} \right]^\mathrm{T}$, and the noise variance σ_w^2, the mean function $\mu(x)$ and variance function $\sigma(x)$ used in (2.26) are given by

$$
\mu(x) = \sum_{i=1}^{|\mathcal{D}|} \alpha_i K(x, x_i), \tag{2.27}
$$

$$
\sigma(x) = K(x, x) - \underline{k}^\mathrm{T} (\mathbf{K} + \sigma_w \mathbf{I})^{-1} \underline{k} \, ,
$$

with $\alpha_i = (\mathbf{K} + \sigma_w \mathbf{I}) \underline{y}$. The properties of the $\mathcal{GP}$ may be discussed for the mean function estimate and the probabilistic model. The mean function $\mu(x)$ of the $\mathcal{GP}$ is the estimate of the mean function g. As $\mu(x)$ in (2.27) is a weighted linear combination of the output values in $\mathcal{D}$ it may be considered a linear smoother, cf. [73]. The smoothness of $\mu(x)$ depends on the kernel choice. The GPR estimate of $g(x) := \mu(x)$ is the minimizer of [152, Sec. 6.2, 7.1]

$$
J[g] = \frac{1}{2} \|g\|_\mathcal{H}^2 + \frac{1}{2\sigma_w^2} \sum_{i=1}^{|\mathcal{D}|} [y_i - g(x_i)]^2 \, . \tag{2.28}
$$

The trade-off problem (2.28) comprises of a regularization and a data fit term. The regularizer[4] is the norm of the g in the reproducing kernel hilbert space (RKHS) $\mathcal{H}$ induced by the $\mathcal{GP}$'s kernel K. The data fit is measured by the squared error, which is relative to a negative log-likelihood of a Normal noise model with variance σ_w^2 [73]. General consistency results, e.g., w.r.t. other loss functions or asymptotically are unknown up to now. The existing results assume well-behaved kernels which allow, e.g., for orthogonal decomposition and are non-degenerate [152, Sec. 7.1]. The probabilistic model in (2.26) consists of Normal densities centered at $\mu(\hat{x})$ for each fixed $\hat{x}$ with input dependent variance. The smoothness of the surface of the probabilistic model $f_{\mathcal{GP}}$ therefore depends on the kernel choice too. Assuming the noise variance is correctly identified the model may only converge to the true probabilistic model relative to the limits of the convergence of the generative model.

Regarding descriptive validity GPR only suffers from negligible side-effects of a wrong kernel choice and kernel parameters if the noise is Normal. A major drawback of a $\mathcal{GP}$ is its incapability of describing multimodal noise densities without reformulation of the problem, i.e., the identification of multimodal noise or a data association problem in conjunction with multiple regressions. Prescriptive validity is achieved by smoothing the generative model, i.e., by minimizing (2.28). Determining the hyperparameters is a model-selection problem, typically involving gradient based maximization of the marginal likelihood of the output values [152], i.e., a target function with potentially many local extrema. The computational complexity is dominated by the fact, that the entire data set $\mathcal{D}$ is stored in the obtained functional representation by default. Evaluating a probabilistic model for a value involves the inversion of a $|\mathcal{D}| \times |\mathcal{D}|$ matrix, which costs $\mathcal{O}(|\mathcal{D}|^3)$ operations. Yet, there is a large variety of sparsification approaches [89, 152] for reducing the complexity by using subsets of the data $\mathcal{D}' \subset \mathcal{D}$, $|\mathcal{D}'| \ll |\mathcal{D}|$. Besides this aspect, the representation of the conditional density function in the form of (2.26) is unfavorable. Even though evaluating (2.26) for certain inputs is straight forward, if a density is given as an input, this computation can only be performed approximately in general. This is very disadvantageous, e.g., in nonlinear filtering or in inference in continuous Bayesian networks [42]. Note that there exist some exceptions [152], e.g., for the squared-exponential kernel, and assumed density solutions [42].

---

[4]The interested reader is referred to [152, 164, 190] for more detailed information about RKHS and regularization properties.

Probabilistic Model   The less restrictive approach to CDE focuses on the recovery of the probabilistic model only. The identification problem is relaxed by disregarding the existence of a generative model, cf. Fig. 2.4. The objective is the identification of the probabilistic model only. Approaches only determining the probabilistic model may be categorized into indirect and direct methods.

Indirect CDE   Indirect methods construct a conditional density function estimate indirectly by using density estimates. This is the approach used in Ex. 2.1, i.e., the relation $f(\underline{y}|\underline{x}) = f(\underline{y}, \underline{x})/f(\underline{x})$ is exploited. The fundamental deficiency of this approach has been pointed out earlier: optimization of the wrong parameters and in general, no closed-form processing, because of the division contained in the probabilistic model, e.g., for the considered density and conditional density function in the form of GM.

Direct CDE   In contrast to the indirect approach, the direct approach aims at the estimation of the conditional density function only. As noted in [78], "[...] a small amount of work on nonparametric kernel conditional density estimation has been done by statisticians and econometrics researchers [...], it appears to have received little or no attention from the machine learning community [...]". In fact, the most important related works are a conditional density approximation [78] and an SVM-like CDE [190, 193]. The former aims at the fast evaluation of existing kernel conditional density estimates. The latter is a straight-forward extension of the structural risk minimization (SRM) principle [164, 191], i.e., estimates are determined based on their estimation quality and their capacity as defined by the norm in the respective function space. Graphically, this can be understood as preferring flat f over highly oscillating f or as minimizing an entropy measure of f.

Comparison   The major differences between the approaches to CDE w.r.t. descriptive and prescriptive validity as well as their efficiency may be summarized as follows. Due to the obvious deficiencies of the approach of subsuming CDE by DE, this approach is not discussed.

Descriptive Validity   The GPR and direct CDE as presented above are both non-parametric approaches, i.e., f is represented in terms of the $\mathcal{D}$ in conjunction with a model. Both approaches will therefore represent the training data well in the limits of the employed model.

The difference between GPR and the SVM-like CDE approaches is that the GPR assumes one underlying mean function g and by default uses a noise term represented by a Normal density. Even though possible, it is far more difficult to integrate multiple g present in the data or multimodal noise than for the indirect approach. The indirect approach suffers from the fact a finite mixture cannot represent a valid conditional density function, because the probability mass constraints cannot be met.

Prescriptive Validity Regarding the prescriptive validity the GPR inherits the properties of the well-understood non-parametric linear smoothing and combines it with a smooth noise density. Given the model assumed by the GPR is appropriate, it delivers well generalizing estimates. The indirect CDE suffers from the restriction of the components' positions. This restriction causes severe degradation of the prescriptive validity in parts of the state where little or no data is present.

Computational Efficiency The GPR has two drawbacks regarding computational efficiency. The representation of the GPR's probabilistic model (2.26) allows for an easy point-wise evaluation, but only for approximate use in a Bayesian estimation framework. For example, the GPR-based approaches to (nonlinear) filtering such as the extensions of the Extended or Unscented Kalman Filter (GP-EKF/UKF) [95, 96, 97] or the analytic moment-based GP (GP-ADF) [41, 42] have to perform an approximation in each step of the recursive estimation. This approximation additionally limits the representation of the posterior state estimates to be normally distributed. In contrast, a representation of f in the form of a GM allows for closed-form Bayesian inference [4, 50, 107] and supports multimodal posterior state distributions. Given the prior density and all probabilistic models are GM, a nonlinear filter with constant time complexity may be derived [107].

Remaining Challenges The overall aim of this thesis is to learn dynamic systems for the application in human-robot-cooperation. It is therefore imperative that these models may be used for recursive state estimation and generalize well. The remaining challenges therefore are:

- A further sparsification of conditional density function representations in GM form. For this reason, an improvement in the capacity of the kernel conditional density function and the existing sparse CDE are necessary in order to allow for further sparsification.

- Like in density estimation, the indirect CDE is limited due to use of a cumulative distribution function which is not well defined for comparing multivariate random variables.

- In general, a combination of the favorable processing properties of the GM representation with the prescriptive validity of the GPR seems desirable.

Contributions of this Thesis The contributions of this thesis may be categorized into extensions of the existing sparse CDE [190] and extensions lifting the default non-parametric to a full parametric optimization, i.e., all parameters of the mixture density are optimized.

Extensions of Non-Parametric Conditional Density Estimation

- A regularization term related to the Rényi entropy is derived and its relation to the norm in the RKHS induced by the mixture estimates kernel is discussed. This regularization term extends the norm in the RKHS by using inhomogeneous kernels.

- A regularized distance-based sparse CDE is derived, which avoids the fallacies of the multivariate extensions of the cumulative distribution function by the modified Cramér-von Mises distance. Using the above regularization term, heteroscedastic GM estimates may be obtained.

Full Parameter Conditional Density Estimation

- The limitation of the non-parametric CDE approaches to estimate only GM with component means identical to $\mathcal{D}$ is lifted by a nested optimization scheme and the introduction of a superficial regularization term. The superficial regularization is based on the interpretation of the roughness of the surface f in terms of the surface curvature. For the bivariate case, the superficial regularization is shown to be an approximate upper bound on the curvature of the

generative model's mean function, a minimization of this regularizer
simultaneously regularizes the mean function.

• A desirable property of a $\mathcal{GP}$ is the modeling of the uncertainty
about the model by means of the covariance of the noise density $f_{\underline{w}}$,
cf. Fig. 2.3. This property is very useful for many applications, such
as sensor scheduling or active sensing and conveys much information
to the practitioner. In order to reflect this property with a CDE
represented as a GM, the GM's component covariances are adapted
to the confidence in the model. This is achieved by an extension with
variable kernels [25] based on the local data density.

2.1.4 Hyperparameter Optimization

Solving the density or conditional density estimation problem not only
involves finding the parameters $\underline{\theta}$ of a Gaussian mixture density (2.7), but
rather solving for

$$\underline{\eta} = [\ \underline{\alpha}^{\mathrm{T}}\ \underbrace{\underline{\mu}^{\mathrm{T}}\ \underline{\Sigma}^{\mathrm{T}}\ \underline{\omega}^{\mathrm{T}}}_{=:\underline{\zeta}^{\mathrm{T}}}\ ]^{\mathrm{T}}, \qquad (2.29)$$

where $\underline{\omega}$ denotes the parameters such as the parameter λ governing the
trade-off between training error and regularization term in the SRM [190]
or the error tolerance ε for the ε-insensitive loss function [107]. The regularized density and conditional density estimation algorithm [107, 190]
will determine only the weights $\underline{\alpha}$ of a Gaussian mixture density. The
other parameters $\underline{\zeta}$ need to be optimized in a meta optimization, using the
algorithm in Sec. 3.4 or Sec. 4.3 as a subroutine. In the following, only $\underline{\zeta}$
are denoted as hyperparameters, i.e., the parameters of $\underline{\theta}$, which are not
optimized by the algorithms in Sec. 3.4 or Sec. 4.3, and the additional parameters, e.g., λ. The optimization of the hyperparameters is important,
as e.g., a progressive $\mathbf{C}_i$ may result in overfitting and dense representations
of the solution and a conservative $\mathbf{C}_i$ may lead to underfitting and produce
sparse representations. Similar to density and conditional density estimation as such, hyperparameter optimization is concerned with the problem of finding a hypothesis explaining the observations and generalizing
to unobserved values. Therefore the hyperparameter optimization problem may be understood as a classical model selection problem [130, 156]
and addressed by the same approaches: assessment of the generalization
properties of the estimate based on theoretical bounds or example results,
i.e., based on data [47, 164]. As for the considered problem no theoretical

bounds on the generalization properties exist up to this point in time, this approach is omitted and left to be subject of future research. Regarding data driven approaches, these may be further categorized as being based on heuristic, Bayesian model selection, or cross-validation.

Heuristic Model Selection   Even though theoretically hardly grounded, enough model selection problems are addressed by the practitioner using heuristic "rules-of-thumb". For example in kernel density estimation, Silverman discusses "[s]ubjective [c]hoice[s]" [179, Sec. 3.4.1] or the so-called rule-of-thumb [179, Sec. 3.4.2] for choosing the smoothing parameter h of the GM. Note, that the rule-of-thumb is one of the most often used kernel width selection methods and typically this rule is applied disregarding whether the underlying assumptions hold or not. More general "educated guess" methods may for example be found in [164, Ch. 7.8], which include advice for transferring parameter settings from already solved to new problems, stopping criteria based on expected error rates or volume assessments.

Bayesian Model Selection   In contrast to the heuristic model selection, Bayesian model selection [47, 123, 152] is based on the idea that models should be compared by the posterior probability of the model given the data $\mathcal{D}$. Adapting [123, Ch. 28] to the given problem, for a fixed set of hyperparameters $\hat{\underline{\zeta}}$, the posterior probability may be calculated by

$$f(\hat{\underline{\zeta}}|\mathcal{D}) \propto f(\mathcal{D}|\hat{\underline{\zeta}}) \cdot f(\hat{\underline{\zeta}}), \tag{2.30}$$

where $f(\hat{\underline{\zeta}})$ is our prior information about the distribution of $\hat{\underline{\zeta}}$ and the likelihood is given by

$$f(\mathcal{D}|\hat{\underline{\zeta}}) = \int_{\mathbb{R}^{\dim(\underline{\alpha})}} f(\mathcal{D}|\underline{\alpha}, \hat{\underline{\zeta}}) \cdot f(\underline{\alpha}|\hat{\underline{\zeta}}) \, \mathrm{d}\underline{\alpha}, \tag{2.31}$$

with $\underline{\alpha}$ the set of parameters not being hyperparameters. Bayesian model selection results in choosing the model which is most likely given the data and our prior information about the hyperparameters. The flaw of this approach is that (2.30) is in general neither analytically nor numerically solvable—at least not in reasonable time [47]. Additionally, the effort for asserting the relevant constraints may be substantial.

Model Selection by Cross-validation The key idea of model selection based on cross-validation [47, 130, 156] is to estimate the generalization performance by not estimating the distribution of the underlying phenomenon explicitly but by using the data as a representative of this distribution. This approach avoids the modeling problems of a Bayesian approach, but is computationally expensive. The key idea is to obtain a robust generalization assessment by partitioning the given data into several disjoint training and validation sets. By repeatedly training and testing on different partitions the assessment shall avoid overfitting and deliver a good approximation as to how the given estimators perform with unseen data. One obtains a "leave-one out" (LOO) estimate of the generalization error if only one sample is left for testing in each iteration. The computational effort is maximal for this type of estimate, as $|\mathcal{D}|$ estimates need to be obtained from $|\mathcal{D}| - 1$ samples. Even though the LOO estimate may be approximated by, e.g., generalized cross-validation [73, 194], the computational effort is demanding. In contrast, if the number of partitions is small, the test effort will be reduced, but the data distribution may deviate strongly from the distribution of full data set, i.e., the assessment of the generalization is inaccurate.

Contributions of this Thesis The hyperparameter optimization depends on the problem given. In this thesis, hyperparameter optimization algorithms for the non-parametric density and conditional density estimation as well as the full parameter conditional density estimation will be presented. The contributions may therefore be understood as solutions to instantiations of the generic hyperparameter optimization for two specific problems.

- The first hyperparameter optimization for non-parametric sparse density and conditional density estimation is presented. Several extensions for the CDE are discussed.

- The first hyperparameter optimization for the full parameter sparse CDE is presented and discussed. The main contributions are analytical calculations and approximations for improved efficiency of the hyperparameter optimization.

2.1.5 Conditional Density Estimation given Samples and Prior Knowledge

In the preceding sections, the CDE from samples $\mathcal{D}$ was discussed. Yet, in reality no measurement sequence performed for obtaining $\mathcal{D}$ is free of defects and the results of consecutive measurement sequences need to be fused. In this case, conditional density estimation w.r.t. $\mathcal{D}$ and prior knowledge, e.g., in the form of already obtained estimates, needs to be considered. Additionally, previously conducted high resolution measurement campaigns, which may have been limited to a certain part of the state space, need to be combined with low-resolution sequences which span a larger state space.

The challenge is to fuse information given in the form of samples with this prior knowledge, which may be given in the form of already compiled generative or probabilistic models. The key idea of the incorporation of prior knowledge is to estimate the conditional density function from the samples and the prior knowledge simultaneously. The approach to introducing prior knowledge into the CDE algorithm depends on the specific type of prior knowledge. For the remaining part of this thesis, only prior knowledge in the form of a generative or a probabilistic model is considered. For prior knowledge available in the form of a generative model, the following model is assumed to be given

$$\underline{y} = \underline{g}(\underline{x}) + \underline{w}, \tag{2.32}$$

with additive, zero-mean noise, where $\underline{g} : \mathbb{R}^{N} \mapsto \mathbb{R}^{M}$, and a noise term $\underline{w} \in \mathbb{R}^{M}$, $\underline{w} \sim f_{\underline{w}}$. If the corresponding probabilistic model is given, the prior knowledge will be represented as

$$f(\underline{y}|\underline{x}) = f_{\underline{w}}\left(\underline{y} - \underline{g}(\underline{x})\right) .$$

The investigated CDE problem will be phrased as a quadratic program (QP) embedded in a nonlinear non-convex hyperparameter optimization algorithm. Estimating the conditional density function from samples and prior knowledge simultaneously requires the induction of the prior knowledge into the QP. As the used QP formulations resemble generic support vector machines (SVM), the approaches to introducing prior knowledge into SVMs [162, Ch. 4] can be applied to conditional density estimation too. There exists a wealth of literature about introducing prior knowledge into SVMs. The relevant approaches are discussed below. The interested reader is referred to [115] for a more detailed overview about incorporating prior knowledge into SVMs for classification and regression tasks. The approaches may be categorized according to the way information is introduced into the QP formalism: adding artificial data, changing the kernel, changing the regularization term, or changing the constraints.

Artificial Data The incorporation of prior knowledge, e.g., invariances, by appending artificial data is discussed, e.g., in [40] and [164, Ch. 11.3]. This approach may be seeminglessly integrated into the proposed CDE algorithms. Given prior knowledge in the form of a compiled model, i.e., information about f for the entire or parts of the state space, only samples thereof may be used by this approach. This approach may be implemented fast but is inefficient.

Mixture Kernel Another approach towards incorporating prior knowledge in the form of invariances was proposed in [163], where the distance measure as implicitly encoded in the kernel was changed to allow for invariance against group transformations and to make use of local correlations. Other approaches based on specialized kernel, exploit that a convex combination of valid kernels yields a valid kernel [178]. These include, product probability kernels [88] and multiple kernel learning [8]. Product probability kernels model the causal dependencies producing the data. In multiple kernel learning the original optimization problem is extended to include the simultaneous determination of the mixture proportions of a set of kernels. The resulting component of f is in itself a mixture kernel. For CDE one would obtain a mixture density of mixture density components.

Regularization Term & Constraints In [184], the regularization term was augmented with a term penalizing the distance between the current estimate f and a given function $\bar{f}$. Estimates f closer to the prior knowledge encoded in $\bar{f}$ will be penalized less than other estimates. A detailed discussion of the properties of the regularization term is given in [164]. A common problem for SVM applied to classification problems, is the availability of prior knowledge in the form of rules from a knowledge base [115]. The rules may be interpreted as constraining the solutions and are therefore added to the optimization problem in the form of additional constraints [124]. In contrast to SVMs used for classification, "rules" interpreted as constraints, need to have real-valued consequences for the CDE optimization problem.

Contributions of this Thesis   In this thesis, only prior knowledge in the form of a given generative and probabilistic model is considered. The contributions are two approaches for introducing the prior knowledge into the CDE approach based on the following approximations.

- For introducing prior knowledge about the generative model, the deviation of the mean of the estimate f from the prior knowledge is penalized. This is achieved by sampling the mean function and penalizing the point-wise deviation by means of the l_1^ε-error.

- In order to incorporate a probabilistic model, the prior knowledge is assumed to be given as a GM. The GM may encode arbitrary conditional density functions, e.g., encoding multimodal noise. This form of prior knowledge is introduced into the CDE by replacing the components in f with a location-based mixture kernel. The kernel is a mixture of the default kernel and the GM encoding the prior knowledge. The mixture proportion is governed by the confidence in the prior knowledge w.r.t. the location in state space.

- Both approaches towards incorporating prior knowledge will be shown to reduce the number of components in f, at the cost of potentially high estimation effort ex ante.

2.2   Intention Recognition

The second part of this thesis is concerned with the application of dynamical systems to intention recognition as means of implicit human-robot-cooperation. The presented approach to intention recognition is not limited to human-robot-cooperation but is applicable to the wide range of tasks, which the permanently increasing number of technical devices embedded in the human's environment address. Any technical device assisting the human in his daily life requires at least a basic understanding of the present and future human behavior in order to support him. Examples are car traffic monitoring [147], surveillance systems [29, 133], airport security systems [7], assistance tools in software, e.g., in office [80] or email software [120], computer games [2, 52], card games like poker [20], wheelchair control [185] or human-robot-cooperation [160, 171], cf. [30] for more applications. Applied to a humanoid robot the intention recognition is input to the overall control loop of the humanoid robot and plays a crucial part in enabling the humanoid robot to behave similar to a human

[160, 172], cf. Fig. 1.1. This demands responsive behavior to the human behavior in real-time and with a level of understanding similar to humans. These properties are mandatory for the humanoid robot to be supportive and may in the future lay the foundation for a further development to a robotic social companion [23, 24, 38]. In the remainder of this section, the problem definition as applicable to the general case, a restricted formulation w.r.t. human-robot-cooperation, the resulting challenges, related work, and the key ideas for addressing these challenge are discussed. The section is concluded with a summary of the main contributions.

2.2.1 Generic Intention Recognition Problem

In this section the definitions necessary for the further discussion are given. The definition of the concept of an intention is non-trivial: Literally, the term intention stems from the latin word intentio, which translates depending on the context to mindfulness, concern, undertaking, or aim [135]. A detailed definition and discussion of the term intention can be found in the field of philosophy, e.g., [5]. For the purpose of this thesis the understanding of an intention as an aim or an undertaking is relevant. The concept of an intention has been embedded into a broader framework of belief-desire-intention (BDI) [22, 34], which has become very popular for the development of software agents in computer science [76]. For the remainder of this thesis the following definition is adopted from [168, German].

Definition 2.1 (Intention, [168]) An intention is a conscious striving towards an aim.

The undertaking of recognizing an intention may therefore be defined as follows.

Definition 2.2 (Intention Recognition) Intention recognition is the process of recognizing the aim of conscious behavior.

One should note two aspects of Def. 2.1. First, Def. 2.1 emphasizes the consciousness of the behavior. The challenge for developing an recognition system is the definition of the relevant conscious behavior, e.g., from a temporal point of view the question is whether the aim of the intentional behavior in the next five minutes, one day, or one month is to be recognized.

Second, Def. 2.1 does not state if only the aim or additionally the "way" how to achieve the aim shall be recognized. The way of achieving a goal is denoted as a plan, i.e., a sequence of actions, and the corresponding recognition problem is defined as follows[5].

Definition 2.3 (Plan) "[...] *The problem of plan recognition is to take as input a sequence of actions performed by an actor and to infer the goal pursued by the actor and also to organize the action sequence in terms of a plan structure. This plan structure explicitly describes the goal-subgoal relations among its component actions. [...]*" [161].

Since the execution of a plan is in each step intentional the terms intention and plan may be used synonymously [103]. Yet, the concept of an intention may also refer to a relevant set only, rendering it the more flexible concept [168, German]. The set of all possible intentions in one moment is restricted by the belief about state of the world. This set is denoted as a situation.

Definition 2.4 (Situation) A situation is a set of conditions enabling a certain behavior.

The set of conditions may be, e.g., social, temporal, or spatial. This definition is based on [26, German] and extends the definition given in [168, German] by the emphasizing that the existence of a situation is prerequisite for intentions. As the conditions of situations need not be mutually exclusive, the set of existing situations is the context of the behavior [168, German]. Just as the prevailing situation is a prerequisite for a set of intentions, the pursuit of an intention changes the situation, i.e., the intention drives actions that change the state of the world.

Definition 2.5 (Action) An action is a manipulation of the state of the world.

An action[6] is a direct effect of an intention and therefore intentional, i.e., directed towards a goal. The type of action is not further specified and may

---

[5]Note that in contrast to the definition of a policy [156] a plan does not describe the transitions between two states-of-the-world but merely one sequence of actions pursued or to be pursued to achieve a goal.

[6]In this thesis the term "action" is used synonymously with motion or motion primitive, e.g., [55, 56, 59].

be as general as moving from one place to another. For example, if in a household setting one leaves the kitchen towards the living room, any kind of situation limited to being inside the kitchen, e.g., a meal preparation, is impossible. The main distinction between an intention and an action is that the action can be (visually) observed and atomic actions may be defined [58], e.g., as a motion "alphabet" [55, 56, 59].

Definition 2.6 (Activity) An activity is a coarse change of the state of the world limited to a restricted spatial area of the world.

In contrast to the fine-grained actions, which are motivated from a generative modeling of human behavior, activities are motivated by the observation that most human behavior can be described coarsely as being contained in certain spaces [136, 157, 199]. This is important for a discrimination of human behavior. The importance of this differentiation for the construction of a fast multi-level recognition system will be shown in Ch. 7.

The central insight of this section is that the definition of the quantity to estimate, i.e., the intention, is difficult for a generic problem setup and requires a definition w.r.t. the considered application. Therefore the exact definition of the intentions to be estimated will be given in the context of the specific experiments in Ch. 7. For the categorization of an intention recognition methods it is furthermore necessary to distinguish whether the intentions of one human shall be estimated or if there is a group of people, e.g., with a "collective" intention [176]. Similar to many persons being present, many instances of technical devices may be present with complimentary or redundant tasks, e.g., each person's mobile phone and laptop may have complimentary tasks but multiple surveillance camera systems may have redundant tasks. If these technical devices were equipped with actuators one might attribute the property of *agency* to these devices and obtain an intention recognition problem in a multi-agent scenario. Another categorization is based on the tasks and their different requirements. For example, the required accuracy and acceptable latency will differ for applications of a devices in a smart home, a mobile device, a robot, or a humanoid robot. In the following section, the considered setup in terms of these categories will be discussed for the intention recognition problem in human-robot-cooperation.

2.2.2 Intention Recognition in Human-Robot-Cooperation

The intention recognition problem discussed in this thesis is part of the Collaborative Research Center 588 "Humanoid Robots - Learning and Co-operating Multimodal Robots"[7] [45, 182]. This project is aimed at developing a humanoid robot to support the human in its daily activities. The example scenario investigated is a household with a standard kitchen in which only the robot and the human are present. In this setting, the intentions of the human shall be estimated in order to allow for close cooperation with the humanoid robot in the household. The estimation is based mainly on the observations made by the robot cameras and the provided domain knowledge, e.g., the objects present. In order to allow for cooperation with the human, e.g., cooperatively loading the dish washer, the intention recognition is required to deliver robust estimates in real-time.

2.2.3 Challenges

The above described setting and defined requirements are challenging for the following reasons:

- The vision-based observations are uncertain, e.g., due to changes in lighting, temporary partial visibility, or even occlusion. Furthermore an uncertain self-localization and inherent unreliable calibration complicate the observation.

- In addition, the estimation problem involves dynamic dependencies, i.e., having set the table, it is more likely to prepare and eat a meal than to clean the kitchen.

- The complexity of the relations is enormous for realistic scenarios. This means that all realistic combinations of edible goods with food processing tools and their various ways of usage on all workspaces have to be accounted for in the model. For example, apples may be peeled, chopped, or die-pressed by different types of knives on and in pots or plates, which may in turn lie on merely all workspaces in the kitchen. Each object-action-place combination may have a distinct meaning.

---

[7]The German name is "Sonderforschungsbereich 588 Humanoide Roboter - Lernende und kooperierende multimodale Roboter" sponsored by the Deutsche Forschungsgemeinschaft (DFG).

2.2.4 Related Work

A lot of research has been performed in the field of intention and plan recognition. This research differs in scope, i.e., recognition of the goal only [19], both goal and plan [60], whereas the plan ranges from low-level movements [20, 58] to hierarchical plans or policies [19, 29, 103]. The problem has been approached, e.g., with formal systems [80, 91], stochastic grammars [133], temporal templates [20], case-based reasoning [52], token-passing [7], a combination of temporal logic with Bayesian networks (BN) [86], Dynamic Bayesian networks (DBN) [2, 33, 103, 147], a combination of Hidden Markov Models (HMM) [150] with grammars or n-grams [55, 58, 57], or Abstract Hidden Markov (Memory) Models [29].

Categorization The existing research may be categorized according to intended or keyhole recognition. Intended recognition occurs in any form of communication, where the addresser has the aim of conveying his intention to the addressee. The addresser is thus cooperative and facilitates intention recognition. In contrast, the intention recognition by surveillance systems [29] or assistance software [80, 120] is based on the observation of the user only, i.e., peeping through a keyhole, e.g., by using a camera or reading mouse and keyboard of a computer. Additionally, the existing research may be categorized as symbolic and probabilistic recognition approaches. Symbolic recognition approaches employ reasoning methods such as automata theory, first order logic, or predicate calculus to deduce the possible intention. The notion of symbolic reasoning emphasizes the absence of any kind of uncertainty in the observation process, i.e., a symbol has been observed with certainty. In contrast, in the probabilistic recognition approaches the intention is inferred not only on the possibility but on the likelihood of the intention given the observations. The approaches allow for modeling uncertainty in the inference and observation process. Hybrid approaches aimed towards combining symbolic and probabilistic recognition exist. As a consequence of the human-robot-cooperation setting and requirements only hybrid or probabilistic keyhole intention recognition approaches are applicable. In the following, the relevant approaches will be discussed.

Hybrid Recognition The key idea underlying the relevant hybrid recognition approaches is to remove the uncertainty in the observation and use the certain observation with the symbolic reasoning. The most relevant approaches are the pending-set approach [60, 65] and the token-passing approach [7]. The key idea of the pending-set approach [60, 65] is to maintain a set of actions which are consistent with a given plan library and the preceding observations, i.e., the actions which have completed. The set is updated using Probabilistic Horn Abduction. This approach allows for a fast detection of plan/goal abandonment [61] and interleaving plans. The token-passing approach [7] may be understood as a Petri network augmented with a sophisticated "feature decision tree" [7]. This decision tree maps uncertain observation to certain causes, which are used as input to the network. The feature decision tree compensates for not observed features by missing value branches. Time consistency is asserted for by memory flags and duration models.

Probabilistic Recognition The key idea underlying the probabilistic recognition approaches is to convert a causal model into a DBN [39, 134] and then infer the intention by performing standard exact or approximate inference methods with the DBN. The most relevant probabilistic approaches are grammar-based approaches [147] and policy-based approaches [29]. The grammar-based approaches [148, 147, 149] use a given grammar of the behavior and generate parse trees from this grammar. This may be understood as using a generative model of the behavior to produce all possible behaviors and compile these into a DBN. As the human behavior is state-dependent the most advanced approaches use a probabilistic state dependent grammar [147, 149] for the generation. Additionally, the policy-based approaches [29] employ a layered structure of the intention. In the lowest-level of the DBN the transition from the past to the current state of the world is modeled given all possible actions. The state space of the random variable corresponds to the elements of the policy [134]. The state of the world is estimated from the observations. Higher level or abstract policies may be modeled by appending these random variables as parents of the lower levels to the DBN. This model is also referred to as an Abstract Hidden Markov (Memory) Model [29].

Comparison w.r.t. Human-Robot-Cooperation The approaches presented above need to be compared with regard to the three challenges: model complexity, uncertain observations, and dynamic dependencies. All of the approaches presented above, are capable to process dynamic dependencies directly. Regarding the processing of uncertain information only probabilistic recognition approaches, which compile a DBN, allow for a consistent uncertainty treatment. The hybrid approaches lack any uncertainty regarding the dynamic dependencies [60] or restrict the uncertainty treatment to the measurement update [7]. All of the approaches suffer from the number of considered states of the world and actions. The hybrid approaches need to account for all possible further execution plots, e.g., all plans consistent with the plan library and the state of the world. The effect on the DBN s compiled by the probabilistic approaches is even more drastic as the state space has to map the policy into its state space. As stated in [147, Ch. 7.11], the state space may contain a full enumeration of all plans. This renders inference already for small problems intractable. In summary, all approaches are incapable of handling the combinatorial explosion inherent in the problem. The probabilistic approaches at least allow for a consistent uncertainty modeling.

2.2.5 Key Idea

As a consequence of the above comparison an extension of the probabilistic approaches is sought, which addresses the combinatorial explosion inherent in the problem. The key insight of the discussion is that even though many object-action-place combinations are possible, only a few are likely. This is not always the case, but many applications have, e.g., spatio-temporal constraints, which may be exploited. These spatio-temporal constraints match the definition of a situation in Def. 2.4. The key idea is therefore to exploit the situation dependencies in the problem to reduce the state-space sizes and therefore to alleviate the combinatorial explosion.

2.2.6 Main Contributions

The main contributions of this thesis w.r.t. the intention recognition as means of non-verbal communication in human-robot-cooperation may be summarized as follows.

- A model-predictive approach is presented to exploit the situational dependencies inherent in the intention recognition problem. This approach is shown to allow for efficient inference in large-scale models and is based on selecting subset models on-line.

- The approach is validated using video-based and extended-range telepresence experiments. Especially the latter experiments are used for showing the properties and restrictions of the approach w.r.t. the scalability due to the reproducible and scalable problem setups.

A theory with mathematical beauty is more likely to be correct than an ugly one that fits some experimental data.

—PAUL DIRAC

3 Non-Parametric Density and Conditional Density Estimation

In this chapter, non-parametric approaches to density and conditional density estimation from samples will be presented as introduced in Ch. 2.1. The samples are given in the form of the empirical probability density function f_D (2.1). The non-parametric approach is limited to estimating mixtures with components collocated with the samples $\mathcal{D}$ only and employs identical parameters for all components. Initially, the two main challenges for density and conditional density estimation as well as the key idea how these may be addressed by regularized non-parametric approaches will be discussed. Consecutively, the elements of a non-parametric approach are presented in Sec. 3.1-3.3, i.e., distance measures, regularization terms as well as constraints. These elements are combined to a generic algorithm in Sec. 3.4 for the estimation of sparse density and conditional density functions. This chapter is concluded with an experimental validation section in Sec. 3.5 and the summary of contributions in Sec. 3.6.

Challenges   The two main challenges for density and conditional density estimation are prescriptive validity and computational efficiency. Regarding the prescriptive validity, the generalization of the estimate to unobserved data is still an open question for mixture density and conditional density estimates. In order to achieve computational efficiency, the considered mixture representation needs to be sparse relative to the training sample size as the computational complexity of any application of the estimate will scale with its number of components.

Key Idea   Both challenges are addressed by optimizing the data fit in terms of a distance measure and the regularization of the estimates' capacity. The application of a distance measure enforces descriptive validity and allows for the identification of redundant components in the mixture as will be shown in the rest of this section. The approach proposed in this section is a Minimum Distance Estimator (MDE) in the sense of Sec. 2.1.2 with regularization. The MDE approach is employed for both density and conditional density estimation. The regularization term ensures prescriptive validity and amplifies the sparseness of the representation as it governs whether a given data point is considered redundant or relevant for the estimate. In the rest of this section, these two elements of the approach will be presented as well as the constraints that need to be asserted to obtain valid density or conditional density functions. The approach is summarized in a generic algorithm in pseudo-code.

3.1   Distance Measures

In this section, the reformulation of the conditional density estimation problem into a density estimation problem and the employed distance measure are discussed.

3.1.1   Reformulation of the Conditional Density Estimation Problem

Before introducing the employed distance measure, the conditional density estimation problem needs to be reformulated into a density estimation problem, in the sense that the conditional density estimate is extended to a joint density of both input and output random variables. This is necessary as no distance measure for conditional density functions is defined and $f_{\mathcal{D}}$ is a joint density of the input and output random variables. Additionally, this reduction allows for a unified treatment of both problems w.r.t. the distance measure. In detail, given the estimate $f(\underline{y}|\underline{x})$ of the considered true conditional density function $\tilde{f}(\underline{y}|\underline{x})$, a joint density function based on the estimate may be obtained by calculating

$$f(\underline{y}, \underline{x}) = f(\underline{y}|\underline{x}) \cdot f(\underline{x}) \,. \tag{3.1}$$

In an MDE approach, the joint density $f(\underline{x}, \underline{y})$ in (3.1) is compared to the given data in the form of the EPDF $f_{\mathcal{D}}(\underline{x}, y)$, cf. Sec. 2.1. The EPDF is an approximation of the left-hand side of (3.1) if the true conditional density function would be used. In (3.1), the density $f(\underline{x})$ corresponds to the prior knowledge about the probability density function of $\underline{x}$. As Vapnik states one "[...] can use [...] better approximations of the density [...]" [190, 7.11]. The quality of this density will impact the quality of the conditional density estimate. Besides a user given $f(\underline{x})$, it may be determined as the marginal distribution of the given data $\mathcal{D}$ directly, i.e., as a Dirac mixture density [190], or as a Gaussian mixture density estimate of this marginal density [107]. The choice of $f(\underline{x})$ influences the computational complexity of the estimation too. It should be noted, that if $f(\underline{x})$ and $f(\underline{y}|\underline{x})$ are mixture densities with L and K components respectively, the number of components in (3.1) is $L \cdot K$ and for a distance measure involving the calculation of f^2, e.g., the integral squared distance, a term with $(L \cdot K)^2$ components has to be formed.

3.1.2   Cumulative Distributions

The preceding section has shown that similar to the density estimation problem an MDE approach to conditional density estimation involves the comparison of two densities only. As introduced in Sec. 2.1.2, many distance measures are applicable for comparing densities. These may be categorized into point-wise and integral distances with the respective advantages and disadvantages discussed in Sec. 2.1.2. Both point-wise and integral distance measures may be calculated w.r.t. the probability density or the cumulative probability distribution function. Since for the considered problem, $f_{\mathcal{D}}$ is defined only at the sample points and undefined in the rest of the state space, a comparison of the density functions is theoretically not sound[1] and neglects the rest of the state space. For this reason, it is common to compare two densities, $\tilde{f}$ and f, based on their respective cumulative probability distribution functions, $\tilde{F}$ and F, i.e.,

$$\mathrm{D}\left(\tilde{f}, f\right) \approx \mathrm{D}\left(\tilde{F}, F\right). \tag{3.2}$$

3.1.3   Localized Cumulative Distribution

In order to compare probability density functions over the entire state space, the cumulative distribution shall be used. Even though the cumulative distribution function is well defined for scalar random variables, there is no canonical extension to the multivariate case. The challenge is the non-uniqueness of an extension, as 2^{N} integration orders are possible in an N-dimensional space. The integration order influences the distances as it yields asymmetric results and therefore biases the outcome of any estimation algorithm [70, 71]. These disadvantages are overcome by the localized cumulative distribution (LCD) [71], i.e., it is symmetric and unique. The key idea is to measure the local probability mass only. The LCD is calculated by integrating the product with symmetric kernels for all positions

---

[1]Point-wise evaluations are not defined for a probability density function w.r.t. a continuous space.

and widths. For the sake of self-containedness, the definition of the LCD from [71] is restated below.

Definition 3.1 (Localized Cumulative Distribution, [71]) *For a multivariate random vector $\underline{x} \in \mathbb{R}^N$ with corresponding probability density function $f : \mathbb{R}^N \to \mathbb{R}_+$, the Localized Cumulative Distribution (LCD) is*

$$\mathrm{F}(\underline{m}, \underline{b}) = \int_{\mathbb{R}^N} f(\underline{x}) \cdot \mathcal{K}_{\underline{b}}(\underline{x}, \underline{m}) \, \mathrm{d}\underline{x} \,, \tag{3.3}$$

with $\Omega \subset \mathbb{R}^N \times \mathbb{R}_+^N$, $\mathrm{F} : \Omega \to [0, 1]$, $\underline{b} \in \mathbb{R}_+^N$, $\mathcal{K}_{\underline{b}}(\underline{x}, \underline{m})$ an admissible kernel, in the sense of [71], centered at $\underline{m} = [\, m^{(1)} \cdots m^{(\mathrm{N})} \,]^\mathrm{T}$ with extent/width $\underline{b}$ and $\mathcal{K} : \Omega \to [0, 1]$.

A typical choice for the kernel is an axis-aligned Gaussian kernel (A.5) with mean $\underline{m}$ and identical width b for all N dimensions [71], i.e.,

$$\mathcal{K}_b(\underline{x}, \underline{m}) = \prod_{k=1}^{\mathrm{N}} \exp\left(-\frac{1}{2} \frac{(x^{(k)} - m^{(k)})^2}{b^2} \right) . \tag{3.4}$$

Even though other choices are possible, only (3.4) is used for the remaining part of this thesis, as the multiplication of a Gaussian kernel with a Gaussian mixture density will give rise to a Gaussian mixture density and may be performed in closed-form for a fixed kernel width b.

Localized Cumulative Distribution of $\tilde{f}$ and f   The LCDs of the density estimate f or its reformulation according to (3.1) and the empirical probability density function $f_{\mathcal{D}}$ in Gaussian mixture form are obtained by multiplying both densities with the kernel

$$\mathcal{K}_b(\underline{x}, \underline{m}) = \sqrt{\det\left(2\pi\boldsymbol{\Sigma}_b\right)} \, \mathcal{N}(\underline{x}; \underline{m}, \boldsymbol{\Sigma}_b) \,, \tag{3.5}$$

with $\boldsymbol{\Sigma}_b = b \cdot \mathrm{diag}(\underline{1})$, i.e., identical kernel width b for all dimensions. For the EPDF given by

$$f_{\mathcal{D}}(\underline{x}) = \sum_{i=1}^{|\mathcal{D}|} w_i \, \delta(\underline{x} - \underline{d}_i) \,, \tag{3.6}$$

with $w_i = 1/|\mathcal{D}|$ for all $1 \le i \le |\mathcal{D}|$ and $\underline{x} \in \mathbb{R}^N$, the LCD is obtained by multiplying (3.6) with (3.5) and integrating over $\underline{x}$. The resulting LCD is a function of $\underline{m}$ and b, i.e., the position and the width of the multiplied kernel, and given by

$$\mathrm{F}_{\mathcal{D}}(\underline{m}, b) = \sum_{i=1}^{|\mathcal{D}|} w_i \sqrt{\det\left(2\pi \Sigma_b\right)} \, \mathcal{N}(\underline{m}; \underline{d}_i, \Sigma_b) \,. \tag{3.7}$$

For fixed parameters $\underline{m}$ and b, the term in (3.7) may be understood as measuring the average overlapping probability mass located at the sample $\underline{d}_i$. Each kernel in (3.7) will attain a value of 1 if $\underline{m} = \underline{d}_i$ and otherwise a value in $[0, 1)$ depending on the distance between the kernel centers relative to the kernel width. The target density—based in case of conditional density estimation on (3.1)—is a Gaussian mixture density (A.1.2), with $\underline{x} \in \mathbb{R}^N$ and L components

$$f(\underline{x}) = \sum_{i=1}^{L} \alpha_i \, \mathcal{N}(\underline{x}; \underline{\mu}_i, \Sigma_i) \,. \tag{3.8}$$

The LCD of (3.8) is obtained by the same operations as for $f_{\mathcal{D}}$ and given by

$$\mathrm{F}(\underline{m}, b) = \sum_{i=1}^{L} \alpha_i \, \sqrt{\det\left(2\pi \Sigma_b\right)} \, \mathcal{N}(\underline{\mu}_i; \underline{m}, \Sigma_i + \Sigma_b) \,. \tag{3.9}$$

3.1.4 Modified Cramér-von Mises Distance

In order to compare two distributions, a distance measure has to be employed. Note, that even though there exists a wealth of distance measures[2] a novel distance measure is required if two LCDs shall be compared. For comparing the LCDs over the entire state space a distance measure extending the l_2-distance[3] between the two distributions $\tilde{\mathrm{F}}$ and F may be derived

$$\mathrm{D}\left(\tilde{f}, f\right) = \int_{\mathbb{R}} \left(\tilde{\mathrm{F}}(x) - \mathrm{F}(x)\right)^2 \mathrm{d}x \,, \tag{3.10}$$

e.g., by weighting or averaging the l_2-distance [189, p. 116]. Given the LCDs $\tilde{\mathrm{F}}$ and F, the modified Cramér-von Mises distance measure (mCvMD)

---

[2]The interested reader is referred to [189] for an overview.

[3]In some parts of the literature this is referred to as *squared integral* or *integral squared distance* (ISD).

was defined in [71]

$$D = \int_{\mathbb{R}^+} w(b) \int_{\mathbb{R}^N} \left(\tilde{F}(\underline{m}, b) - F(\underline{m}, b) \right)^2 d\underline{m}\, db\,, \qquad (3.11)$$

as a modification of the standard Cramér-von Mises distance, where the l_2-distance is calculated w.r.t. all kernel positions $\underline{m} \in \mathbb{R}^N$ and widths $b \in \mathbb{R}^+$. The function $w(b)$ in (3.11) is introduced in order to assert for convergence of the integral. For the remaining part of this thesis,

$$w(b) = \begin{cases} \frac{1}{b^{N-1}} & ,\ b \in [0, b_{\max}] \\ 0 & ,\ \text{elsewhere} \end{cases},$$

will be used. The interested reader is referred to [71] for more information. The maximum kernel width $b_{\max}$ is set to a sufficiently large size in order to capture even low frequency variation in the densities, e.g., a multiple of the maximum distance between two samples in $\mathcal{D}$.

3.1.5   Properties and Restrictions

In summary, the distance calculation between two density and conditional density functions may be reduced to the calculation of the distance between two density functions. Due to the non-uniqueness and the asymmetry of the straight-forward extension of the scalar cumulative distribution function to the multivariate case, the LCD is employed. In consequence, the l_2-distance of the cumulative distributions is replaced by the mCvMD and thus the shortcomings of the cumulative distribution functions are overcome. The properties and restrictions applying when using the mCvMD are listed below:

- The mCvMD is a modification of the l_2-distance and therefore considers the difference of the two distributions over the entire state space and emphasizes differences relative to the local probability mass, i.e., differences in the tails of the distributions are less important.

- For all densities considered in this thesis, the integral in (3.11) over $\underline{m}$ may be solved analytically using equation (A.7). In general, the integral b may be calculated numerically only and for numerical reasons the kernel width is upper bound, i.e., $b \leq b_{\max}$ is assumed to hold. Note, that the integral will converge for a fixed $b_{\max}$.

- The choice of integration points by a numerical integration algorithm may be understood as an automatic kernel width selection, conveying insight about the data distribution.

- As discussed above, the squared term involved in calculating the mCvMD may be too expensive to compute due to the $L \cdot K$ components and approximations may be required.

- Even though not theoretically proven, it was observed that for density and conditional density estimation no additional constraints were necessary for asserting non-negativity and the amount probability mass. This may be understood as being automatically ensured by aligning the estimate to a positive density with correct probability mass.

A straight-forward but computationally intractable MDE approach minimizing the mCvMD in Sec. 3.1.4 w.r.t. all parameters of each mixture components is presented in Appendix A.3. In the following section, the regularization term for the non-parametric approach is derived.

3.2 Regularization

Unregularized Minimum Distance Estimators have an important short-coming: they are prone to overfitting [130]. As already mentioned in Sec. 2, both, the density and conditional density estimation problem are ill-posed as an infinite amount of solutions may represent the given data arbitrarily well. Maximizing the descriptive validity of an estimate f may be achieved by maximizing the likelihood of f given the $\mathcal{D}$. Yet, maximizing the likelihood or any distance will result in poor prescriptive validity as the estimation disregards all parts of the state space not (densely) populated by data. One possible approach to improving the prescriptive validity, is the use of additional information in form of a preference bias when solving the estimation problem. This information is typically introduced into the estimation algorithm by means of penalty terms. These terms measure properties of the solution, which influence the generalization property. The challenge is to determine a measure for the generalization property. Intuitively, a density or conditional density function capable of high oscillations can model arbitrary noise, thus overfit the data. Whereas, a "flat" density or conditional density function may underfit the data. The key idea is to find a measure related to the roughness[4] of the surface of the density and conditional density function. In the next sections, the regularization using the norm of f in the respective reproducing kernel hilbert space, a generalization of the regularization term based on the Rényi-entropy, and the properties as well as the restrictions of these approaches are presented. Note, the following derivation of the regularization terms are identical for density and conditional density estimation.

3.2.1   Regularization using the Reproducing Kernel Hilbert Space

The key idea of a regularization in a Hilbert space may be understood as measuring the distance of the density or conditional density function estimate to a constant or flat function by means of the spectrum of eigenfunctions. In the following, an inner product of two Gaussian components in a Hilbert space is derived based on the eigen-decomposition of a Gaussian density function. Using this pairwise inner product, the inner product of two Gaussian mixture densities is derived. Finally, a roughness term as a function of the weights of the considered Gaussian mixture is obtained. These results are compiled and in part reproduced from [51, 164, 190, 194]. A scalar Normal density with mean x_i and standard deviation σ possesses the expansion [190]

$$f(x) := \mathcal{N}(x; \mu, \sigma) = \sum_{n=1}^{\infty} \lambda_n\, \phi_n(x)\, \phi_n(\mu)\,,$$

with weights λ_n and eigenfunctions ϕ_n. In [51, p. 22 and 23], the Fourier decomposition is employed for a scalar Gaussian component with $\sigma = 1$ yielding

$$\lambda_n = A\, e^{-n^2/2}\,, \qquad \phi_n(x) = e^{2\pi i n x}\,, \qquad \phi_n(\mu) = e^{-2\pi i n \mu}\,,$$

where the λ_n decrease with increasing n. The function $f(x)$ may be represented as

$$f^c(x) = \sum_{n=1}^{\infty} c_n \phi_n(x)\,. \tag{3.12}$$

---

[4]The term roughness is used in this context, to avoid the confusion of (surface) smoothness with differentiability. Gaussian mixture densities are convex combinations of normal densities, which are infinitely often continuously differentiable.

Two Gaussian density functions $\tilde{f}$ and f therefore differ in their eigenvalue spectra only. For a Gaussian kernel, the following inner product and the set of functions representable by (3.12) define a reproducing kernel hilbert space (RKHS) $\mathcal{H}$, i.e.,

$$< \tilde{f}^{\tilde{c}}(x), f^c(x) >_{\mathcal{H}} = \sum_{n=1}^{\infty} \frac{\tilde{c}_n\, c_n}{\lambda_n} \,.$$

The self-similarity is given by

$$< f(x), f(x) >_{\mathcal{H}} = \sum_{n=1}^{\infty} \frac{c_n^2}{\lambda_n} \,, \tag{3.13}$$

showing that the kernel choice defines the roughness of the density function in terms of the eigenvalues of the spectrum. This derivation may be generalized to Gaussian mixture densities. In analogy to (3.12), one obtains for a mixture of L-components [190]

$$f(x) = \sum_{i=1}^{L} \alpha_i \, \mathcal{N}(x; \mu, \sigma)$$

$$= \sum_{i=1}^{L} \alpha_i \sum_{n_i=1}^{\infty} \lambda_{n_i} \phi_{n_i}(x) \phi_{n_i}(\mu)$$

$$= \sum_{i=1}^{L} \alpha_i \sum_{n_i=1}^{\infty} c'_{n_i} \phi_{n_i}(x) \,. \tag{3.14}$$

Inserting (3.14) into (3.13) gives rise to the self-similarity for a GMM

$$< f(x), f(x) >_{\mathcal{H}} = < \sum_{i=1}^{L} \alpha_i \, \mathcal{N}(x; x_i, \gamma), \sum_{j=1}^{L} \alpha_j \, \mathcal{N}(x; x_j, \gamma) >_{\mathcal{H}}$$

$$= \sum_{i=1}^{L} \alpha_i \sum_{j=1}^{L} \alpha_j < \mathcal{N}(x; x_i, \gamma), \mathcal{N}(x; x_j, \gamma) >_{\mathcal{H}}$$

$$= \sum_{i=1}^{L} \sum_{j=1}^{L} \alpha_i \, \alpha_j \, \mathcal{N}(x_i; x_j, \gamma)$$

$$= \underline{\alpha}^{\mathrm{T}} \mathbf{K} \, \underline{\alpha} \,. \tag{3.15}$$

The vector-valued formulation of the self-similarity (3.15) will be used in the remaining part of this section. The above results hold for scalar Gaussian kernels. For the sake of brevity, any further discussion w.r.t. generalization to more powerful kernel functions or the necessary conditions for a kernel to possess such an expansion are out-of-the-scope of this thesis. The interested reader is referred to [51, 194] for more information. The above derivation was used for the case that all kernels are identical. For density and conditional density estimation this is restrictive and in the next section it will be shown, that from an entropy perspective [177] a similar regularization term may be obtained that is meaningful for arbitrarily aligned kernels.

3.2.2   Regularization using the Negative Rényi-Entropy

The regularization term in (3.15) is based on the idea that the roughness of a function f is measured by the norm in the function space $\mathcal{H}$ induced by the kernel. This may be understood as measuring the oscillation of the density or conditional density function surface. Alternatively, this may be understood measuring the deviation of the estimate from a flat or constant function. As entropy measures [177] colloquially quantify the deviation of a function from a constant function, they may be employed as regularization terms. In this setting, the entropy term needs to be maximal, i.e., one wishes to determine the least informative estimate. A common entropy measure for continuous random variables is the Rényi-Entropy.

Definition 3.2 (Rényi Entropy)   *The Rényi entropy [35] is defined as*

$$H_{\mathcal{R}}(\underline{x}, r) = \frac{1}{1-r} \log \int_{\mathbb{R}^N} f^r(\underline{x}) \, \mathrm{d}\underline{x}, \qquad (3.16)$$

with $r \in [0, \infty] \setminus 1$.

More details of the Rényi entropy, e.g., convergence to the Shannon entropy in the limit, can be found in [35]. As the parameters $\underline{\theta}$ of the "flattest" function are desired, one minimizes the negative Rényi-entropy.

Choosing $r = 2$ for its similarity to the l_2-distance, gives

$$
\begin{aligned}
\underline{\theta}^* &= \arg\min_{\underline{\theta}} \left[-H_{\mathcal{R}}(\underline{x}, 2) \right] \\
&= \arg\min_{\underline{\theta}} \left[\log \left(\int_{\mathbb{R}^{\mathrm{N}}} f^2(\underline{x}) \, \mathrm{d}\underline{x} \right) \right] \\
&= \arg\min_{\underline{\theta}} \int_{\mathbb{R}^{\mathrm{N}}} f^2(\underline{x}) \, \mathrm{d}\underline{x},
\end{aligned}
\tag{3.17}
$$

where the logarithm may be omitted due to its monotonicity. The minimization of (3.17) not only minimizes the negative Rényi entropy, but has similar to the RKHS a meaning in a function space. Because probability density functions are square-integrable, the l_2-space of all probability density functions allows for the definition of the inner product, thus

$$
< \tilde{f}(x), f(x) >_{l_2} = \int_{\mathbb{R}^{\mathrm{N}}} \tilde{f}(\underline{x}) \cdot f(\underline{x}) \, \mathrm{d}\underline{x}.
\tag{3.18}
$$

The self-similarity in (3.18) may be computed for an arbitrary Gaussian mixture density f by

$$
\begin{aligned}
\int_{\mathbb{R}^{\mathrm{N}}} f(\underline{x}) \cdot f(\underline{x}) \, \mathrm{d}\underline{x} &= \int_{\mathbb{R}^{\mathrm{N}}} \left(\sum_{i=1}^{L} \alpha_i \, \mathcal{N}(\underline{x}; \underline{\mu}_i, \Sigma_i) \right)^2 \mathrm{d}\underline{x} \\
&= \sum_{i=1}^{L} \sum_{j=1}^{K} \alpha_i \, \alpha_j \int_{\mathbb{R}^{\mathrm{N}}} \mathcal{N}(\underline{x}; \underline{\mu}_i, \Sigma_i) \, \mathcal{N}(\underline{x}; \underline{\mu}_j, \Sigma_j) \, \mathrm{d}\underline{x} \\
&= \sum_{i=1}^{L} \sum_{j=1}^{K} \alpha_i \, \alpha_j \, \mathcal{N}(\underline{\mu}_i; \underline{\mu}_j, \Sigma_i + \Sigma_j) \\
&= \underline{\alpha}^{\mathrm{T}} \mathbf{K} \, \underline{\alpha}.
\end{aligned}
\tag{3.19}
$$

The terms in (3.19) may be further simplified if a homoscedastic Gaussian mixture density is considered, e.g., a Parzen window, or all components have identical weights [62].

Properties and Restrictions

In this section, two regularization terms were introduced. The first regularizer function corresponds to the norm in the reproducing kernel hilbert space induced by the component function of the mixture density. This

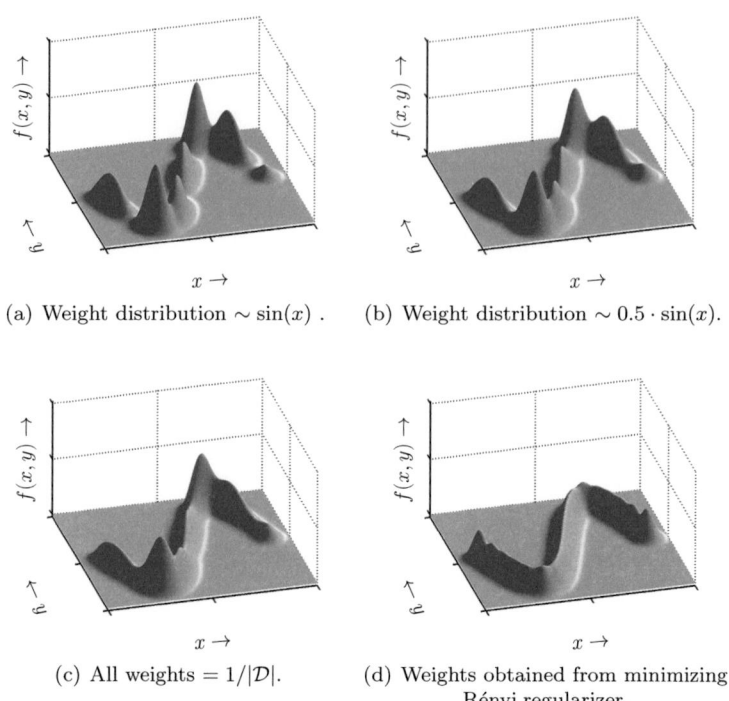

(a) Weight distribution $\sim \sin(x)$.   (b) Weight distribution $\sim 0.5 \cdot \sin(x)$.

(c) All weights $= 1/|\mathcal{D}|$.   (d) Weights obtained from minimizing
Rényi regularizer.

Figure 3.1: Joint GMM density functions plotted for various weight distributions: the weights are (a) sinusiodally distributed, (b) sinusiodally distributed with lower bandwidth, (c) all identical, and (d) determined to minimize (3.15). The means are 100 equidistant sample points of a sine function and the covariance are identical.

regularizer intuitively measures the oscillation of the density or conditional density function estimate. As this regularizer is derived for a mixture of components of the same scale, a regularization motivated by the entropy minimization idea was introduced, which avoids this shortcoming. The term may be calculated for mixture densities with components differing in every parameter. It is not only related to an estimate of the second-order Rényi entropy, but may also be understood as the norm in the space of square integrable functions. The effect of the regularization is depicted in Fig. 3.1, where the joint probability density functions for several weight distributions are contrasted with the weight distribution obtained by minimizing (3.19).

- Although both terms differ in their derivation and motivation, the effective calculation is almost identical. Both terms were shown to be representable as functions of the weight vector only and may be calculated in vector-matrix form. As the component functions for the RKHS approach are identical, this regularizer is slightly more efficient to calculate.

- Intuitively, both regularization terms measure the distance to a flat function. As will be shown in the experimental validation, minimizing this property prevents the lumping of probability mass. For example, in conditional density estimation turning points of the generative model may have a high local data density, cf. Fig. 3.1.

- For fixed covariances, the components' locations which minimize any of the two regularizers will be maximally distributed, i.e., spread apart. This trivial minimization of the regularization terms will been shown in Ex. 4.1.

3.3 Constraints

In the previous sections, the components for density and conditional density estimation have been presented, which ensure that the estimates fit the data and generalize well. A requirement for any density and conditional density estimation algorithm is to additionally assert that the results are valid density and conditional density functions. A function is a valid density function if the constraints

$$ f(\underline{x}) \geq 0, \forall \underline{x} \in \mathbb{R}^N , \qquad \int_{\mathbb{R}^N} f(\underline{x}) \, \mathrm{d}\underline{x} = 1 . \qquad (3.20) $$

are satisfied, i.e., f returns valid probabilities and the probability mass integrates to one. A function is a valid conditional density function if the following constraints

$$ f(\underline{y}|\underline{x}) \geq 0, \forall \underline{x} \in \mathbb{R}^N , \forall \underline{y} \in \mathbb{R}^M , \qquad \int_{\mathbb{R}^N} f(\underline{y}|\underline{x}) \, \mathrm{d}\underline{y} = 1 , \forall \underline{x} \in \mathbb{R}^N . \quad (3.21) $$

are satisfied, i.e., f returns valid probabilities and the probability mass integrates to one.

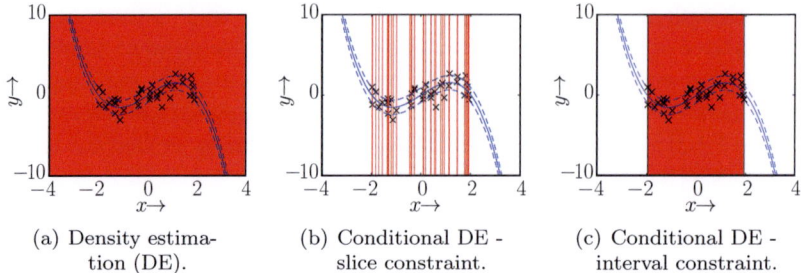

(a) Density estima-
tion (DE).

(b) Conditional DE -
slice constraint.

(c) Conditional DE -
interval constraint.

Figure 3.2: Mass constraints for density and conditional density estimation: for density estimation the integration of the mass over the entire state space (red area) is asserted (a). For conditional density estimation the mass constraint may be asserted for "slices" (red lines) aligned with the sample points (b) or the over the considered part (red area) of the state space (b).

Non-Negativity Constraint For both density and conditional density functions, the first constraint asserts the non-negativity of the probabilities returned by either the density or conditional density function. Because in this work density and conditional density functions are represented by Gaussian mixture densities (A.8) only, the non-negativity may be asserted by restricting the weights

$$\alpha_i \geq 0, \qquad\qquad 1 \leq i \leq L. \qquad\qquad (3.22)$$

If the constraint (3.22) is satisfied, both the density and conditional density function values are sums of evaluations of normal densities, which are weighted by positive factors. Therefore, the density and conditional density function values have to be positive[5].

Mass Constraint In contrast to the non-negativity constraint, the mass constraints in (3.20) and (3.21) cannot be treated uniformly for density and conditional density estimation. For density estimation the mass constraint in (3.20) may be satisfied by trivially adding the following constraint for

---

[5]This constraint is overly strict, as the evaluation of a Gaussian mixture density may still be positive even if some components are negative. The given constraint satisfies the necessary condition and can be enforced easily.

the weights $\underline{\alpha} = [\alpha_1 \dots \alpha_L]^{\mathrm{T}}$, $\alpha_i \in \mathbb{R}_+$

$$\sum_{i=1}^{L} \alpha_i = \underline{1}^{\mathrm{T}}\underline{\alpha} = 1, \qquad (3.23)$$

which in conjunction with (3.22) also implies $\alpha_i \leq 1$ as an upper bound on the weights. Any Gaussian mixture density adhering to these weight constraints fulfills the mass constraint in (3.20), cf. Fig. 3.2 (a). Asserting the mass constraint for conditional densities is more challenging as the integral condition in (3.21) needs to be satisfied for all fixed input values $\underline{x} \in \mathbb{R}^{\mathrm{N}}$. Even if the values are restricted to an interval $\mathcal{I} = [\underline{x}_{\min}, \underline{x}_{\max}]$ and $\underline{x} \in \mathcal{I}$, an infinite number of mixture components would be necessary to fulfill the mass constraint. If the conditional density function is extended to a joint density, similar to Sec. 3.1.1, the necessary mass constraint is

$$\int_{\mathbb{R}^{\mathrm{N}}} \int_{\mathbb{R}^{\mathrm{M}}} f(\underline{y}|\underline{x})\, f(\underline{x}) \; \mathrm{d}\underline{y}\,\mathrm{d}\underline{x} \stackrel{!}{=} 1, \qquad (3.24)$$

and for the conditional density function in the form of a mixture of $f_i(.|.)$ one obtains

$$\int_{\mathbb{R}^{\mathrm{N}}} \int_{\mathbb{R}^{\mathrm{M}}} \left(\sum_{i=1}^{L} \alpha_i\, f_i(\underline{y}|\underline{x}) \right) f(\underline{x})\; \mathrm{d}\underline{y}\,\mathrm{d}\underline{x} = \int_{\mathbb{R}^{\mathrm{N}}} \sum_{i=1}^{L} \alpha_i'\, f_i'(\underline{x}) \; \mathrm{d}\underline{x} \stackrel{!}{=} 1.$$

The density $f(\underline{x})$ may be replaced with $f_{\mathcal{D}}(\underline{x})$, giving rise to the approximate constraint [190]

$$\sum_{d=1}^{|\mathcal{D}|} \left(\sum_{i=1}^{L} \alpha_i'\, f_i'(\underline{x}_d) \right) = \underline{\alpha}^{\mathrm{T}}\underline{s} \stackrel{!}{=} 1, \qquad (3.25)$$

where $\underline{s}$ is obtained by rearranging the sums. The approximate constraint (3.25) enforces that the probability mass of slices conditioned on $\underline{x}$-positions of the samples sums to one, cf. Fig. 3.2 (b). The mass constraint in (3.21) is met only approximately, as the probability mass is only measured at a set of distinct $\hat{\underline{x}}$. Asserting (3.25) is cumbersome as it involves the summation over point-evaluations of the conditional density function. Additionally, (3.25) only enforces the mass constraint in total, i.e., the sum of evaluations at $\mathcal{D}$ not the mass of each slice is constrained. This may be understood as asserting that the probability mass w.r.t. the interval $\mathcal{I}$ of

Table 3.1:   Overview of the constraints to be asserted in density and conditional density estimation.

Estimate	Non-Negativity Constraint	Mass Constraint	
Density	$\underline{0} \prec \underline{\alpha} \, (\prec \underline{1})$	$\underline{\alpha}^{\mathrm{T}} \underline{1} = 1$	
		Slices	**Interval**
Cond. Density	$\underline{0} \prec \underline{\alpha} \, (\prec \underline{1} \cdot \mathcal{I})$	$\underline{\alpha}^{\mathrm{T}} \underline{s} = 1,$	$\underline{\alpha}^{\mathrm{T}} \underline{1} = \mathcal{I}$

the state space populated by the data approximately. In the following, a simpler interval-based approximation to (3.24) is proposed, cf. Fig. 3.2 (c)

$$\int_{\mathcal{I}} \int_{\mathbb{R}^N} f(\underline{y}|\underline{x}) \, \mathrm{d}\underline{y} \, \mathrm{d}\underline{x} = \mathrm{vol}\,(\mathcal{I}) \ .$$

For a conditional density function represented as a mixture density, this gives rise to

$$\int_{\mathbb{R}^N} \sum_{i=1}^{L} \alpha_i' \, f_i'(\underline{x}) \, \mathrm{d}\underline{x} = \underline{\alpha}^{\mathrm{T}} \underline{1} = \mathrm{vol}\,(\mathcal{I}) \ , \qquad (3.26)$$

which resembles the mass constraint for the density estimation problem. Note, that the mass constraint in (3.26) imposes an upper bound on the weights, similar to the density estimation case. This constraint is simple to assert as it only involves the calculation of the interval size $\mathrm{vol}\,(\mathcal{I})$. Tab. 3.1 gives an overview of the constraints to be asserted in density and conditional density estimation presented in this section.

3.4   Density and Conditional Density Estimation Algorithm

Up to this section, the three components of the non-parametric density and conditional density estimation algorithm have been introduced: a distance term, a regularization term, and the necessary constraints to obtain valid estimates. In this section, an algorithm will be composed from the components presented in the previous sections, which may be used generically for both density and conditional density estimation and addresses the problem of insufficient generalization capabilities as well as sparseness of the mixture representation. The key idea is that the estimation process for both problems corresponds to a weight optimization. In the rest of this section, the composition of the optimization problem, i.e., the target function and constraints, the pseudo-code of the algorithm as well as the properties and restrictions of the approach are discussed.

Setting up the Optimization Problem   The optimization problem consists of two steps. First, a problem-specific preprocessing converts the distance and the regularization term into quadratic forms. Second, the target function of the optimization problem is composed and the constraints are determined. The initial step of the preprocessing concerns only the conditional density estimation as the conditional density $f(y|\underline{x})$ is extended into a density $f(\underline{x})$, where for the sake of brevity the notation is abused by setting $\underline{x} := [\,y^{\mathrm{T}}\ \underline{x}^{\mathrm{T}}\,]^{\mathrm{T}}$. Consecutively, the LCDs of $\mathrm{F}_{\mathcal{D}}(\underline{x})$ and $\mathrm{F}(\underline{x})$ of $f_{\mathcal{D}}(\underline{x})$ and $f(\underline{x})$ for both density and conditional density estimation are determined. Using the notation introduced in Ch. 2.1.2, all parameters of $f(\underline{x})$ are

$$\underline{\theta} = [\ \underline{\alpha}^{\mathrm{T}}\ \ \underline{\mu}^{\mathrm{T}}\ \ \underline{\Sigma}^{\mathrm{T}}\ ]^{\mathrm{T}}\,. \tag{3.27}$$

In this non-parametric approach, the means $\underline{\mu}$ are collocated with the samples $\mathcal{D}$, the parameters of the covariances of all GM components are identical and obtained from hyperparameter optimization, cf. Sec. 5. Thus, only the weights $\underline{\alpha}$ in (3.27) are optimized. This allows for a simplification of the expressions for the LCDs (3.7) and (3.9) as well as the mCvMD (3.11)

$$D = \int_{\mathbb{R}^+} w(b)\left(\underline{\alpha}^{\mathrm{T}}\mathbf{P}_1\,\underline{\alpha} - 2\,\underline{\alpha}^{\mathrm{T}}\underline{P}_2 + \mathrm{P}_3\right)\mathrm{d}b\,. \tag{3.28}$$

In (3.28), P_1-P_3 denote the closed-form solutions to the m-integrals of the terms arising from expanding the binomial. In general, the integral over b in (3.28) may be solved numerically only. A further simplification can be achieved by omitting the term P_3, as it is independent of the weights $\underline{\alpha}$, thus it will only influence the absolute value of the distance measure but not the extrema w.r.t. $\underline{\alpha}$. For the remaining part of this thesis, this term will be neglected[6]. These calculations and transformations yield

$$D = \underline{\alpha}^{\mathrm{T}} \mathbf{Q}_1 \underline{\alpha} - 2 \underline{\alpha}^{\mathrm{T}} \underline{Q}_2 , \qquad (3.29)$$

with

$$\mathbf{Q}_1(i,j) := \int_{\mathbb{R}^+} w(b) \, \mathbf{Q}_1^{(i,j)}(b) \, \mathrm{d}b ,$$

$$\underline{Q}_2(i) := \int_{\mathbb{R}^+} w(b) \, Q_2^{(i)}(b) \, \mathrm{d}b ,$$

The expressions for elements of the matrix $\mathbf{Q}_1$ and the vector $\underline{Q}_2$ may be found in [105]. The distance term (3.29) for both densities and conditional densities is a quadratic function of the weights $\underline{\alpha}$. As described in Sec. 3.2, the regularization term will be calculated identically for density and conditional density functions. Similar to the distance term, the regularization term for both, the RKHS (3.15) and the negative Rényi-entropy-based term (3.19) is obtained as quadratic function of the weights $\underline{\alpha}$. In the second step, the target function $\mathrm{T}(\underline{\alpha})$ is calculated as a weighted combination of the distance and regularization terms

$$\mathrm{T}(\underline{\alpha}) = \underbrace{\underline{\alpha}^{\mathrm{T}} \mathbf{Q}_1 \underline{\alpha} - 2 \underline{\alpha}^{\mathrm{T}} \underline{Q}_2}_{\text{Distance term}} + \underbrace{\lambda \cdot \underline{\alpha}^{\mathrm{T}} \mathbf{K} \underline{\alpha}}_{\text{Regularization term}}$$

$$= \underline{\alpha}^{\mathrm{T}} (\mathbf{Q}_1 + \lambda \mathbf{K}) \underline{\alpha} - 2 \underline{\alpha}^{\mathrm{T}} \underline{Q}_2 . \qquad (3.30)$$

The parameter $\lambda \in \mathbb{R}^+$ in (3.30) is obtained from hyperparameter optimization, cf. Ch. 5, and governs the combination of both terms, i.e., for $\lambda = 0$ the target function corresponds to an unregularized MDE approach optimizing only $\underline{\alpha}$. The larger the λ value, the more emphasis is put onto the regularization. The third component of the optimization problem, are the constraints necessary for asserting the validity of the densities and conditional densities. By minor transformations, the non-negativity and mass constraints for densities and conditional densities as a function of the weight, may be generically given in the form of

$$\underline{0} \preceq \underline{\alpha} \preceq \underline{1} \cdot c_p , \qquad\qquad \underline{\alpha}^{\mathrm{T}} \underline{w} = c_m , \qquad (3.31)$$

where the respective constants $c_p, c_m \in \mathbb{R}$ and $\underline{w} \in \mathbb{R}^{\mathrm{N}}$ need to be set according to Tab. 3.1. The density and conditional density estimation problems formulated as a quadratic program of the weights $\underline{\alpha}$ using the above derived generic expressions for the target function (3.30)

---

[6]If the absolute value of the distance measure needs to be calculated the expression P3 may be derived based on [71].

and the constraints (3.31) may be summarized in the following optimization problem

$$\min_{\underline{\alpha}} \quad \underline{\alpha}^{\mathrm{T}}\left(\mathbf{Q}_1 + \lambda \mathbf{K}\right)\underline{\alpha} - 2\underline{\alpha}^{\mathrm{T}}\underline{Q}_2 \tag{3.32}$$

$$\text{s.t.} \quad \underline{0} \preceq \underline{\alpha} \preceq \underline{1} \cdot c_p,$$

$$\underline{\alpha}^{\mathrm{T}}\underline{w} = c_m.$$

The properties of the solution depend on the matrix $(\mathbf{Q}_1 + \lambda \mathbf{K})$. The most important property is the positive (semi-)definite[7] of a matrix. Using Corollary A.2, the positive semi-definiteness of matrix $(\mathbf{Q}_1 + \lambda \mathbf{K})$ may be proven by showing that both $\mathbf{Q}_1$ and $\mathbf{K}$ are obtained from dyadic products. This can be seen for $\mathbf{Q}_1$ and $\mathbf{K}$ in the derivation of (3.29) and for $\mathbf{K}$ can be seen for the regularization by the norm in RKHS in (3.15) as well as for the regularization by Rényi-entropy in (3.19). As shown in Corollary A.1, the addition of two p.s.d. matrices yields a p.s.d. result, i.e., the proposed optimization problem is a convex quadratic problem.

Algorithm   The entire algorithm is summarized in Alg. 1. Given a set of samples $\mathcal{D}$ and the hyperparameters, i.e., the estimate's component means and covariances $\{\underline{\mu}_i, \boldsymbol{\Sigma}_i\}$ as well as the trade-off parameter λ, the algorithm determines the weights $\underline{\alpha}^*$ minimizing the target function (3.30) w.r.t. the constraints (3.31) for density or conditional density estimation. The structure of Alg. 1 is as follows. Initially, the starting values for the weights are set similarly to the standard KDE, e.g., to uniform weights. Consecutively, the three main components of the algorithm are computed, i.e., the distance term, the regularization term, and the constraints. If a conditional density shall be estimated, the reformulation needs to be calculated prior to determining the distance term. The regularization term may be calculated independent of the type of estimation problem. The constraints are set according to Sec. 3.3. The resulting quadratic program (QP) may then be solved by any standard solver for this type of problem. Finally, weights smaller than a given tolerance, e.g., $1e^{-4}$, are removed from the obtained vector of weights $\underline{\alpha}^+$, yielding the reduced weight vector $\underline{\alpha}^*$. The reduced components are negligible for the overall density or conditional density function due to their tiny weight. The result of the algorithm is a Gaussian mixture density with weights $\underline{\alpha}^*$ and the set of given means and covariances $\{\underline{\mu}_i, \boldsymbol{\Sigma}_i\}^*$ associated with the non-reduced weights.

---

[7]The interested reader is referred to Def. A.2 for a definition of p.(s.)d.

Algorithm 1 Regularized Density and Conditional Density Estimation.

1: **Input:** $\mathcal{D}$, hyperparameters, i.e., $\{\underline{\mu}_i, \Sigma_i\}$ and λ

2: Assign $\underline{\alpha}_0 \leftarrow$ E.g. $\underline{1} \cdot \frac{1}{|\mathcal{D}|}$ ▷ Initial Values

3: [Calculate $f(\underline{x})$, $f(\underline{y}, \underline{x}) = f(\underline{y}|\underline{x}) \cdot f(\underline{x})$]   ▷ Reformulation

4: Calculate $\mathbf{Q}_1, \underline{\mathbf{Q}}_2 \leftarrow \mathrm{D}\,(\mathrm{F}, \mathrm{F}_{\mathcal{D}})$ w.r.t. $\underline{\alpha}$

5: Calculate $\mathbf{K} \leftarrow$ regularization term   ▷ Preprocessing

6: Calculate c_p, c_m for the constraints

7: $\underline{\alpha}^+ \leftarrow$ COMPOSE AND SOLVE $\mathrm{QP}(\underline{\alpha}_0, \mathbf{Q}_1, \underline{\mathbf{Q}}_2, \mathbf{K}, c_p, c_m)$ ▷ Standard solver

8: $\underline{\alpha}^* \leftarrow$ REDUCE$(\underline{\alpha}^+)$

9: **Output:** $f \sim \mathrm{GMM}\{\underline{\alpha}^*, \{\underline{\mu}_i, \Sigma_i\}^*\}$

10: **function** REDUCE$(\underline{\alpha}')$ ▷ Removing obsolete components

11:     $\underline{\alpha}'' \leftarrow \underline{\alpha}' \geq \varepsilon$ ▷ E.g. $\varepsilon = 1\mathrm{e}^{-4}$

12: **end function**

Properties and Restrictions   The descriptive validity, prescriptive validity, and computational efficiency of the proposed regularized density and conditional density estimation may be summarized as follows:

- A solution to the problem for density estimation exists and may be attained as the Parzen window estimate is in the feasible set of solutions [190]. For conditional density estimation a similar solution may be obtained by assigning an identical weight to all components in the estimate. As by construction $(\mathbf{Q}_1 + \lambda\mathbf{K})$ is p.s.d., cf. (A.34), the solution of the QP will be a minimum of the target function. For the stricter case of $(\mathbf{Q}_1 + \lambda\mathbf{K})$ being p.d. this minimum will be unique. In the former case, there is a set of solutions with identical values of the target function.

- The descriptive validity may be investigated w.r.t. a small or an asymptotic amount of data. For $\lambda = 0$, the density and conditional density estimation algorithms return estimates that fit the data best w.r.t. the given distance and hyperparameters. For an asymptotic amount of data for density estimation the classical consistency arguments of kernel density estimation may be employed. For conditional density estimation, these same results apply w.r.t. each fixed input value. In the proposed algorithms, the parameters of all components are identical. This property restricts the set of estimates and limits the algorithm's capacity to model the data especially for small data sets.

- Regarding the prescriptive validity, the probability mass is located at the data points only. This is a strong restriction of the capability of the model and limits its generalization to parts of the state space, which are only populated by a few data points, e.g., gaps where a generative model was not sampled. In the absence of data the uncertainty is maximal. By definition, the mean function values in those parts of the state space align with the last components' mean values due to the exponentially decreasing influence of the components.

- The computational effort for obtaining the solution to the QP depends on the number of variables L being optimized. The complexity depends on the used implementation and may have a complexity as lows as polynomial in L. Due to the formulation in matrix/vector-form and the locality inherent in the problem, the estimation algorithm lends itself to parallelization. For more information the interested reader is referred to Appendix A.4.3.

- As the optimization fulfills (A.34), the optimization problem is a constrained convex quadratic problem. These problems may be solved in polynomial time w.r.t. the number of optimization variables and constraints, cf. Appendix A.4.3.

3.5 Experimental Validation

In this section, the derived generic non-parametric estimation algorithm shall be compared to existing approaches. This comparison needs to be performed for density and conditional density estimation separately as the data is generated in a different manner, i.e., a different experimental setup is required, and the estimator needs to be compared to different state of the art estimators.

3.5.1 Density Estimation

In the following, the experimental setup, the evaluation criteria, relevant implementation details regarding the employed estimators, and the results for density estimation are presented.

Experimental Setup   In contrast to conditional density estimation, the data for density estimation does not correspond to noisy measurements of a deterministic dependency, but are samples from an unknown density function $\tilde{f}$. In order to determine the performance for estimating multimodal densities, 2D Gaussian mixture densities were automatically produced by sampling the parameters of each component uniformly at random from the intervals

$$\tilde{\alpha}_i \in [\,0.01\,,\,1\,]\,, \qquad \underline{\tilde{\mu}} \in [\,1\,,\,2\,] \times [\,5\,,\,7\,]\,, \qquad \tilde{\mathbf{C}} = \mathbf{D}^{\mathrm{T}}\mathbf{D} \qquad (3.33)$$

with $\mathbf{D}_{ij} \in [\,0.25\,,\,0.4\,]$. The constrained random generation of $\tilde{\mathbf{C}}$ in (3.33) asserts that the covariance matrices are p.d. From each generated mixture 150 samples are drawn for training and testing.

Evaluation Criteria   The quality of the density estimates obtained for the Gaussian mixtures estimated from the data generated according to (3.33) is assessed by the following criteria:

- The prescriptive validity is quantified by determining a test set of 150 samples by sampling the random Gaussian mixture and determining the negative log-likelihood of this test set.

- The number of components is a measure of computational efficiency as the number of components governs the computational complexity of any further application of a mixture, e.g., w.r.t. a Bayesian estimation framework.

Implementation Details   The following implementations and parameter settings were used for the different estimators:

- Expectation Maximization (EM) was employed as a parametric density estimator. As discussed in Ch. 2, the main drawbacks of EM are the model selection problem—as the number of components has to be specified in advance—and no direct account for the generalization properties. For the comparison four settings EM1 - EM4 were used, i.e., the number of components was either fixed to the number of components obtained from the proposed approach (EM1 & EM2) or determined by optimizing the widely used Akaike Information Criterion (AIC) in (EM3 & EM4). In order to improve the generalization properties, a matrix $\mathbf{1} \cdot \epsilon$ was added to $\tilde{\mathbf{C}}$ (EM2 & EM4). The minimal covariance was introduced yielding smoother estimates. The implementation of EM for Gaussian mixture densities by Matlab^{TM} was used.

- As a nonparametric estimator the default kernel density estimator (KDE) was employed. Several bandwidth selection rules were used for the comparison, e.g., Silverman's rule of thumb (ROT), a plug-in estimator w.r.t. the MISE criterion (HALL), a leave-one-out likelihood criterion (LCV), and a k-th nearest neighbor distance measure (LOC). The KDE toolbox for Matlab^{TM} from [85] was used for the comparison.

- The approach resembling the proposed algorithm most is the Reduced Set Density Estimator (RSDE) [63]. This approach performs a sparsification ex post of the KDE estimate. Therefore, reduced estimates of the kernel density estimates were calculated too. Given the HALL, LCV and LOC estimates, the respective RSDE estimates are denoted by REH, RER, and REL. The RSDE implementation is contained in the toolbox [85], too.

- For the proposed approach the LCD distance and the Rényi-based regularization term are used. The $b_{\max}$ was set to ten times the largest data spread over all dimensions. The parameter λ balances between the distance and the regularization term was initialized with $\lambda_0 = 0.25$ and optimized with the constraints $\lambda \in [0.01, 100]$. For the hyperparameter optimization the algorithm based on k-fold cross-validation minimizing the negative log-likelihood, as proposed in Ch. 5 was employed. This approach is referred to as LCD.

Results   The results of ten random experiments generated according to (3.33) in terms of the proposed performance measures are given in Fig. 3.3. The results show, that the generalization capability of the approach is better than the results of EM and KDE except for ROT. Yet, the ROT estimate has on average ca. 30 % more components than the proposed approach. In general, the results for the RSDE estimator are sparser than

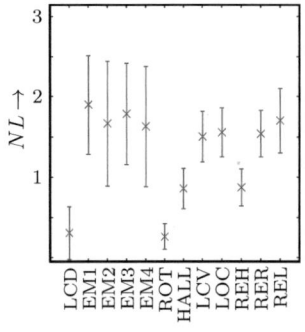

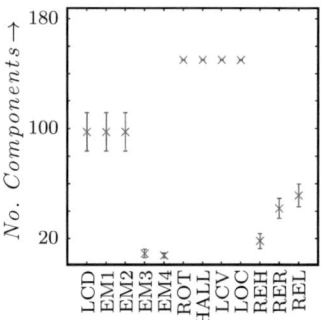

(a) Neg. Log-Likelihood scores.   (b) Number of components.

Figure 3.3: Mean and standard deviation of the negative Log-Likelihood scores and number of components achieved by different density estimation algorithms' results for ten Monte Carlo experiments.

LCD, but the quality is worse. This is due to the fact that the results of RSDE given the generated densities are almost unimodal. The reason for this is that the bandwidth selection performs badly for multimodal densities. In contrast to KDE and RSDE, EM captures the present multimodalities well but suffers from the model selection problem and the quality of the solution varies largely.

3.5.2 Conditional Density Estimation

The procedure for evaluating the quality of the conditional density estimation algorithm differs from the setup for evaluating the density estimation algorithms in that the data is generated differently, the set of estimators and their respective implementation differs as well as the evaluation needs to be performed differently to account for the semantic differences.

Experimental Setup   In the case of density estimation, the space of Gaussian mixture densities was sampled w.r.t. certain restrictions. As conditional density estimation is concerned with the estimation of a probabilistic model possibly derived from a deterministic functional dependency perturbed by a noise term, the space to sample from is the space of dependencies and noise terms. In order to discuss the proposed approach, experiments based on the following exemplary nonlinear system perturbed

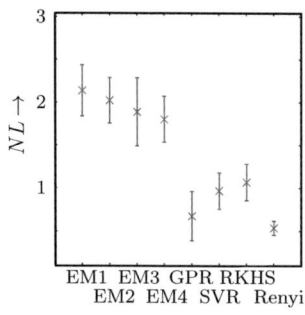
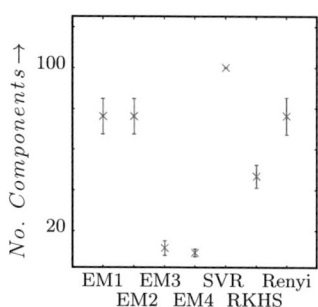

(a) Neg. Log-Likelihood scores. (b) Number of components.

Figure 3.4: Mean and standard deviation of the negative Log-Likelihood scores and number of components achieved by different conditional density estimation algorithms' results for ten Monte Carlo experiments.

by additive Normal noise are presented.

$$y = x + \sin(x^3) + w \ , \qquad w \sim \mathcal{N}(0, 0.15) \, . \tag{3.34}$$

The nonlinear mean function oscillates with varying frequencies. For example, the system is almost linear around $(0,0)$ and oscillates strongly elsewhere. For learning the conditional density function 100 samples are obtained by sampling x uniformly at random for the interval $[-3, 3]$ and y according to normally distributed noise term w.

Evaluation Criteria The quality of the estimates is assessed according to the criteria below:

- The prescriptive validity is quantified only by determining a second set of 100 samples used for testing and calculating the log-likelihood of this test set.

- The number of components is used as a measure of computational efficiency for the conditional density function estimates.

Implementation Details As mentioned before, the set of considered estimators differs from the density estimation case as density estimators are only theoretically applicable to conditional density estimation, cf. Ex. 2.1.

The bandwidth selection rules as presented in Sec. 2.1.2 render an application of KDE or the respective RSDE estimator inadequate. As EM fits the Gaussian mixture component covariances locally, i.e., without reference to an assumed overall density over the input dimensions, EM will yield meaningful results and is therefore included in the comparison as a representative of the subsumption approach to conditional density function estimation.

- EM was employed for the comparison with four settings EM1 - EM4 for both, the estimation of $f(\underline{y}, \underline{x})$ and $f(\underline{x})$. The number of components was either fixed to the number of components obtained from the proposed approach to conditional density estimation (EM1 & EM2) or determined by optimizing the common Akaike Information Criterion (AIC) [129, 53] (EM3 & EM4). In order to improve the generalization properties, a matrix $\mathbf{1} \cdot \epsilon$ was added to $\tilde{\mathbf{C}}$, i.e., the minimal covariance was introduced yielding smoother estimates (EM2 & EM4). The implementation of EM for Gaussian mixture densities by Matlab^{TM} was used for all experiments.

- As the state of the art conditional density function estimator for additive Gaussian noise, the Gaussian Process Regression (GPR) was used. The default parameter settings and hyperparameter optimization was used for all experiments. The GPR implementation from [152] for Matlab^{TM} with default parameter settings was used for the experiments.

- The proposed nonparametric approach was implemented by means of an support-vector regression (SVR) with the l_1-distance between the estimate and the EPDF at the sample points and the RKHS regularizer, as proposed in [107]. Additionally, implementations using the LCD in conjunction with the RKHS or Rényi regularizer were proposed. For the hyperparameter optimization the k-fold cross-validation-based algorithm minimizing the negative log-likelihood, as proposed in Sec. 5 was employed.

Results   The results of ten random experiments based on samples of the system (3.34) w.r.t. the proposed performance measures are reported in Fig. 3.4. These show that the subsumption approach as represented by EM produces overfitting results. This can be seen especially at the turning points of the underlying sine function. GPR produces results with almost ground truth quality. Yet, without any further sparsification a GPR will have a function representation, i.e., the non-parametric mean and covariance functions, containing the entire training data set. The proposed approach yields drastically better generalization results than EM and only slightly worse results than the GPR. The implementation using LCD and the Rényi-entropy based regularizer produces even better results than the GPR. Yet, even though the resulting Gaussian mixture densities are not as sparse as the results of the AIC-based EM, cf. Fig. 3.4 (b), there is a significant reduction in the number of components, i.e., $20\% - 50\%$ less components.

3.6 Main Contributions

The main contributions of this thesis w.r.t. non-parametric density and conditional density estimation are summarized in the following list.

- The proposed weight optimization of densities and conditional densities produces sparse and well-generalizing estimates w.r.t. the state of the art. Given the hyperparameters, the arising optimization problem may be solved efficiently by standard QP solvers.

- A novel entropy-based regularization term was derived, which is more general than the regularization by the norm in the RKHS.

- The introduction of the LCD and the modified l_2-norm, i.e., the mCvMD, removes the fallacies of the default extensions of the standard cumulative distribution functions for density and conditional function estimation.

- Due to its non-parametric nature, the approach is limited due to the assumption of identical parameters for all components and the limitation to $\{\underline{\mu}_i\}_{1 \leq i \leq |\mathcal{D}|} = \mathcal{D}$.

- The arising optimization problem may be solved efficiently as it is a constrained convex quadratic problem. The problem may therefore be solved in polynomial time w.r.t. the number of optimization variables and constraints.

It is easier to perceive error than to find truth,
for the former lies on the surface and is easily seen,
while the latter lies in the depth,
where few are willing to search for it.
—JOHANN WOLFGANG VON GOETHE

4 Full Parameter Identification

In the last section, density and conditional density estimation of sparse Gaussian mixture densities or conditional densities were considered. The proposed approach improved the respective state of the art by offering a good compromise between sparseness and quality. This chapter is concerned with further improvements of the conditional density estimation algorithms.

Challenge The quality of the conditional density estimation algorithms presented in Ch. 3 is limited due to the restriction of the estimates to Gaussian mixture densities with means identical to the data points and identical parameters for all components of the mixture density. The limitation to fixed mean positions prohibits a good approximation of the true conditional density by the mixture density in parts of the state space where little or no data is located. The restriction to identical parameters for all components allows for an efficient implementation of the algorithms, but does not reflect variations in the local data distributions.

Key idea The aim of this chapter is to increase the model's capacity to allow for improved generalization. In the rest of this chapter, an approach for lifting each restriction is presented. The key ideas are the introduction of a curvature-based regularization term allowing for a simultaneous regularization of the mean function and the probabilistic model as well as a local data-driven calculation of the component covariances. As the extension to variable mean positions and variable kernel covariances requires a fundamentally different interpretation for density and conditional density estimation this chapter is limited to conditional density estimation. In the rest of this chapter, approaches for introducing variable means and kernel covariances will be presented and summarized in an algorithm in Sec. 4.3.

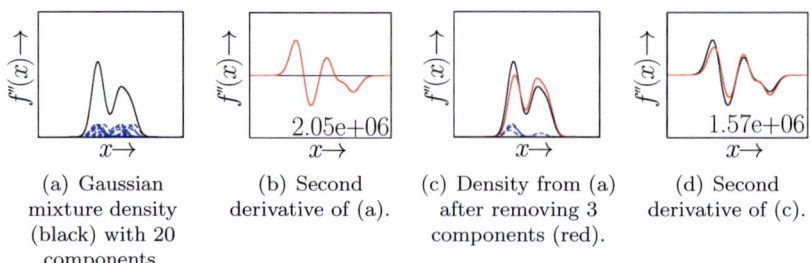

(a) Gaussian mixture density (black) with 20 components.

(b) Second derivative of (a).

(c) Density from (a) after removing 3 components (red).

(d) Second derivative of (c).

Figure 4.1: Effect on the second derivative for a minimal change in the shape: both (a) and (c) are bimodal probability density functions. In (c) three components were removed from (a).

4.1   Variable Mean Positions

The proposed conditional density estimation involves finding the parameters of a Gaussian mixture density[1] and the hyperparameters $\underline{\omega} = [\,\lambda\;\varepsilon\,]^{\mathrm{T}}$ of the optimization problem, i.e.,

$$\underline{\theta} = [\;\underline{\alpha}^{\mathrm{T}}\;,\;\;\underline{\mu}^{\mathrm{T}}\;,\;\;\underline{\Sigma}^{\mathrm{T}}\;,\;\;\underline{\omega}^{\mathrm{T}}\;]^{\mathrm{T}}\,. \tag{4.1}$$

Using Alg. 1 from Ch. 3, $\underline{\alpha}$ may be efficiently determined. The set of mean positions were set to $\{\underline{\mu}\} = \mathcal{D}$, thus $|\{\underline{\mu}\}| = |\mathcal{D}|$, and considered hyperparameters of Alg. 1. Extending the set of mean positions to the entire state space, i.e., $\underline{\mu}_i \in \mathbb{R}^N$, introduces two model selection problems: (a) the number of components, because not necessarily $|\{\underline{\mu}\}| = |\mathcal{D}|$, and (b) the mean locations. One advantage of Alg. 1 is the automatic determination of the number of components by the algorithm itself. This property may be exploited when determining variable means, because redundant components will be removed when using Alg. 1 as an inner loop of a hyperparameter optimization. In principle, it would be possible to add an arbitrary number of variable means to the optimization problem and let Alg. 1 determine the optimal number of components. Because the hyperparameter optimization is a costly nonlinear function minimization, it is advisable to keep the number of variable means low. Additionally, the regularization terms presented in Sec. 3.2 and used in Alg. 1 cannot be used when optimizing mean positions as trivial minimization may be shown, e.g., w.r.t. mean positions for fixed kernel covariances, cf., in Ex. 4.1. In

---

[1]A definition of a Gaussian mixture density is given in (A.30).

the following, a regularizer is proposed, that avoids this fallacy and penalizes conditional density estimates based on the curvature of the density's surface.

Example 4.1: Trivial Minimizer of RKHS-based and Rényi-based Regularization Terms.
Assume the following scalar Gaussian mixture density with two components to be given

$$f(x) = \alpha_1 \, \mathcal{N}(x; \mu_1, \sigma_1) + (1 - \alpha_1) \, \mathcal{N}(x; \mu_2, \sigma_2),$$

with fixed $\underline{\alpha} = [\alpha_1 \ (1 - \alpha_1)]$, $\underline{\alpha}^T \underline{1} = 1$, $\alpha_i \in [0, 1]$, fixed $\sigma_1, \sigma_2 \in \mathbb{R}^+$, $\sigma_1 = \sigma_2$, and $\mu_2 = \mu_1 + \varepsilon$. The Rényi-based regularization term according to Sec. 3.2.2 is

$$\begin{aligned}
\underline{\alpha}^T \mathbf{K} \underline{\alpha} = & \, \alpha_1^2 \, \mathcal{N}(\mu_1; \mu_1, \widehat{\sigma}) + \alpha_1 \alpha_2 \, \mathcal{N}(\mu_1; \mu_1 + \varepsilon, \widehat{\sigma}) \\
& + (1 - \alpha_1)^2 \, \mathcal{N}(\mu_1 + \varepsilon; \mu_1 + \varepsilon, \widehat{\sigma})
\end{aligned} \tag{4.2}$$

$$= \left(\alpha_1^2 + (1 - \alpha_1)^2\right) \, \sqrt{(2\pi)}\widehat{\sigma} + \alpha_1(1 - \alpha_1) \mathcal{N}(\mu_1; \mu_1 + \varepsilon, \widehat{\sigma}), \tag{4.3}$$

with fixed $\widehat{\sigma} \in \mathbb{R}^+$. From (4.3) it follows that

$$\max \varepsilon \equiv \arg \min_{\varepsilon} \ \underline{\alpha}^T \mathbf{K} \underline{\alpha}, \tag{4.4}$$

holds, thus minimizing the regularizer means maximizing the distance between both components. The same argument holds for the regularization in terms of the norm in RKHS. ∎

4.1.1 Superficial Regularization

The aim of introducing variable means for the components in the target function of Alg. 1 is to improve the generalization in parts of the state space where little or no data is located. If only the mean function of the generative model shall be recovered from the data, determining function values of the mean function at positions, where no data is located corresponds to a classical regression. This problem may be solved with any (non-)parametric regression algorithm, cf. [73]. These algorithms have a justification in their own right, but since in conditional density estimation, not the mean function of the generative model, but the probabilistic model is required, they may not be employed.

Key Idea   The key idea is to extend the smoothness assumptions underlying the (non-)parametric regression algorithm for the mean function to the surface of the conditional density. By assessing the quality merely of the conditional density surface, there is no need for an underlying generative model and the conditional density function representation may be arbitrary. The measure of roughness which is implicitly minimized by a regression method, e.g., splines [77] or smoothing splines [73], is the curvature. The curvature $K(\cdot)$ of a curve $g : \mathbb{R} \to \mathbb{R}$ in the plane for a point $p \in \mathbb{R}$ is defined by

$$K\left(g(p) \right) = \frac{\frac{\partial^2 g(p)}{\partial^2 p}}{\left(1 + \left(\frac{\partial g(p)}{\partial p}\right)^2\right)^{\frac{3}{2}}}. \qquad (4.5)$$

As only the cumulated strength of the curvature at this point and not the direction of the curvature is of interest, the squared or absolute value of (4.5) is considered

$$K^2\left(g(p) \right) = \frac{\left(\frac{\partial^2 g(p)}{\partial^2 p}\right)^2}{\left(1 + \left(\frac{\partial g(p)}{\partial p}\right)^2\right)^3} \leq \left(\frac{\partial^2 g(p)}{\partial^2 p}\right)^2, \qquad (4.6)$$

and bounded from above by neglecting the denominator of (4.5) in (4.6). For the overall curve,

$$K^2(g) = \int_{\mathbb{R}} K^2\left(g(p) \right) \, \mathrm{d}p \leq \int_{\mathbb{R}} \left(\frac{\partial^2 g(p)}{\partial^2 p}\right)^2 \, \mathrm{d}p, \qquad (4.7)$$

is an upper bound of the curvature. Regression methods, e.g., smoothing splines, minimize a target function consisting of a data fit term and (4.7), cf. [73, p. 151]. As a result smooth, minimally oscillating functions are obtained. The sensitivity of the second derivative as an element of the upper bound on the curvature (4.7) to the smoothness of the surface is visualized in Fig. 4.1. In Fig. 4.1, the difference in the second derivative of two scalar bimodal GMM is depicted before and after removing a number of components. Regarding conditional density functions, it is intuitive that for additive Gaussian noise, smooth, minimally oscillating mean functions correspond to smooth, minimally oscillating conditional density function surfaces. Lifting the curvature-based regularization from the mean function to the function's surface corresponds to using a regularization term measuring the curvature of this surface. In the remaining part of this section, a regularization term for 2D surfaces will be derived and discussed.

4.1.2 Superficial Regularizations for 2D Conditional Density Functions

A 2D conditional density function in this section denotes a function f : $\mathbb{R} \times \mathbb{R} \rightarrow [0, 1]$ with scalar in- and output dimension. The surface of f is a 2D surface in a 3D space. In contrast to the point-wise curvature of a line, the curvature of a surface is not uniquely defined [31]. The canonical curvature definitions arise from different combinations of the curvatures of plane curves defined by the intersection of the surface with two normal planes at a given point $p = (x, y) \in \mathbb{R}^2$. The mean curvature averages and the Gaussian curvature multiplies the minimal and the maximal curvature [31]. For the sake of brevity, some abbreviations are introduced, e.g., the considered Gaussian mixture function may be written as vector product

$$f(y|x) = \sum_{i=1}^{L} \alpha_i \, \mathcal{N}(y; \mu_{y,i}, \sigma_{y,i}) \, \mathcal{N}(x; \mu_{x,i}, \sigma_{x,i}) = \underline{\alpha}^{\mathrm{T}} \underline{f}(y, x) \,, \qquad (4.8)$$

with weights $\underline{\alpha} = [\alpha_1 \ldots \alpha_L]^{\mathrm{T}}$, $\alpha_i \in \mathbb{R}^+$ and the vector of normal components $\underline{f}(y, x)$ in (4.8)

$$\underline{f}(y, x) = [\, f^1(y, x) \ldots f^L(y, x)\,]^{\mathrm{T}} \,, \qquad (4.9)$$

where each component is defined by

$$f^i(y, x) = \mathcal{N}(y; \mu_{y,i}, \sigma_{y,i}) \, \mathcal{N}(x; \mu_{x,i}, \sigma_{x,i}) \,.$$

For the calculation of the curvature, partial derivatives of (4.9) need to be calculated w.r.t. a point p, i.e., a pair of input and output values

$$\frac{\partial}{\partial m} f(y|x) = f_m(y|x) \,, \qquad \frac{\partial}{\partial m} \underline{f}(y, x) = [f_m^1(y|x) \ldots f_m^L(y, x)]^{\mathrm{T}} \,,$$
$$f(y|x) \equiv f(\underline{p}) \,. \qquad (4.10)$$

Using these definitions, the signed Gaussian curvature for a point $\underline{p}$ is given by

$$K_G(\underline{p}) = \frac{f_{xx}(\underline{p}) \, f_{yy}(\underline{p}) - f_{xy}^2(\underline{p})}{\left(1 + f_x^2(\underline{p}) + f_y^2(\underline{p})\right)} \,.$$

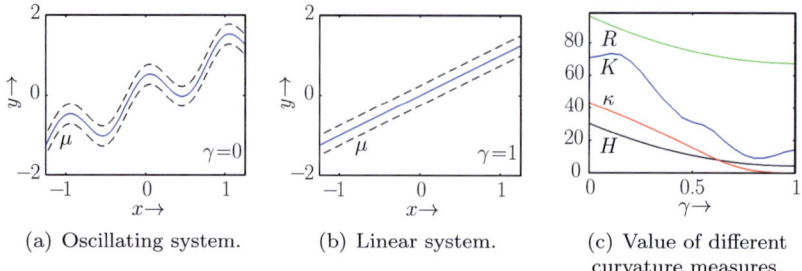

(a) Oscillating system. (b) Linear system. (c) Value of different curvature measures.

Figure 4.2: Relationship of the curvature of the mean function and probabilistic model w.r.t. different measures is exemplified by evaluating the curvature measures for an oscillating system (a) progressing towards a linear system (b). The values of the numerically calculated integral squared curvature measures for varying progression parameters γ (red) are depicted in (c), i.e., Gaussian curvature K (blue), mean curvature H (black), the superficial regularizer's value R (scaled, green), and curvature of the generative model κ. Graphics taken from [109].

The pointwise squared Gaussian curvature is upper bound by neglecting the denominator

$$K_G^2(\underline{p}) \leq \left[\, f_{xx}(\underline{p})\, f_{yy}(\underline{p}) - f_{xy}^2(\underline{p})\,\right]^2 ,$$

and for the overall surface of f the upper bound of the Gaussian curvature is given by

$$K_G^2(f) = \int_{\mathbb{R}^N} K_G^2(\underline{p})\, \mathrm{d}\underline{p} \leq \int_{\mathbb{R}^N} \left[\, f_{xx}(\underline{p})\, f_{yy}(\underline{p})\,\right]^2 \mathrm{d}\underline{p}. \tag{4.11}$$

In order to incorporate the regularizer into Alg. 1, $K_G^2(f)$ needs to be minimized w.r.t. the weights with all other parameters fixed. The following regularizer w.r.t. the weights is proposed.

Definition 4.1 (Scalar Superficial Regularizer, [109]) *For a conditional density $f(y|x)$ with scalar in- and output $x, y \in \mathbb{R}$, given in the form of (4.8) with*

$$\underline{f}(x,y) = \begin{bmatrix} \mathcal{N}(y; \mu_{y,1}, \sigma_{y,1}) & \cdot & \mathcal{N}(x; \mu_{x,1}, \sigma_{x,1}) \\ & \vdots & \\ \mathcal{N}(y; \mu_{y,L}, \sigma_{y,L}) & \cdot & \mathcal{N}(x; \mu_{x,L}, \sigma_{x,L}) \end{bmatrix},$$

the superficial regularizer R is defined w.r.t. the weights $\underline{\alpha}$ as

$$R := c\,\underline{\alpha}^{\mathrm{T}}\,\mathbf{R}\,\underline{\alpha}\,, \tag{4.12}$$

with c constant w.r.t. the weights $\underline{\alpha}$. The entries of the matrix R are calculated by

$$\mathbf{R}_{ij} = \sum_{k=1}^{L} \int_{\mathbb{R}^2} f_{xx}^{(i,k)}(\underline{p})\, f_{yy}^{(i,k)}(\underline{p})\, f_{xx}^{(k,j)}(\underline{p})\, f_{yy}^{(k,j)}(\underline{p)}\ d\underline{p}\,,$$

with

$$f_m^{(i,k)}(\underline{p}) =$$
$$\frac{\partial}{\partial m}\mathcal{N}(x;\mu_{x,i},\sigma_{x,i})\cdot\mathcal{N}(y;\mu_{y,i},\sigma_{y,i})\cdot\mathcal{N}(x;\mu_{x,k},\sigma_{x,k})\cdot\mathcal{N}(y;\mu_{y,k},\sigma_{y,k})\,.$$

For the purpose of this thesis, the constant c in the quadratic form (4.12) is neglected. The most important properties of (4.12) are given in the following theorem.

Theorem 4.1 (Properties of the scalar Superficial Regularizer, [109]) The superficial regularizer, introduced in Def. 4.1, has the following properties:

1. R is an approximation of an upper bound of $K_G^2(f)$, as defined in (4.7).

2. For a generative model perturbed by zero-mean Gaussian additive noise, the superficial regularizer of the probabilistic model is a linear transform of an upper bound of the squared curvature of the generative model.

The proofs for Theorem 4.1 are given in Appendix A.4.2. The key idea behind the proof of the first property is a series of approximation of the squared curvature of the entire surface of the scalar conditional density function f. For the second property, a point-wise upper bound on the curvature of the generative model is extended to the entire surface. In analogy to Sec. 3.4, the definiteness properties of the superficial regularization matrix $\mathbf{R}$ can be shown by an application of Lemma A.2. Based on (4.12), it is shown in Appendix A.2, that $\mathbf{R}$ is obtained from dyadic product and thus, $\mathbf{R}$ is p.s.d. When using the same distance matrix as in

Sec. 3.1, the same properties of the solution w.r.t. uniqueness and attainment of a solution as well as the computational efficiency of the solution algorithm as for the conditional density estimation algorithm in Sec. 4.12 hold. The application of the regularization term will be shown in Alg. 4.3.

4.1.3   Properties and Restrictions

The properties and restrictions of the superficial regularization may be summarized as follows:

- The insight given by Theorem 4.1 is that the regularization with the term proposed in Def. 4.1 regularizes an approximate upper bound of the curvature of the generative model's mean function and the conditional density function's surface simultaneously. The generalization properties of a regularized mean function can therefore be achieved by regularizing the surface only. This relation is visualized in Fig. 4.2, where a system progressing from an oscillating to a linear mean function is shown. The values of the upper bound on the curvature for the probabilistic model and other numerically calculated integral squared curvature measures are depicted.

- Theorem 4.1 needs to be put into perspective with the underlying assumptions. These assumptions include that the noise disturbance needs to be additive and that the approximation quality needs to be high, which corresponds to a high number of components in the resulting conditional density.

- Another restriction is that the superficial regularizer does not distinguish between in- and output dimensions, requiring additional regularization of the probability mass distribution over the input dimension.

- The regularization term in Def. 4.1 is defined for scalar in- and output dimensions only. This definition needs to be extended to include the higher-dimensional cases.

4.2   Variable Kernel Covariances

In this section, the limitation to identical kernel covariances as used in Ch. 3 is removed to improve the capacity of the model and allow for a modeling of the model uncertainty due to a locally varying distribution of the data used for the conditional density estimation.

4.2.1 Related Work

The idea of adapting the covariances of the kernel functions corresponding to probability density functions has found wide-spread use in kernel density estimation [25, 158, 179]. For the remaining part of this section, the terms (locally) adaptive [158, 179] or variable kernel parameters [25] are used synonymously as in kernel density estimation. The first approach towards alleviating the shortcomings of using a common kernel covariance as described in Sec. 3.4 was given in [25]. The key idea is to scale the width of each kernel with the l_2-distance $h_i := l_2(\underline{x}^{k,i} - \underline{x}_i)$ of this kernel's mean $\underline{x}_i$ to its k-th nearest neighboring sample $\underline{x}^{k,i}$

$$f(\underline{x}) = \sum_{i=1}^{|\mathcal{D}|} \frac{1}{|\mathcal{D}| \, h_i^{\mathrm{N}}} \, \mathcal{K}(\underline{x}; \underline{x}_i, h_i) \,,$$

similar to the k-th nearest neighbor density estimator [122]. This choice is known to be asymptotically equivalent to scaling with the likelihood of the data point $\underline{x}_i$ [179, 187], i.e.,

$$h_i = f(\underline{x}_i)^{-1/\mathrm{N}} \,. \tag{4.13}$$

As a result, the kernel width will be small in areas densly populated by samples and will be large in low density areas. This may be understood as modeling the model uncertainty as more change in the density function's shape is allowed in areas with a high density of samples. Since [25], a lot of research has been pursued leading to a categorization of variable kernel approaches into sample-based and balloon estimators [158, 187]. The sample-based estimators extend to the idea of [25], whereas the balloon estimators scale the kernel covariance relative to the evaluation point and not to the component's mean. Variable kernel density estimation is still an active research field, e.g., in computer vision, where incremental and online estimation algorithms are investigated [28, 110, 131]. In the remaining part of this section, the sample-based covariance estimator presented in [28] is extended for the application to conditional density estimation.

4.2.2   Key Idea

The key idea of determining the variable kernel covariances is to calculate the kernel covariances relative to the local data density. This implies a decomposition w.r.t. the in- and output dimensions of $\boldsymbol{\Sigma}_i$ into independent matrices $\boldsymbol{\Sigma}_{i,x} \in \mathbb{R}^{N \times N}$ and $\boldsymbol{\Sigma}_{i,y} \in \mathbb{R}^{M \times M}$, i.e.,

$$\boldsymbol{\Sigma}_i = \left[\begin{array}{cc} \boldsymbol{\Sigma}_{i,y} & \mathbf{0} \\ \mathbf{0} & \boldsymbol{\Sigma}_{i,x} \end{array} \right] .$$

The submatrices have different semantics and are calculated separately. In principle both $\boldsymbol{\Sigma}_{i,y}$ and $\boldsymbol{\Sigma}_{i,x}$ might be estimated for each component independently. In this thesis, the idea of the scalable kernel is adopted [25], as this approach reduces the computational effort to the optimization of two submatrices only and the calculation of the scale parameter, i.e.,

$$\boldsymbol{\Sigma}_i = \phi_i \left[\begin{array}{cc} \boldsymbol{\Sigma}_y^{\mathcal{D}} & \mathbf{0} \\ \mathbf{0} & \boldsymbol{\Sigma}_x^{\mathcal{D}} \end{array} \right] + \mathbf{I}\,\varepsilon , \qquad (4.14)$$

where ϕ_i captures the local data density and the submatrices $\boldsymbol{\Sigma}_y$ and $\boldsymbol{\Sigma}_x$ may be understood as a basis kernel capturing the average covariance w.r.t. the input and output dimensions. The last term in (4.14) adds a tiny value ε to $\boldsymbol{\Sigma}_y$ and $\boldsymbol{\Sigma}_x$, in order to avoid singular covariances. There exist many ways for estimating the basis kernels $\boldsymbol{\Sigma}_y$ and $\boldsymbol{\Sigma}_x$. Some of which are considered in the section about initial values in Ch. 5. Note that $\boldsymbol{\Sigma}_y$ and $\boldsymbol{\Sigma}_x$ may be used without any further optimization too. This approach is the default procedure used in KDE [179]. If on the other hand, e.g., the variance in the sample covariance for any of the directions is too high, the above estimates may serve as an initial value for an optimization, e.g., w.r.t. cross-validated log-likelihood scores as proposed in Ch. 5. The submatrices $\boldsymbol{\Sigma}_y$ and $\boldsymbol{\Sigma}_x$ are scaled relative to $\mathcal{K}$ of k-nearest neighboring samples to the respective $\underline{\mu}_i$

$$\phi_i = g\left(\; \{\, l_2(\, [\underline{x}_k\ \underline{y}_k]^{\mathrm{T}}, \underline{\mu}_i \,) \,\}_{k \in \mathcal{K}} \; \right) .$$

The function $g : \mathbb{R}^{N+M} \mapsto \mathbb{R}$ may be, e.g., the average or maximal distance to each sample in the k-neighborhood. Combining all elements gives rise to the data-dependent adaptive kernel covariance $\boldsymbol{\Sigma}_i$ for each component of the Gaussian mixture density. The sections about variable mean positions and kernel covariances are summarized in an algorithm in the following section.

4.2.3   Properties and Restrictions

The two main properties and restrictions of the variable kernel covariances are listed below.

- The presented approach is an extension of existing variable kernel approaches for density estimation to conditional density estimation. The variable kernel covariances removes the restriction to identical parameters for all components and allows for reflecting variations in the local data distributions.

- Without further assumptions, the number of variables of the optimization problem depends on the dimensionality of the considered spaces due to the variable kernel covariances.

4.3   Algorithm

In this section, the nested optimization scheme for optimizing all parameters of a Gaussian mixture is stated based on the preceding sections. The proposed optimization scheme is composed of an outer and inner loop: the inner loop optimizes the weights and the outer loop optimizes the means, covariances of the Gaussian mixture density as well as hyperparameters $\underline{\omega}$

$$\underline{\theta} = [\quad \underbrace{\underline{\alpha}^{\mathrm{T}}}_{\text{Inner loop}} \quad , \quad \underbrace{\underline{\mu}^{\mathrm{T}}, \Sigma^{\mathrm{T}}}_{\text{Outer loop}} , \quad \underbrace{\underline{\omega}}_{\substack{\text{Hyperparameter} \\ \text{Optimization}}} \quad]^{\mathrm{T}} . \tag{4.15}$$

Outer Loop   The outer loop comprises of the determination of the adaptive kernel covariances for each component, the solution of the inner loop, and the update of the components' means based on the function value of the inner loops target function. The adaptive kernel covariances are determined as described in Sec. 4.2 for the given components' mean position. Having determined each component's mean and covariance as well as the hyperparameters, the inner loop, i.e., the weight optimization, may be performed. The target function value ν is minimized using a default function minimization algorithm w.r.t. $\underline{\mu}$. The adaptive kernel covariances are determined separately and analytically, without any further optimization. In order to determine the hyperparameters $\underline{\omega}$, e.g., cross-validation–based methods as proposed in Sec. 5 may be used.

Inner Loop The inner loop of the optimization scheme consists of composing and solving a convex quadratic program, similar to Alg. 1 for conditional density estimation. The major difference from this inner loop to Alg. 1 is the calculation of the regularization and the distance terms. The distance measure needs to be calculated w.r.t. a Gaussian mixture density with non-identical covariance matrices. As a regularization term, the superficial regularization term presented in Sec. 4.1.1 needs to be calculated. Additionally, the regularization term and the distance measure term need to be combined to form the target function of a convex quadratic program. The constraints of the arising quadratic program are identical to Alg. 1 as the conditions for a GMM to be estimated do not differ from Alg. 1.

Start Values The above algorithm corresponds to the solution of a nonlinear and non-convex optimization problem. It is advisable to carefully choose the start values for the optimization.

- As described in Sec. 4.1, the number of mean positions will be automatically reduced by the QP of the inner loop of the overall optimization scheme. Due to the complexity of the optimization scheme, an iterative test is proposed whether additional components improve the solution. Otherwise a heuristic needs to be adopted, e.g., sampling from the largest adaptive covariances for $\{\underline{\mu}\} = \mathcal{D}$, until a threshold, e.g., on the determinant of the covariances, is reached.

- In order to reduce the computational effort, the variable means may be set to $\{\underline{\mu}\} = \mathcal{D} \cup \mathcal{V}$, so that only the additional set $\mathcal{V}$ needs to be determined, by, e.g., an adaptive kernel covariance based sampling scheme.

- Fundamental to the further optimization is the determination ε and the size of neighborhood k employed for calculation of the variable kernel covariances in each optimization step. These parameters may be determined a priori and their calculation corresponds to a model selection problem, which may be solved as described in Sec. 5. The other hyperparameters may be determined as proposed for Alg. 1 and shown in Ch. 5.

4.3.1 Efficient Implementation

The computational complexity of the proposed algorithm depends on the number of optimization variables and constraints in the outer and inner loop. In order to obtain an efficient implementation, an approach to reduce the computational burden is proposed for each loop.

- In the outer loop, for m means $\underline{\mu}_i \in \mathbb{R}^N$, an $(m \cdot N)$-dimensional optimization problem arises. As proposed for the start values, setting $\{\underline{\mu}\} = \mathcal{D} \cup \mathcal{V}$ lends itself to the reduction to a $(|\mathcal{V}| \cdot N)$-dimensional optimization problem, with $|\mathcal{V}| \ll m$, if the means of the components located at $\mathcal{D}$ are not optimized. Because a 20-dimensional optimization problem arises for ten components with means in $\mathbb{R}^2$, an iterative optimization scheme is proposed, where the means are iteratively optimized one after the other until convergence.

- A similar scheme may be pursued for the optimization of the weights $\underline{\alpha}$ in the inner loop. All but a small "chunk" of variables $\underline{\alpha}_v$ is considered constant $\underline{\alpha}_c$, i.e., $\underline{\alpha} = [\underline{\alpha}_v^T \ \underline{\alpha}_c^T]^T$. The target function of the QP (3.32) then allows for a decomposition into a smaller problem

$$
\underline{\alpha}^T \mathbf{Q} \, \underline{\alpha} - 2\underline{\alpha}^T \underline{q} = \underline{\alpha}^T \begin{bmatrix} \mathbf{Q}_{vv} & \mathbf{Q}_{vc} \\ \mathbf{Q}_{cv} & \mathbf{Q}_{cc} \end{bmatrix} \underline{\alpha} - 2\underline{\alpha}^T \begin{bmatrix} \underline{q}_v \\ \underline{q}_c \end{bmatrix}
$$
$$
= \underline{\alpha}_v^T \mathbf{Q}_{vv} \, \underline{\alpha}_v + \underline{\alpha}_v^T \left[2\mathbf{Q}_{vc} \underline{\alpha}_c - 2\underline{q}_v \right] + c, \quad (4.16)
$$

with a scalar term combining all summands independent of $\underline{\alpha}_v$. The constraints of the QP may be reformulated analogously. The QP in (4.16) has only length$(\underline{\alpha}_v) \ll$ length$(\underline{\alpha})$ optimization variables, but will require the iterated solution of chunks containing all $\underline{\alpha}$ until convergence to obtain a solution. For this approach no optimality or convergence have been proven up to now. This approach is equivalent to the "chunking" method for a fast solution of the QPs arising in large SVMs [138, 164].

4.3.2 Properties and Restrictions

In the following, the properties of the proposed conditional density estimation are discussed.

- The proposed method of optimizing the variable mean positions required the introduction of a novel superficial regularizer to avoid a trivial minimization of the regularization term. The superficial regularizer was proposed for two-dimensional problems and shown to be related to an upper bound on the curvature of the generative model

---

Algorithm 2 Nested Conditional Density Estimation Algorithm.

1: **Input:** $\mathcal{D}$, $\underline{\omega}$

2: Calculate $\underline{\theta}_{k=0}$ ▷ Initial Values

3: **repeat**   ▷ Outer Loop

4:     $(\underline{\alpha}_k, \nu_k) \leftarrow$ OPTIMIZEWEIGHTS$(\mathcal{D}, \underline{\mu}_k, \underline{\Sigma}_k, \underline{\omega})$

5:     $\underline{\mu}_{k+1} \leftarrow$ UPDATE$(\underline{\mu}_k, \underline{\omega})$ ▷ Update variable means

6:     Calculate $\underline{\Sigma}_{k+1}$ from $\mathcal{D}$ ▷ Update variable covariances

7: **until** $\Delta(\nu_{k-1}, \nu_k) < \varepsilon$

8: **function** OPTIMIZEWEIGHTS$(\mathcal{D}, \underline{\mu}_k, \underline{\Sigma}_k, \underline{\omega})$ ▷ Inner Loop

9:     $\underline{\theta} \leftarrow \underline{\alpha}, \underline{\mu}_k, \underline{\Sigma}_{k+1}$

10:     Calculate $D(\mathcal{D}, \underline{\theta})$ and $R(\underline{\theta})$ ▷ E.g. (4.12)

11:     Calculate constraints

12:     Compose and solve QP

13:     **return** Weights $\underline{\alpha}_k$, value of ν_k

14: **end function**

15: **Output:** $f \sim$ GMM $\{\underline{\alpha}_k, \underline{\mu}_k, \underline{\Sigma}_k\}$

---

disturbed by additive Gaussian noise. Minimizing the superficial regularizer may thus be understood as minimizing an approximate upper bound on a common measure of curvature for the mean function of the generative model. Using the superficial regularizer the deficient approximation of the approaches in Ch. 3, where data is distributed scarcely was overcome and the generalization performance may be improved.

- The extension of the existing variable kernel approach used in density estimation to variable kernel covariances for conditional density estimation allows for a representation of the model uncertainty. The local data density scales the kernel covariance, so that in areas with plenty of data more peaked conditional densities are allowed, whereas for low density parts of the state space large, i.e., more conservative covariance extensions reflect the model uncertainty.

- A caveat is the computational complexity of the given approach as discussed in Sec. 4.3.1. A naive implementation of the proposed

Table 4.1: Average neg. log-likelihood scores
and component numbers for Exp. 4.4.1.

	EM1	EM2	GPR	Rényi	SF	SF+XV
NL	14.7577	25.4307	0.79627	0.83297	0.72647	0.56547
$\pm \sigma$	± 5.7847	± 9.6808	± 0.062536	± 0.62414	± 0.1773	± 0.11966
# Comp.	67.3	67.3	N/A	66.1	67.3	66.5

overall optimization problem, i.e., a simultaneous optimization of all
means' positions yields an optimization problem with a number of
optimization variables scaling with the number of the variable kernel
means and the dimensionality of the estimation problem. The proposed efficient implementation alleviates this problem, but is greedy,
order-dependent, and not guaranteed to converge. The same statement holds for the proposed "chunking" method. It should be noted
that chunking is one of the most common methods for solving the
QPs arising in SVMs.

Alg. 2 summarizes this chapter by combining the implementation of the
outer and inner loop of the nested optimization scheme into one algorithm.
This algorithm takes only the data as input and returns the estimated
conditional density in the form of a Gaussian mixture density.

4.4 Experimental Validation

The experimental validation resembles the evaluation setup in Sec. 3.5.2 for
non-parametric conditional density estimation presented in the preceding
chapter. For the evaluation, the identical system is employed, but in order
to test the generalization capabilities an artificial "gap" was created by
not sampling a part of the system. Additionally, the application of the
presented approach to nonlinear filtering is investigated for the benchmark
Kitagawa growth process [42, 93]. In the following, the experimental setup
as deviating from Sec. 3.5.2 is presented.

4.4.1 Conditional Density Estimation

In the following, the experimental setup, evaluation criteria, implementation details, and results for conditional density estimation are presented.

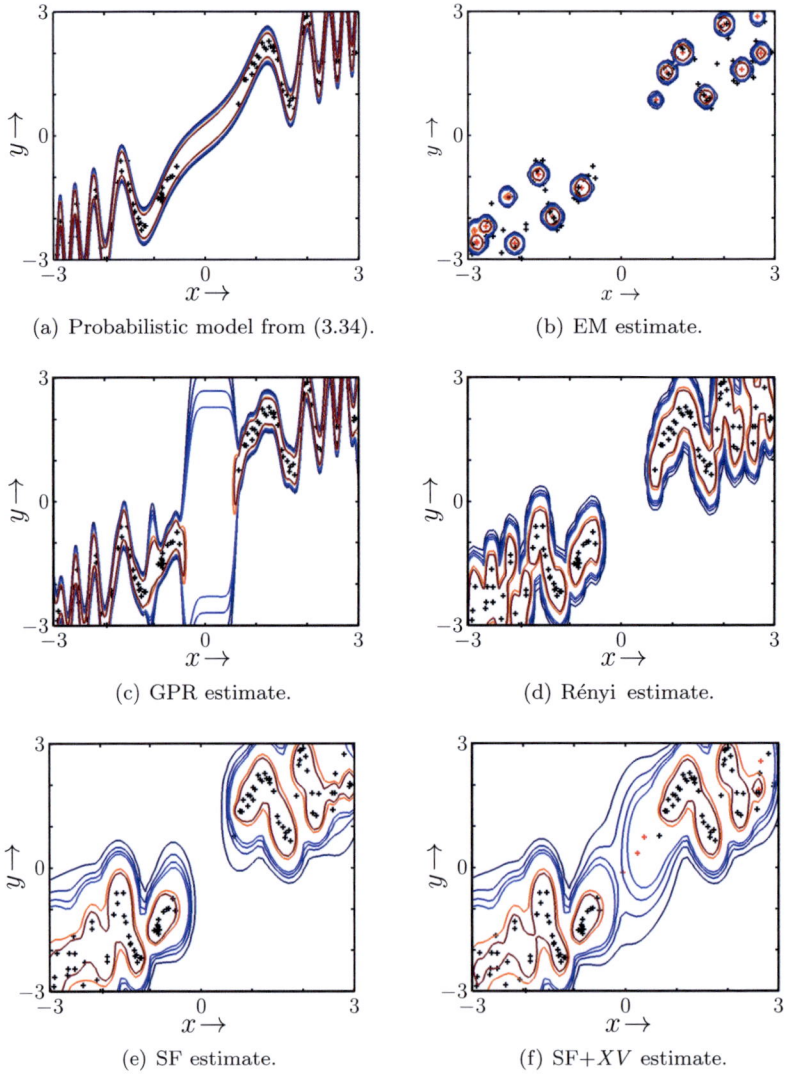

(a) Probabilistic model from (3.34).

(b) EM estimate.

(c) GPR estimate.

(d) Rényi estimate.

(e) SF estimate.

(f) SF+XV estimate.

Figure 4.3: Plots of the $[0.025, 0.05, 0.075, 0.1, 0.35, 0.45]$ probability contours (a) of the true underlying probabilistic model and (b)-(f) exemplary unnormalized estimates for the experiment in Sec. 4.4.1. Crosses mark samples (black) and component variable means (red). The results are based on [109].

Experimental Setup   For the evaluation of the conditional density estimation, a probabilistic model derived from the following exemplary nonlinear functional dependency perturbed by a noise term is sampled. This system is identical to the system in Sec. 3.5.2

$$y = x + \sin(x^3) + w \ , \qquad\qquad w \sim \mathcal{N}(0, 0.15) \,. \qquad (4.17)$$

The conditional density estimators are given 100 samples as input, which are obtained by sampling x uniformly at random for the intervals $[-3, -0.5]$ and $[0.5, 3]$ as well as the corresponding y according to the normally-distributed noise term w. The generalization performance of the estimators is investigated for the not sampled interval $[-0.5, 0.5]$.

Evaluation Criteria   The quality of the estimates is assessed according to the criteria below:

- The prescriptive validity is quantified by determining a second set of samples from $[-1, 1]$, i.e., half of the sampling interval overlaps with the sampling interval of the training samples and the rest is sampled in an interval for which the estimators are not given any data. For testing, the negative log-likelihood of this test set is calculated

- The computational efficiency of the conditional density function estimates is quantified by the number of components in the estimate. This differs from Sec. 3.5.2 as for the proposed full-parameter optimization some means are freely placeable and the inner loop of the optimization will remove components irrelevant of their positioning.

Implementation Details   The estimators used for this comparison are identical to the set of estimators considered in Sec. 3.5.2, i.e., different variants of EM (EM1-2), the standard GPR and the non-parametric approach with LCD distance measure and Rényi regularizer. Regarding the approach proposed in this chapter, two parameter sets were considered. In order to show the benefit in optimizing the variable means, the proposed regularizer and variable covariances were used with the constraint of fixing all components' means to $\mathcal{D}$ (SF) and adding five variable means to this set as well as optimizing these (SF+XV). Except for this difference, the employed parameters are identical, i.e., the size of the considered neighborhood for the variable covariance was $k = 10$, $\varepsilon = 0.02$, the $b_{\max}$ value for the LCD was set to ten times the largest distance between two

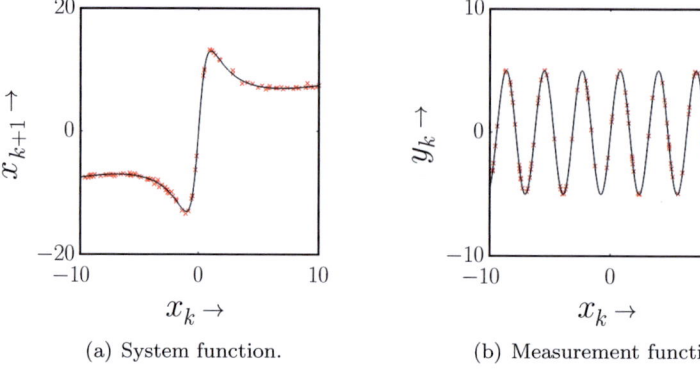

(a) System function.   (b) Measurement function.

Figure 4.4: System (a) and measurement function (b) of the Kitagawa growth process [93] used in Exp. 4.4.2.

sample points, an initial $\sigma_x = 0.05$ as well as the trade-off parameter was set to $\lambda = 0.5$. For determining the variable means' initial positions a greedy splitting procedure was adopted. The largest variable covariance was determined and the variable mean was located half-way between the component's mean and the nearest neighboring sample. This step was repeated for all variable means.

Results The results w.r.t. the prescriptive validity are given in Tab. 4.1 and show that EM produces drastically worse conditional density estimates than all other approaches. The reason for this can be seen in Fig. 4.3 (b). EM appears to overfit the estimate at the turning points of the oscillating function, where clusters of data points are located. Thus, no continuous function is recovered and the estimate deviates strongly from the true underlying system Fig. 4.3 (a). The quality of GPR, the non-parametric Rényi approach, and full parametric SF approach yield comparable results with no significant advantage for either of the estimators, cf. Tab. 4.1. This resembles the results from Sec. 3.5.2 and shows that the superficial regularizer allows for the same level of generalization as the Rényi regularizer. GPR produces results of similar quality. Yet, the variance of the results shows that the GPR produces high quality results more consistently. The overall best results are obtained from SF+XV. These results improve on SF and have a variance in the estimation, which is second only to the GPR. Note, that only SF+XV and GPR are capable

Table 4.2: Negative log-likelihood scores for the growth process [93]. The results are averages over ten experiments.

	$\mathbf{NL}^{0.25}$	$\pm\sigma$	$\mathbf{NL}^{0.5}$	$\pm\sigma$	$\mathbf{NL}^{0.75}$	$\pm\sigma$
EKF	921.7	± 168.7	$2.9e+04$	± 1585.9	$2.7e+05$	± 4036.5
UKF	60.8	± 1.9	628.4	± 31.0	2399.8	± 63.4
GP-UKF	62.7	± 4.9	429.3	± 54.2	1717.1	± 95.5
GP-ADF	59.3	± 3.1	283.6	± 23.4	1066.8	± 42.8
GMF-SF	55.9	± 3.5	246.5	± 57.1	775.6	± 296.8
GMF-SF+XV	53.8	± 1.8	187.2	± 19.4	489.5	± 77.6

of interpolating the underlying functional dependency at intervals, where no data is located, cf. Fig. 4.3 (b)-(d). Regarding the computational efficiency, the GPR will have a function representation entailing all samples if not further sparsification is performed. In contrast, the other approaches produce GMM with ca. 30-40 % less components. The results presented in this section are based on [109].

4.4.2 Nonlinear Filtering Application

As the conditional density estimation algorithm proposed in this chapter will be used for nonlinear filtering, results for a nonlinear Gaussian filtering benchmark application and an experiment for filtering with multimodal posterior densities are presented.

(a) Kitagawa growth process

The benchmark problem considered is the Kitagawa growth process [93], which has been used for comparing especially $\mathcal{GP}$-based filters, e.g., in [42, 107, 109].

Experimental Setup The process comprises the following nonlinear system model

$$x_{k+1} = 0.5\,x_k + \frac{25\,x_k}{1+x_k^2} + w_k\,, \tag{4.18}$$

and the nonlinear sinusoidal measurement model

$$\boldsymbol{y}_k = 5\,\sin(2\,\boldsymbol{x}_k) + \boldsymbol{v}_k\,. \tag{4.19}$$

Identical to [42], the stationary process noise is set to $\boldsymbol{w}_k \sim \mathcal{N}(w, 0.2)$ and $\boldsymbol{v}_k \sim \mathcal{N}(v_k, 0.01)$.

Evaluation Criteria   For the evaluation, a second data set was generated. Given a fixed prior normal density $f(x_0)$, the successive state distribution $f(x_1)$ was calculated and a measurement $\hat{y}_1$ sampled. This generation process was performed for 200 prior normal distributions with equidistantly sampled mean $\mu_0 \in [-10, 10]$, but fixed noise $\sigma_0 = 0.5$. In order to assess the quality of the results two criteria are employed.

- The distribution of the negative log-likelihood score (NL) of the true state for the estimated $f(x_1)$ is given in three quartiles. The NL shows how well the true state is explained by the estimates.

- The Mahalanobis distance $\mathcal{M}(x)$ [125] between the true and the estimated state is given as a measure of the estimate's uncertainty, i.e., estimates close to the true state will be considered far away, if the uncertainty about the state is high.

In summary, lower values indicate better performance for both scores.

Implementation Details   For the comparison, the Extended Kalman Filter (EKF), Unscented Kalman Filter (UKF), the GP-based UKF, i.e., the GP-UKF, and the GP-based analytic moment based filter (GP-ADF) were used as state of the art nonlinear filters. The EKF, UKF, GP-UKF and GP-ADF implementations of [42] were used with default parameter settings. For testing, the quality of the proposed conditional density estimates for nonlinear filtering, a Gaussian mixture filter was employed. In this filter the system and measurement model are GMM. The implementation from [107] was used. Similar to Sec. 4.4.1 the system model was trained with SF and SF+XV and the measurement model was trained with SF only.

Results   The numerical results for both benchmark nonlinear Gaussian filtering experiment in Tab. 4.2 and Tab. 4.3 show that the proposed GMM filter based on the estimated GMM yields results better than EKF, UKF,

Table 4.3: Mahalanobis distance results for the growth process [93].

	$\mathcal{M}(\mathbf{x})$	$\pm\sigma$
EKF	$2.1e + 06$	$\pm 3.0e + 06$
UKF	1025.6	± 4499.2
GP-UKF	3623.9	± 41986.9
GP-ADF	22.6	± 36.6
GMF-SF	12.1	± 13.3
GMF-SF+XV	7.2	± 7.1

and GP-UKF. Only the GP-ADF produces comparable results. Additionally, the results show that the introduction of the variable means improves the results for the Kitagawa experiment. The reason for this improvement is that the system model, cf. Fig. 4.4 (a) is almost a jumping system around $(0,0)$. As the samples used for training are uniformly distributed this jump is undersampled. Thus, the optimization of the means w.r.t. the superficial regularization alleviates this problem as the variable means "fill" the gap.

(b) Multimodal Posterior Densities

The Kitagawa growth process was used for comparing with Gaussian filters. In order to show the capability of the proposed GMM-based filter to estimate multimodal posterior densities the following nonlinear cubic sensor model [72, 107] is considered

$$\boldsymbol{x}_{k+1} = 2\,\boldsymbol{x}_k - 0.5\,\boldsymbol{x}_k^3 + \boldsymbol{w}_k \,, \quad \boldsymbol{w}_k \sim \mathcal{N}(0, 0.175)\,. \tag{4.20}$$

For training, 100 samples were generated according to (4.20). As only the capability to estimate multimodal posterior densities shall be investigated the GMM conditional density for the system model is estimated using the SVR approach described in Sec. 3.5.2. Given the prior density

$$f(x_0) = \mathcal{N}(x_0; 0.4, 0.8)\,, \tag{4.21}$$

the prediction capacity of the resulting Gaussian mixture filter (SVDF) [107] is compared to the GP-ADF for four consecutive prediction steps without any measurements.

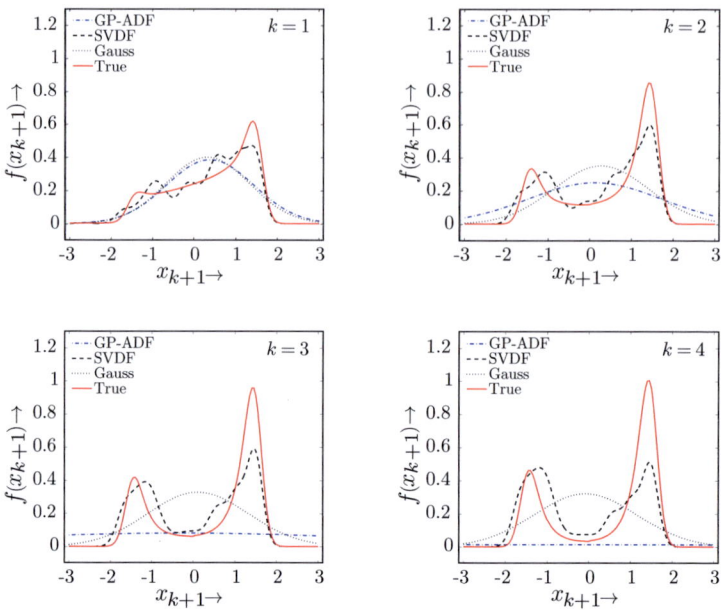

Figure 4.5: Posterior densities after 1,2,3, and 4 prediction steps: true posterior density (red, solid), the GP-ADF estimated posterior density (blue, dash-dotted), the SVR-based estimate (SVDF) (black, dash), and a moment-matched Gaussian approximation of the SVR-based estimate (black, dotted). Graphics taken from [107].

Results Fig. 4.5 shows the prediction results for the cubic sensor system (4.20). This example shows that the GMM filter captures the modes well, whereas the GP-ADF as a prototypical nonlinear Gaussian filter degenerates. Note that even a moment-matching approximation of the GMM yields better results than the GP-ADF. The results presented in this section are reproduced in part from [107, 109].

4.5 Main Contributions

The main contributions of this chapter may be summarized as follows w.r.t. descriptive and prescriptive validity as well as computational efficiency.

- In this section, a conditional density estimation algorithm was proposed that overcomes the limitation of the estimates to Gaussian mixture densities with means identical to the data points and identical parameters for all components of the mixture. These restrictions reduced the capacity of approaches proposed in Ch. 3 and therefore limited the quality of the obtainable conditional density estimates, i.e., the descriptive validity.

- The proposed approach improved the prescriptive validity by simultaneously smoothing the mean function of the estimate and smoothness of the conditional density function surface by means of the superficial regularization term. Additionally, an account for the model uncertainty in the estimate was introduced by means of data-dependent covariances. As was shown in the experimental validation, both measures improve the generalization capability of the obtained estimate.

- Regarding the computational efficiency, the resulting conditional densities are sparser than the estimates produced by the more restrictive approach presented in Ch. 3, but the training algorithm is more expensive. The conditional densities produced by the proposed approach are more efficient for the use with a nonlinear filtering online, but take longer to train offline.

- For the potential application of the conditional density estimator, i.e., nonlinear filtering, the proposed approach has been shown to produce comparable or better results in nonlinear Gaussian filtering than GP-based filters. Additionally, the proposed GMM-based filter is capable of supporting multimodal posterior densities, which is not possible for all assumed Gaussian filters.

5 Hyperparameter Optimization

The density or conditional density estimation algorithms presented in Ch. 3 and Ch. 4 solve their respective estimation problems w.r.t. a set of predefined hyperparameters. Since the solutions and therefore the quality of the solutions depend on the hyperparameters, the determination of the hyperparameters is crucial to the density and conditional density estimation. In this chapter methods for the optimization of the hyperparameters w.r.t. to scalar objective functions will be derived. Most of the optimization methods are applicable to density and conditional density estimation. The specific differences will be considered where necessary.

Challenge Let the set of all parameters of the generic optimization problem be given identically to the problem definition (2.29) by the following vector

$$\underline{\theta} = [\ \underline{\alpha}^{\mathrm{T}}\quad \underline{\mu}^{\mathrm{T}}\quad \underline{\Sigma}^{\mathrm{T}}\quad \underline{\omega}^{\mathrm{T}}\ ]^{\mathrm{T}}. \tag{5.1}$$

The hyperparameters $\underline{\zeta}$ are the parameters in $\underline{\theta}$, which are not optimized by the respective algorithm presented in Ch. 3 or Ch. 4. The exact set $\underline{\zeta}$ depends on the specific algorithm. Similar to the underlying problem, the challenge is the determination of $\underline{\zeta}$ is ill-posed and needs to be performed w.r.t. a given measure of generalization. For example, a covariance Σ, e.g., with a small value of $\det(\Sigma)$, may result in overfitting and dense representations of the solution or may lead to underfitting for large values and produce sparse representations, cf. Fig. 5.1. Furthermore, the optimization problem to be solved is nonlinear and nonconvex and has many local extrema in general.

Key Idea As motivated in Sec. 2.1.4, the hyperparameter optimization problem may be understood as a classical model selection problem and addressed by approaches ranging from heuristics over Bayesian approaches to cross-validation. In this chapter, a data-driven approach to hyperparameter optimization for density and conditional density estimation based on cross-validation (CV) [47, 130, 156] is presented. The key idea of this approach is the assessment of the generalization performance of the estimator

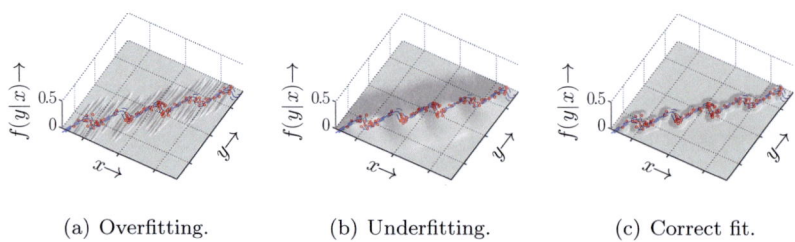

(a) Overfitting.   (b) Underfitting.   (c) Correct fit.

Figure 5.1: Three different noise levels for an exemplary system. In (a), the noise is too small in x-direction to approximate the underlying functional dependency well and the noise too large in the y-direction. In (b), the noise value is too large so that the oscillation of the function can be hardly seen. In (c), the correct noise level was used.

w.r.t. the distribution of the underlying phenomenon as manifesting in the data. In order to obtain a robust assessment, the assessment is performed iteratively on hold-out data.

5.1 Overall Optimization Scheme

In this thesis, hyperparameter optimization is considered as a generic constrained optimization problem. The optimization comprises of four components: the optimization variables ζ, a measure of generalization, a generic function minimization procedure, and the constraints of the optimization variables. The key idea is to create a measure of generalization and to perform a generic function minimization thereof w.r.t. the hyperparameters ζ. In the following, the generalization measure based on a performance score on a hold-out sets will be derived, the constraints on ζ will be introduced, and combined with a generic function minimization scheme.

5.2 Generalization Measure

A data-driven measure of generalization performance is CV [47, 130, 156]. The most common type of CV is so-called k-fold CV. In k-fold CV, the data $\mathcal{D}$ is partitioned into k equally sized subsets $\mathcal{F}_i \subset \mathcal{D}$. For estimating the generalization performance, training $\mathcal{T}_j$ and validation $\mathcal{V}_j$ sets are constructed for each fold

$$\mathcal{D} = \bigcup_{i=1:k} \mathcal{F}_i \,, \qquad \mathcal{F}_i \cap \mathcal{F}_j = \emptyset \,, \qquad \mathcal{T}_j = \bigcup_{\substack{i=1:k, \\ i \neq j}} \mathcal{F}_i \,, \qquad \mathcal{V}_j = \mathcal{F}_j \,. \qquad (5.2)$$

In (5.2), the j-th fold is used for validation and all other folds are merged into the training set. If a merger like (5.2) is performed for each of the k folds, k distinct training and testing data sets are obtained, cf. Fig. 5.2 (left). The generalization performance of an estimator is assessed by considering the estimator's performance on each fold, i.e., by training the estimator with each training set and evaluating its performance on the respective testing set for each of the k folds, cf. Fig. 5.2 (right). Typically generalization performance of the estimator is calculated as the average performance $\bar{\nu}$ over all k folds, other choices are possible, e.g., a least regret choice, cf. [130, Ch. 5]. In order to assess the estimator's score, which is trained on the training set $\mathcal{T}_j$, on the validation set $\mathcal{V}_j$ the log-likelihood (2.9) is employed[1]

$$\bar{\mathcal{L}}(\mathcal{V}_j) = \sum_{i=1}^{|\mathcal{V}_j|} \log f_{\mathcal{T}_j}(\underline{x}_i) \,, \qquad\qquad \forall \underline{x}_i \in \mathcal{V}_j \,,$$

$$\bar{\mathcal{L}}(\mathcal{V}_j) = \sum_{i=1}^{|\mathcal{V}_j|} \log f_{\mathcal{T}_j}(\underline{y}_i | \underline{x}_i) \,, \qquad\qquad \forall (\underline{x}_i, \underline{y}_i) \in \mathcal{V}_j \,. \qquad (5.3)$$

The definition of the log-likelihood in (5.3) differs for density estimation (left) and conditional density estimation (right). Other measures for assessing the estimator's performance are applicable too and only need to substitute the log-likelihood score in the overall algorithm.

5.3 Function Minimization

Using the obtained approximation of the generalization performance $\bar{\nu}$, the hyperparameters $\underline{\zeta}^*$ are obtained by minimizing $\bar{\nu}$ w.r.t. $\underline{\zeta}$ using standard function minimization algorithms [12]. Note, that the specific choice of the generalization measure may facilitate or prohibit some function minimization approaches, e.g., due to non-differentiability of the measure. Having optimized the hyperparameters, the final estimate $\underline{\zeta}^*$ is obtained by using

---

[1]The interested reader is referred to Appendix A.2.2 for more information about the log-likelihood as a distance measure.

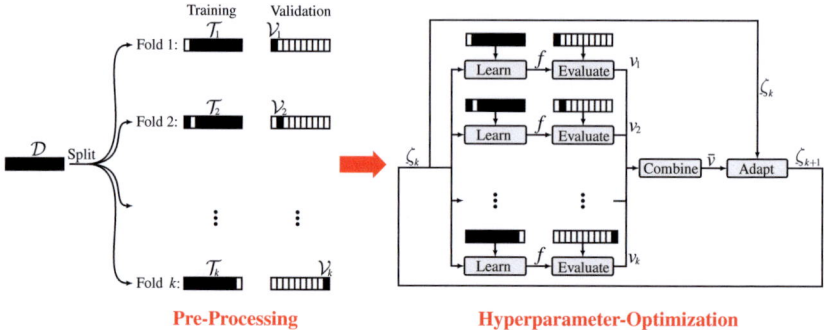

Figure 5.2: Illustration of the pre-processing used for the cross-validation (left) and the hyperparameter optimization algorithm (right) as explained below and formalized in Alg. 3.

$\underline{\zeta}_k$ and then performing density or conditional density estimation using the entire data set. The generic CV optimization scheme[2] is summarized in the Alg. 3. Given an initial parameter estimate $\underline{\zeta}_0$, the number of folds k, and $\mathcal{D}$, Alg. 3 returns the optimal hyperparameters $\underline{\zeta}^*$ and the Gaussian mixture density or conditional density f^*.

5.4   Constraints and Reformulations

The algorithms for density and conditional density estimation proposed in Ch. 3 and Ch. 4 use different sets of hyperparameters. The weights $\underline{\alpha}$ are estimated by the algorithms in both chapters and also the non-negativity and mass constraints of $\underline{\alpha}$ are imposed by these algorithms. For the other parameters in $\underline{\theta}$ the constraints are presented below. Wherever necessary, the difference in constraints w.r.t. density or conditional density estimation is explained.

Means $\underline{\mu}$: The means of the estimate are defined as the concatenation of all mean vectors $\underline{\mu}_i$ of the estimated mixture density representation in the density or conditional density, i.e.,

$$\underline{\mu}^{\mathrm{T}} := [\,\underline{\mu}_1^{\mathrm{T}} \ \cdots \ \underline{\mu}_L^{\mathrm{T}}\,]^{\mathrm{T}}. \tag{5.4}$$

---

[2]More information, other CV variants, and respective pseudo-code can be found in [130, Ch. 5] and [47, Ch. 9].

In the non-parametric approaches to density and conditional density estimation presented in Ch. 3, both the number of components $L = |\mathcal{D}|$ and the mean locations $\underline{\mu}_i = \underline{d}_i$, $\underline{d}_i \in \mathcal{D}$ are fixed. Therefore, the means were not variable and not subject to any constraints. The advantage of the full parameter conditional density estimation proposed in Ch. 4 was the removal of this restriction by allowing a set of means $\mathcal{M}_v$ to be freely chosen, i.e., $L \neq |\mathcal{D}|$, typically, $L = |\mathcal{D}|+|\mathcal{M}_v|$ and the mean locations $\underline{\mu}_i \in \mathcal{D} \cup \mathcal{M}_v$, $\mathcal{M}_v \subset \mathbb{R}^{N+M}$. As discussed in Ch. 4 the typical restrictions are due to computational limitations. It was the purpose of the optimization of the component locations $\mathcal{M}_v$ to improve the expressiveness of the estimator in parts of the state space where little or no data is given and a non-parametric approach is inadequate. All of the above statements do not constitute constraints. In general, an optimization of each component in $\mathcal{M}_v$ w.r.t. a non-convex and nonlinear objective function, i.e., an objective function with many local extrema, would be performed over the entire state space. As this is impractical, the mean position may be constrained to fixed regions of the state space to incorporate prior knowledge into the estimation process.

Covariances $\underline{\Sigma}$: A valid covariance matrix needs to be symmetric and positive definite [18]. It is non-trivial to ensure these properties in a constrained optimization, where the optimization variables are the vectorized elements of the different covariance matrices, i.e.,

$$\underline{\Sigma} := \left[\sigma_1^{(1,1)} \; \cdots \; \sigma_1^{(N,N)} \; \cdots \; \sigma_L^{(1)} \; \cdots \; \sigma_L^{(N,N)} \right]^{\mathrm{T}}, \qquad (5.5)$$

with $\sigma_i^{(1,1)}, \dots, \sigma_i^{(N,N)}$ the elements of the covariance matrix $\Sigma_i \in \mathbb{R}^{N \times N}$. In order to assure positive definiteness of the symmetric matrix, the optimization variables may be substituted against the elements of the square root formulation of the covariance matrix

$$\mathbf{T}_i = \Sigma_i^{1/2}, \qquad\qquad \Sigma_i = \mathbf{T}_i \cdot \mathbf{T}_i.$$

Using the elements of $\mathbf{T}_i \in \mathbb{R}^{N \times N}$ as optimization variables and constructing Σ_i for the evaluation of the estimate guarantees both constraints. Asserting for both constraints may be trivially achieved if the covariance matrices are axis-aligned, i.e., $\Sigma_i = \mathrm{diag}(\underline{\sigma}_i)$ with $\underline{\sigma}_i \in \mathbb{R}_+^N$ the vector of variances along each of the N-dimensions. By construction, Σ_i will be symmetric. If $\underline{0} \prec \underline{\sigma}_i$ is satisfied the

---

Algorithm 3 Hyperparameter Optimization by Cross-Validation.

1: **Input:** $\mathcal{D}$, $\underline{\zeta}_0$, k

2: Initialize $\underline{\zeta}_t \leftarrow \underline{\zeta}_0$

3: $\{\mathcal{T}_i, \mathcal{V}_i\}_{i=1:k} \leftarrow$ Partition $\mathcal{D}$ $\triangleright$ Create $\mathcal{T}_{1:k}$, $\mathcal{V}_{1:k}$

4: **repeat** $\triangleright$ Standard function minimizer

5:     **for** $i = 1 : k$ **do**

6:        $\underline{\theta}_t \leftarrow$ Estimation$(\mathcal{T}_i, \underline{\zeta}_t)$ $\triangleright$ (Conditional) Density Estimation

7:        $\nu_i \leftarrow$ Evaluate$(\mathcal{V}_i, \underline{\theta}_t)$ $\triangleright$ E.g. Log-likelihood Score

8:     **end for**

9:     $\bar{\nu} \leftarrow$ Average or Minimum/Maximum $(\{\nu_i\}_{i=1:k})$

10:    $\underline{\zeta}_{t+1} \leftarrow$ Update$\left(\nu_t, \underline{\zeta}_t\right)$

11: **until** $\varepsilon < \nu_t - \nu_{t-1}$

12: $\underline{\zeta}^* \leftarrow \underline{\zeta}_{t+1}$

13: **Output:** $f^* \sim$ GMM $\{\underline{\alpha}_k, \underline{\mu}_k, \underline{\Sigma}_k\}|_{\underline{\zeta}^*}$

---

covariance matrix will be positive definite too. Note, that there is no difference in the optimization for covariances between density and conditional density estimation. The interpretation of the elements of $\mathbf{\Sigma}_i$ and therefore the structure of $\mathbf{\Sigma}_i$ deviates largely. In the case of density estimation $\mathbf{\Sigma}_i$ is a dense matrix in general. For conditional densities, the in- and output dimensions should be independent of each other, i.e., the covariance matrix will consist of one block matrix encoding the correlation w.r.t. the input and one encoding the correlations w.r.t. output dimensions.

Trade-off Parameter λ: The parameter $\lambda \in \mathbb{R}_+$ adjusts the trade-off between the distance term $\mathbf{Q}_1$ and the regularization term $\mathbf{K}$ in the target functions of the QPs constituting the main part of the algorithms presented in Ch. 3 and Ch. 4, e.g., in (3.32) of Sec. 3.4

$$\underline{\alpha}^{\mathrm{T}}\left(\mathbf{Q}_1 + \lambda\mathbf{K}\right)\underline{\alpha} - 2\underline{\alpha}^{\mathrm{T}}\underline{Q}_2 \,.$$

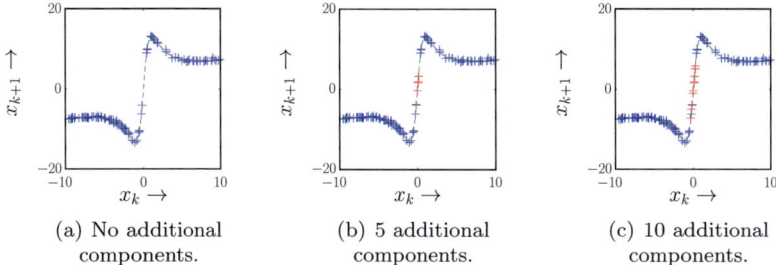

(a) No additional components.

(b) 5 additional components.

(c) 10 additional components.

Figure 5.3: Example for the initial values of variable means in the sense of Ch. 4. The system (mean function [dashed gray] and samples [blue crosses]) is identical to (4.18) and the initial positions for the variable means (red crosses) were obtained by the described greedy reduction of the maximum trace of the adaptive covariances.

In the above formulation, $\lambda = 0$ will remove the regularization term from the target function. This effectively converts the regularized nonparametric density or conditional density estimator into an unregularized estimator, i.e., in the case of Sec. 3.4 to a kernel density estimator with mere weight optimization. A high value of λ will enforce a stronger regularization relative to the distance between estimate and the empirical density or conditional density. The only necessary constraint is the positivity of λ, i.e., a lower bound $\lambda > 0$. Yet, if a maximum value for λ is known, it may be used as an upper bound[3].

For the sake of easier interpretation and numerical stability it is useful to normalize the regularization term, e.g., with a kernel estimate of the Rényi-entropy and the distance. A normalized lambda might be calculated as $\lambda\prime = \lambda \cdot N$ with

$$N \approx \frac{\underline{n}^{\mathrm{T}} \mathbf{Q}_1 \underline{n}}{\underline{n}^{\mathrm{T}} \mathbf{K} \underline{n}}, \qquad\qquad \underline{n} = \underline{1} \cdot \frac{1}{L}.$$

Loss Insensitivity ε: In some implementations of the algorithms presented in Ch. 3 and Ch. 4 the ε-insensitive loss function [36, 164,

---

[3]Note, that some function minimization implementations even require both a lower and an upper bound to be provided.

165, 190] is employed for point-wise comparisons

$$l_1^\varepsilon(a, b) = \begin{cases} 0 & , |a - b| \le \varepsilon \\ |a - b| - \varepsilon & , \text{else} \end{cases}. \tag{5.6}$$

This loss-function penalizes deviations between the two values a and b if they exceed ε. This insensitivity allows for some noise in the estimates, but still penalizes strong deviations. For example, this robust loss function is used in [107] for the point-wise comparison of an empirical cumulative distribution function with the cumulative function constructed from the estimator's result. The level of noise ignored by the loss-function is a hyperparameter, which needs to be optimized. It is lower bound by 0, as an absolute negative difference cannot be obtained. The upper bound differs for density and conditional density estimation. In the case of density estimation the upper bound is $u_\varepsilon = 1$. For conditional density estimation, the upper bound depends on the distribution of the components in input and output dimensions, thus may be $u_\varepsilon = vol(\mathcal{I})$ in the worst case. For both density and conditional density estimation it is favorable to introduce any available prior knowledge into the estimation process.

5.5 Initial Values

As discussed before, the hyperparameter optimization yields a non-convex and nonlinear optimization problem with many local extrema. In order to achieve fast convergence to a high-quality solution a good initial value for the hyperparameters is advisable. In the following list some heuristics, which were found to be useful are devised.

Means $\underline{\mu}_0$ The optimization of the locations of additional means arises only in the conditional density estimation algorithm proposed in Ch. 4. There are two initial values to be set: the number of variable components and their location. The determination of both initial values should be considered simultaneous and is an optimization problem in itself for which an approximation is proposed. The informal reasoning for optimizing components' locations was the improved capacity of the estimator especially in areas of the state space which are populated by no or little data, cf. Fig. 5.3. This intuition may be formalized by an upper bound on the maximum size u_Σ of the variable covariances $\boldsymbol{\Sigma}_i$ on each component, e.g., in terms of the trace

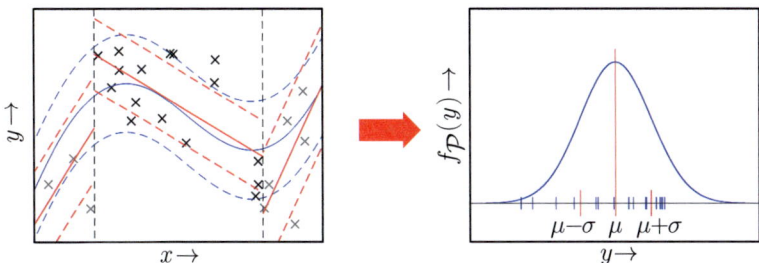

Figure 5.4: Example for determining the initial value of the basis kernel's covariance in **y**-direction for data (crosses) sampled from an oscillating system (blue) with normal additive noise (blue, dashed). Initially the state space is partitioned in **x**-direction (dashed gray lines), a robust linear regression estimate (red solid line) is estimated (left), and σ of the data (crosses) in each partition normalized by the regression is calculated (right). For visualization a normal density was plotted over the partition's data (blue, right) and the σ-bounds for the regression estimate are depicted (left, dashed red lines). The overall σ is then determined by averaging all partitions' σ.

of Σ_i. Determining the number of components to be optimized may then be determined by a greedy iterative approach: In each step, an additional component's $\underline{x}$-position is sampled or calculated as the mean of a k-nearest neighbor sample set of the component of the current estimate with the largest covariance trace. This procedure is repeated until the covariance size falls below a user-defined threshold. The latter approach is shown in Fig. 5.3 (b) and (c) for different numbers of means. If only one functional dependency is present in the data, the y-locations of the variable components may be obtained by standard regression procedures [73]. Otherwise a nearest neighbor density estimator may be employed.

Covariances $\underline{\Sigma}_o$ The initial values for the covariance differ for density and conditional density estimation as for conditional density estimation an underlying functional dependency may be assumed as well as there is a semantic difference for the input and output dimensions.

For density estimation, the results from the kernel density estimation literature as presented in Sec. 2.1.2 or obtainable from the classical

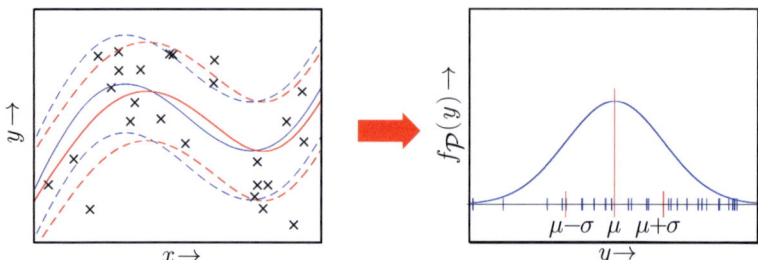

Figure 5.5: Example for determining the initial value of the basis kernel's covariance in y-direction for data (crosses) sampled from an oscillating system (blue) with normal additve noise (blue, dashed). Initially, a nonlinear regression estimate, i.e., a cubic smoothing spline with $p = 0.9$ (red solid line), is estimated (left), and σ of the data normalized by the regression function is calculated (right). For visualization a normal density was plotted over the partition's data (blue, right) and the σ-bounds for the regression estimate are depicted (left, dashed red lines).

texts [87, 140, 153] and more recent overviews [49, 179] may be employed for determining the initial values. Note that in the literature the kernel width is typically calculated a priori and not optimized.

For conditional density estimation, a decomposition of $\mathbf{\Sigma}_0$ into independent submatrices for the input dimensions $\mathbf{\Sigma}_{0,x} \in \mathbb{R}^{N \times N}$ and output dimensions $\mathbf{\Sigma}_{0,y} \in \mathbb{R}^{M \times M}$, i.e.,

$$\mathbf{\Sigma}_0 = \begin{bmatrix} \mathbf{\Sigma}_y & \mathbf{0} \\ \mathbf{0} & \mathbf{\Sigma}_x \end{bmatrix}, \tag{5.7}$$

needs to be considered. Different approaches for the calculation of the $\mathbf{\Sigma}_y$ may be considered given information about the data present. For example, if the data corresponds to a functional dependency perturbed by additive Gaussian noise, i.e., not more than one dependency and no multimodal noise are present, a mean function $\mu : \mathbb{R}^N \mapsto \mathbb{R}^M$ may be determined by standard regression methods [73]. Using this mean function, an estimate of the noise, e.g., by calculating the variance or the y values normalized w.r.t. the regression function may be obtained. This procedure is demonstrated in Fig. 5.4 for an approach, which partitions the state space and performs a robust regression of a linear mean function in each partition

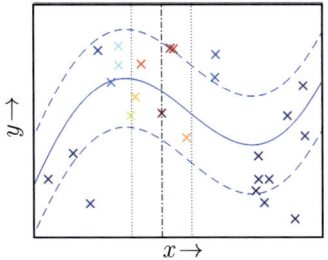
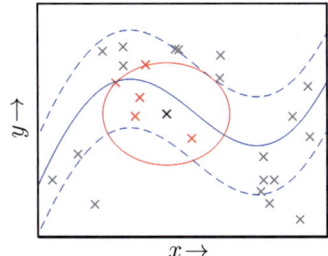

(a) Kernel-weighted contribution of
one sample in the data density
estimator (5.8) w.r.t. the x-direction.

(b) K-nearest neighbors (red crosses)
for one sample (black cross), which are
used for a density estimate, cf. (5.9).

Figure 5.6: Example for determining the initial value of the basis kernel's covariance in y-direction for data (crosses) sampled from an oscillating system (blue) with normal additive noise (blue, dashed). The overall σ is calculated by an averaged covariance calculation w.r.t. each data point. The contribution of each data point is either the local covariance as obtained by using the sample as a sample mean and performing a kernel-weighted covariance calculation (left, dotted and dash dotted lines indicate the kernel $\mu \pm \sigma$ bounds) or by calculating a k-nearest neighbor (red crosses, red outline) estimate of the data density (right).

and in Fig. 5.5 for an approach based on estimating a cubic smoothing spline mean function. Alternatively, the noise may be estimated by local kernel averaging, which gives rise to the following estimator

$$\Sigma_y^{\mathcal{D}} = \frac{1}{|\mathcal{D}| - 1} \sum_{j=1}^{|\mathcal{D}|} w(\underline{x}_i, \underline{x}_j) \left[\underline{y}_j - \underline{y}_i \right] \left[\underline{y}_j - \underline{y}_i \right]^{\mathrm{T}}, \qquad (5.8)$$

i.e., the sample covariance with the samples weighted according to their distance to the position of the i-th component in x-direction by a function $w : \mathbb{R}^N \times \mathbb{R}^N \mapsto [0,1]$, e.g., by a kernel function [28]. This approach and a classical kernel-weighted approach are shown in Fig. 5.6. A similar approach has been derived in [28] for density estimation. If multiple functional dependencies are present in the data and the data cannot be associated certainly with one dependency only, the above approach is inapplicable. The sample covariance would be centralized for one of the present mean functions only and the data produced by other dependencies will increase the covariance size. For this reason, an approach may be considered, which does not assume any functional dependency, but considers the local data density only. This density estimate is calculated based on the k-nearest neighbors $\{ \underline{y}_j^{(i)} \}_{1 \leq j \leq k}$ of $\underline{y}_i$

$$\Sigma_y^{\mathcal{D}} = \frac{1}{|\mathcal{D}|} \sum_{i=1}^{|\mathcal{D}|} \left(\sum_{j=1}^{k} l_2(\underline{y}_j^{(i)}, \underline{y}_i) \right) . \tag{5.9}$$

The resulting $\Sigma_y^{\mathcal{D}}$ is then obtained by averaging the local data densities (5.9). Note, that the number of neighbors k, needs in turn to be determined by general model selection procedures. For calculating Σ_x, regression approaches are not applicable, as the marginal density $f(\underline{x})$ is a uniform distribution over the considered part of the state space in the optimal case. Therefore, Σ_x is estimated based on the k-nearest neighbors $\{ \underline{x}_j^{(i)} \}_{1 \leq j \leq k}$ of $\underline{x}_i$, in analogy to the calculation of Σ_y in (5.9)

$$\Sigma_x^{\mathcal{D}} = \frac{1}{|\mathcal{D}|} \sum_{i=1}^{|\mathcal{D}|} \left(\sum_{j=1}^{k} l_2(\underline{x}_j^{(i)}, \underline{x}_i) \right) . \tag{5.10}$$

Trade-off Parameter λ_o The necessity of regularization as governed by λ depends on the data distribution. As a derivation of a data-dependent regularization is out of the scope of this thesis, the simple rule-of-thumb that regularization should depend on the number of data present is proposed. It is therefore proposed to employ the following heuristic

$$\lambda_0 = p \cdot \frac{1}{|\mathcal{D}|} , \tag{5.11}$$

where p is the maximum amount of regularization expected as an initial value, e.g., $p = 0.5$, which is weighted by the number of data. With $|\mathcal{D}| \to \infty$ the initial amount of regularization converges 0. This formalizes that in this case the density or conditional density estimation problem is no longer ill-posed, i.e., regularization is not necessary.

Loss Insensitivity ε_0 Because ε encodes the tolerated amount of noise in the solution, the initial value may be the initial estimate of this

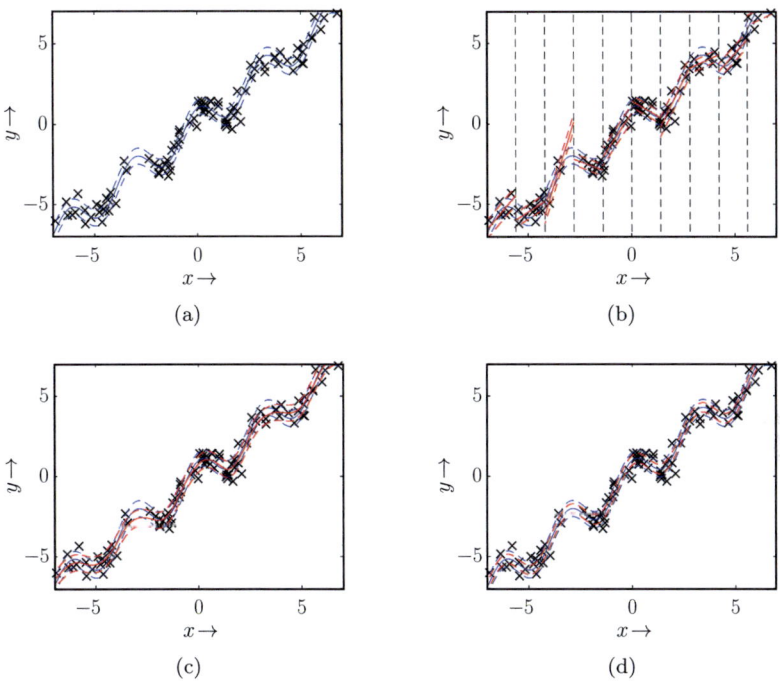

Figure 5.7: Larger view of the basis kernel's covariance as shown in Fig. 5.4, Fig. 5.5, and Fig. 5.6 (left) for the same data and system (a). The partitioning, the respective linear regression estimates with their σ-bounds corresponding to Fig. 5.4 are depicted in (b). The result using the nonlinear regression from Fig. 5.5 is given in (c) and for the data-driven kernel-weighted approach of Fig. 5.6 in figure (d).

tolerance level. For density and conditional density estimation ε may be either the point-wise accepted difference in probability or cumulative distribution between the estimated and the empirical function. Intuitively, the tolerance shall be given as a percentage p, e.g., 10%, depend on the number data $|\mathcal{D}|$ given, and be relative to the maximum deviation $u_{\max}$, e.g., a function like

$$\varepsilon_0 = p \cdot u_{\max} \cdot \frac{1}{|\mathcal{D}|}, \tag{5.12}$$

and the initial value obtained from instantiating (5.12) converges to 0 for $|\mathcal{D}| \to \infty$.

5.6 Properties and Restrictions

The most important properties of each of the four components of the over-all optimization scheme—the optimization variables, the objective function measuring the generalization, the generic function minimization procedure, and the constraints on the optimization variables— are summarized in the following list.

- The complexity of the hyperparameter optimization depends on the setup, i.e., the number of optimization variables and the number of folds considered as well as the initial values. In general, all components' positions may be optimized in one large optimization problem. Since determining only all positions corresponds to solving an $L \cdot (M + N)$-dimensional optimization problem, this becomes intractable already for small problems [181]. Note, that a naive optimization of each covariance matrix requires the optimization of $\mathcal{O}\left([M + N]^2\right)$ variables. As the number of optimization variables, specifically the number of variable means has been discussed in Ch. 4, only the setup of the hyperparameter optimization is considered in the remaining part of this list. If $k = |\mathcal{D}|$, one obtains a "leave-one-out" estimate of the generalization error. The computational effort is maximal for this type of estimate, as $|\mathcal{D}|$ estimates need to be obtained from $|\mathcal{D}| - 1$ samples. In contrast, if k is small, e.g., $k = 5$, only 5 estimates need to be obtained, but the data distribution in the folds may deviate strongly from the distribution of the full data set, i.e., the estimate of the generalization capability will become inaccurate. The same reasoning holds, if $|\mathcal{D}|$ is small and already omitting one sample biases the estimate.

- The objective function is the cross-validated negative log-likelihood score. This score is not appropriate in the case of scarce data and may require an augmentation with prior knowledge, e.g., in the form of smoothness assumptions may be necessary.

- From a theoretical point of view, no statements about convergence speed or even convergence may be given for the considered nonlinear and non-convex problem. This is an inherent property of the density and conditional density estimation problem. We refer the interested reader to [200, 202], where this problem is discussed in depth in the context of the EM algorithm as such and for EM applied to GMM estimation. Local convergence may be guaranteed at most for GMM estimation with EM [202].

- The complexity of evaluating the density or conditional density estimate may be considered independent of the hyperparameter optimization given that the hyperparameter optimization yields non-trivial estimates. For example, if the hyperparameter optimization underfits the true phenomenon too few and if it overfits too many components will be chosen. Typically, this is not the case or may be avoided easily.

- The constraints are necessary to obtain valid estimates, yet they allow for an introduction of prior knowledge into the estimation algorithm too. This is for example the case if it is known that the variance in one dimension is bound due to physical reasons governing the data generation process. This fact may be exploited by setting tighter bounds on the allowed maximum variance for this dimension.

- The initial values allow for an easy introduction of prior knowledge into the estimation problem too. Any prior knowledge, e.g., about the noise due to multiple tracks present in the data may be exploited. A poor choice of the initial values for ζ may result in long training times, w.r.t. the employed function minimizer, and potentially poor quality estimates.

- Each heuristic for determining the initial values shown in Fig. 5.4, Fig. 5.5, and Fig. 5.6 depends on the specific parameters. For a larger state space, the partitioning scheme of the linear regression approach will deliver only good results if the partitions contain enough data as can be seen in Fig. 5.7 (b), where some regression estimates are too smooth or too steep. Similarly, the nonlinear regression smoothes too strongly in Fig. 5.7 (c), e.g., around $(2.5, 3)$, and the kernel-weighted density estimation underfits the noise in Fig. 5.7 (d). The sensitivity to the parameter choices for these three approaches is given in Fig. 5.8, where the number of partitions, the smoothing parameter, and the kernel size were varied for a set of 100 MC runs. The results show that only a good parameter choice will provide an initial value close to the desired true value.

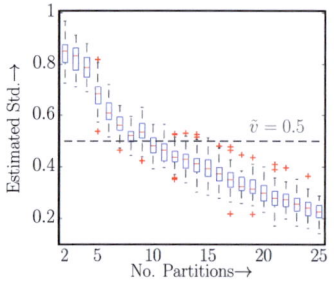

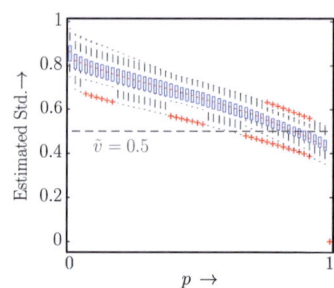

(a) Boxplots of the standard deviations estimated by the linear-regression approach w.r.t. number of partitions.

(b) Boxplots of the standard deviations estimated by the nonlinear-regression approach w.r.t. parameter p.

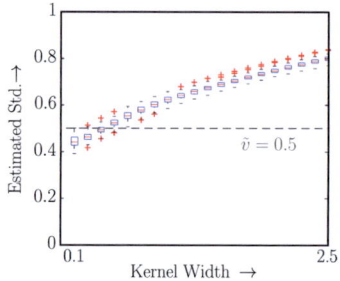

(c) Boxplots of the standard deviations estimated by the data-driven kernel-weighted approach w.r.t. kernel width.

Figure 5.8: Boxplots of the standard deviations estimated by the different approaches w.r.t the respective parameters. Each boxplot summarizes the statistics of 100 MC runs for an approach with a fixed parameter setting. For the linear-regression approach the number of partitions, which are averaged to obtain σ is varied. For the nonlinear regression approach, the trade-off parameter p is varied—$p = 0$ corresponds to a least-squares linear model fit and $p = 1$ yields the cubic spline interpolation. For the data-driven kernel-weighted approach, the degree of locality is varied by varying the width of the employed Gaussian kernel.

5.7 Main Contributions

The contributions of the presented hyperparameter optimization can be summarized w.r.t. descriptive and prescriptive validity as well as computational efficiency as follows.

- The descriptive and prescriptive quality of the given approach is theoretically limited due to the amount of data given and the chosen cross-validation procedure, because the partitioning scheme may prohibit the consideration of a data distribution as represented in the full data set. Practically, the approach is limited by the amount of computation investable in hyperparameter optimization scheme.

- The bottleneck of the algorithm presented in this section is the computational complexity. Assuming the fixed computational complexity of the algorithms for density and conditional density estimation, which are used as a subroutine in Alg. 3, the computational effort of the hyperparameter optimization is dominated by the CV and the convergence properties of the nonlinear function minimization algorithm. For applications, where this computational cost is not acceptable, the proposed algorithm may serve as a benchmark for developing faster, e.g., approximative approaches.

- The presented hyperparameter optimization approach is generic, because—except for minor details—the algorithm may be employed for any density and conditional density estimation. This algorithm resembles cross-validated approaches for KDE [179], but extends these to hyperparameters needed for the regularized estimation scheme. The approach may therefore be understood as a blend of these approaches and hyperparameter optimization for SVMs [165]. As to the best of our knowledge, the given description of hyperparameter optimization, which is an extended and improved version of [107], is the first of this kind for conditional density estimation.

You don't understand anything
until you learn it more than one way.
—MARVIN MINSKY

6 Conditional Density Estimation given Samples and Prior Knowledge

In this section, the problem of conditional density estimation from samples and prior knowledge is investigated[1]. This problem arises because the results of previous measurement sequences or expert/domain knowledge may be available and shall be used in conjunction with the data to solve the conditional density estimation problem. For example previously conducted high resolution measurement sequences, which may have been limited to a certain part of the state space, need to be combined with samples from a low-resolution sequence, which are scattered in a larger fraction of the state space. As will be shown in this chapter, the use of these additional sources of information is advantageous especially for the generalization performance.

Challenges The challenge in using both prior knowledge and data is that the prior knowledge typically will not be given as additional samples but in the form of already compiled generative or probabilistic models. Because of its advantageous properties the type of the conditional density function shall remain unchanged and the computational overhead for using the prior knowledge shall be minimized in training and testing.

Key Ideas The key ideas for the incorporation of the prior knowledge are to use a favorable approximation of the prior knowledge and to estimate the conditional density from the samples and the approximation simultaneously. In the following, the introduction of prior knowledge will be restricted to one specific approximation for a generative and a probabilistic model with scalar input and output dimension each. Both approximations may approximate the prior knowledge arbitrarily well, whereas a higher approximation quality always is accompanied by higher computational complexity. In the following, conditional density estimation with data and prior knowledge of the generative model in the form of

---

[1] The results presented in this chapter are an extended version of the results presented in [108].

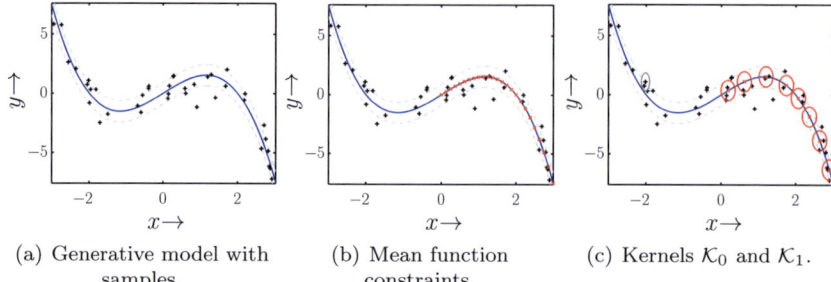

(a) Generative model with samples.

(b) Mean function constraints.

(c) Kernels $\mathcal{K}_0$ and $\mathcal{K}_1$.

Figure 6.1: (a) The true mean function (solid, red) with σ bounds (dashed,gray) and samples drawn accordingly are shown. (b) A discretization of the mean function from equidistant sampling in x-direction is depicted (red). (c) The σ bounds for the default kernel $\mathcal{K}_0$ (gray) and for each component of the mixture kernel $\mathcal{K}_1$ (red) are depicted.

mean function constraints or of the probabilistic model in form a Gaussian mixture density kernel approximating the given probabilistic model will be demonstrated.

6.1   Mean Function Constraints

Mean function values are the key information conveyed by prior knowledge in the form of a generative model. Let the generative model be given with additive, zero-mean Normal noise

$$y = g(\boldsymbol{x}) + \boldsymbol{w}, \qquad (6.1)$$

with $g : \mathbb{R} \mapsto \mathbb{R}$, $\boldsymbol{w} \in \mathbb{R}$, and a Normal noise term $\boldsymbol{w} \sim f_w$. The mean function of (6.1) gives the location of the expected values of the density $f(y|\hat{x})$, for fixed $\hat{x} \in \mathbb{R}$.

Key Idea   The key idea of incorporating (6.1) into the conditional density estimation algorithm is the minimization of the distance D between the expected values of the estimate f and the mean function values $\hat{y} = g(\hat{x})$ for all fixed $\hat{x} \in \mathbb{R}$, i.e.,

$$\min \int_{\mathbb{R}} \mathrm{D}\left(\int_{\mathbb{R}} y\, f(y|x)\, \mathrm{d}y, g(x) \right) \mathrm{d}x. \qquad (6.2)$$

The calculation of the expectation cannot be performed analytically in general and a minimization of (6.2) for an interval, i.e., a restricted part of the state space, involves an infinite number of point-wise evaluations, the following approximation to (6.2) is proposed

$$\min \sum_{c=1}^{C} \mathrm{D} \left(\int_{\mathbb{R}} y \, f(y|\hat{x}_c) \, \mathrm{d} y \,, \, g(\hat{x}_c) \right) , \qquad (6.3)$$

where $\hat{x}_c \in \mathbb{R}$, $g(\hat{x}_c) \in \mathbb{R}$, and $\{(\hat{x}_c, g(\hat{x}_c))\}_{1 \le c \le C} \subset \mathbb{R} \times \mathbb{R}$ correspond to C sample points obtained from discretizing the values of g. Any sampling algorithm may be employed for obtaining the samples, e.g., Monte Carlo or distance-measure based approaches. Each sample corresponds to a constraint on the expected values of the estimate for one fixed input value.

Incorporation In order to introduce the prior knowledge about the mean function into Alg. 1, a term penalizing the distance in (6.3) needs to be added to the QP in (3.32) as a function of the weights $\underline{\alpha}$ of the mixture conditional density f. For each of the C fixed sample points $\hat{x}_i$, one may calculate the expectation using the following simplifications

$$\int_{\mathbb{R}} y \, f(y|\hat{x}_c) \, \mathrm{d} y = \sum_{i=1}^{L} \alpha_i \, f_i^x(\hat{x}_c) \left(\int_{\mathbb{R}} y \, f_i^y(y) \, \mathrm{d} y \right)$$

$$= \sum_{i=1}^{L} \alpha_i \, c_y \, f_i^x(\hat{x}_c)$$

$$= \underline{\alpha}^{\mathrm{T}} \underline{f}_y^{x,i}(\hat{x}_c) , \qquad (6.4)$$

and instantiating D in (6.3) with the l_1^ε-loss function yields for the c-th sample point

$$\left| \int_{\mathbb{R}} y \, f(y|\hat{x}_c) \, \mathrm{d} y - g(\hat{x}_c) \right| = \left| \underline{\alpha}^{\mathrm{T}} \underline{f}_y^{x,i}(\hat{x}_c) - g(\hat{x}_c) \right| < \varepsilon + \xi_c . \qquad (6.5)$$

In (6.5), the slack variable ξ_c captures the error for the c-th sample point, i.e., the deviation between the expected and the mean function value exceeding the tolerated deviation ε. The absolute value in (6.5) may be resolved into one constraint measuring positive and one measuring negative deviation. For each of the C samples, (6.5) may be incorporated into the QP in (3.32) by adding a positive and a negative case of the left-hand side of (6.5) as constraints and the sum of the errors to the target function, i.e., the parts marked red and blue below

$$\min_{\underline{\kappa}} \quad \underline{\kappa}^{\mathrm{T}} \mathbf{P} \, \underline{\kappa} - 2\underline{\kappa}^{\mathrm{T}} \underline{p} + \underline{\kappa}^{\mathrm{T}} \underline{s} \,, \tag{6.6}$$

$$\text{s.t.} \quad 0 \preceq \underline{\kappa} \preceq \underline{l}_p \,,$$

$$\underline{\kappa}^{\mathrm{T}} \underline{w} = c_m \,,$$

$$\underline{\kappa}^{\mathrm{T}} \mathbf{H} \preceq \underline{1} \varepsilon \,.$$

In (6.6), $\mathbf{P}$, $\underline{p}$, $\underline{l}_p$, as well as $\underline{w}$ are identical to the matrices and vectors used in (3.32) except that they are zero-padded to fit the $\underline{\kappa}^+$ and $\underline{\kappa}^-$ as the slack variables ξ are not used in the calculation of the distance and regularization term in (3.32). Additionally, the following vectors are used

$$\underline{\kappa} = [\underline{\alpha}^{\mathrm{T}} \; \xi_1^+ \; \cdots \; \xi_c^+ \; \xi_1^- \; \cdots \; \xi_c^-]^{\mathrm{T}} \,, \qquad \underline{s} = [\underline{0}^{\mathrm{T}} \; \underline{1}^{\mathrm{T}} \; \underline{1}^{\mathrm{T}}]^{\mathrm{T}} \,. \tag{6.7}$$

As can be seen from (6.6), introducing prior knowledge about the generative model in the way presented above requires only minor changes to both the nonparametric and the full-parameter conditional density estimation algorithms presented in Ch. 3 and Ch. 4 respectively. This is due to the fact that the calculation of the distance as well as regularization terms remains independent of the slack variables and the constraints as well as the term in the target function only require zero-padding.

6.2   Location-based Mixture Kernel

In the last section, prior knowledge about the mean function was introduced into (3.32) in the form of constraints. It is more difficult if not only the mean function but a probabilistic model is given with unknown function g, i.e., only the left-hand side of the following model is given

$$f(y|x) = f_w \left(y - g(\underline{x}) \right) \,. \tag{6.8}$$

If information about (6.8) shall be incorporated into Alg. 1. The incorporation depends on the specific representation of the probabilistic model in (6.8). As Gaussian mixture densities are universal approximators, it is assumed for the rest of this section that (6.8) is given as or approximated by a Gaussian mixture density. As the prior knowledge is already a probabilistic model, the challenge is to decide how the estimate f combines prior knowledge with the samples.

Key Idea The key idea of incorporating a probabilistic model in the form of a Gaussian mixture density into Alg. 1 is to create a kernel, which combines the default kernel $\mathcal{K}_0$ and a kernel $\mathcal{K}_1$ encoding the prior knowledge using the sample information. The key requirements are listed below:

- The combined kernel needs to be a valid kernel, in the sense of Appendix A.1.5 or [178].

- The combination shall be a function of the sample location in state space, reflecting our belief in the accuracy of the prior knowledge.

These requirements are fulfilled if the resulting combined kernel is a convex combination of the kernels $\mathcal{K}_0$ and $\mathcal{K}_1$, where the mixing proportions depend on the sample location in state space. This location-based mixture kernel is a valid kernel as a convex combination of valid kernel functions is a valid kernel function, cf. Appendix A.1.5 or [178]. This location-based mixture kernel may be understood as modeling the causal dependency which kernel is valid in which part of the state space. This resembles a product probability kernel [88]. Furthermore, this approach may be considered a multiple kernel approach [8] without learning the mixture weights too.

Incorporation Following this key idea, the mixture kernel including the mixing function needs to be specified. For the definition of the mixture kernel it is assumed that the default kernel $\mathcal{K}_0$ and the kernel $\mathcal{K}_1$ based on the prior-knowledge represented as a Gaussian mixture model are given. The mixture kernel $\mathcal{K}$ for the location $[u \; v]^{\mathrm{T}} \in \mathbb{R}^2$ is then given by

$$
\mathcal{K}\left(\begin{bmatrix} x \\ y \end{bmatrix}, \begin{bmatrix} u \\ v \end{bmatrix} \right) =
$$
$$
\left[\mathcal{K}_0\left(\begin{bmatrix} x \\ y \end{bmatrix}, \begin{bmatrix} u \\ v \end{bmatrix} \right) \; \mathcal{K}_1\left(\begin{bmatrix} x \\ y \end{bmatrix}, \begin{bmatrix} u \\ v \end{bmatrix} \right) \right] \cdot \underline{s}\left(\begin{bmatrix} u \\ v \end{bmatrix} \right), \quad (6.9)
$$

with

$$
\underline{s}\left(\begin{bmatrix} u \\ v \end{bmatrix} \right) = \left[\mathrm{P}\left(k = 0 \middle| \begin{bmatrix} u \\ v \end{bmatrix} \right) \; \mathrm{P}\left(k = 1 \middle| \begin{bmatrix} u \\ v \end{bmatrix} \right) \right]^{\mathrm{T}}, \quad (6.10)
$$

where $k = 0$ ($k = 1$) denotes the weight or mixing proportion for $\mathcal{K}_0$ ($\mathcal{K}_1$). The mixing function $\underline{s} : \mathbb{R}^2 \to [0, 1] \times [0, 1]$ may be an arbitrary function

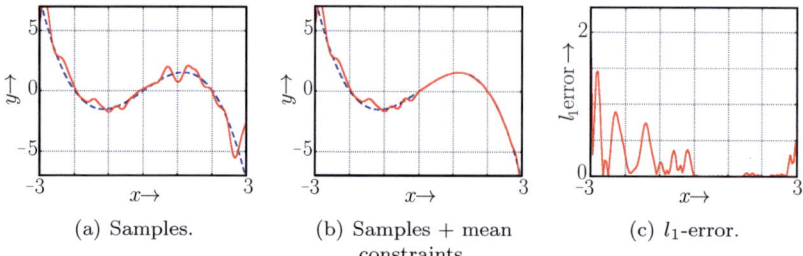

(a) Samples.   (b) Samples + mean   (c) l_1-error.
                          constraints.

Figure 6.2: Means of the true system (dashed, blue) and expectations of the conditional density estimate (red, solid) conditioned on fixed x (a) in case only samples are given, (b) if samples and the mean constraints over $[0,3]$ are given, and (c) the error in terms of the l_1-distance of the conditional expectations to the true mean function. The depicted results were obtained by a modification of the LCD-based approach [105].

yielding valid convex combinations, i.e., satisfies the following condition for all points in $\mathbb{R}^2$

$$\underline{1}^{\mathrm{T}} \underline{s} \left(\begin{bmatrix} u \\ v \end{bmatrix} \right) = 1 \,. \tag{6.11}$$

The mixture kernel (6.9) is a valid kernel, cf. Appendix A.1.5, and needs to be used in the calculation of the distance term D, the regularization term R, and the constraints. Since (6.9) replaces the default kernel, the representation of f is changed too.

6.3 Experimental Validation

In the following, the experimental setup, the evaluation criteria, implementation details, and the results for conditional density estimation with prior knowledge given as mean function constraints and a Gaussian mixture approximation of the probabilistic model are presented.

Experimental Setup In order to demonstrate the advantage of the incorporation of prior knowledge into conditional density estimation the probabilistic model corresponding to the following functional dependency with additive zero-mean noise is used as a ground truth system

$$y = 2\,x - 0.5\,x^3 + w\,, \quad w \sim \mathcal{N}(0, 0.9)\,. \tag{6.12}$$

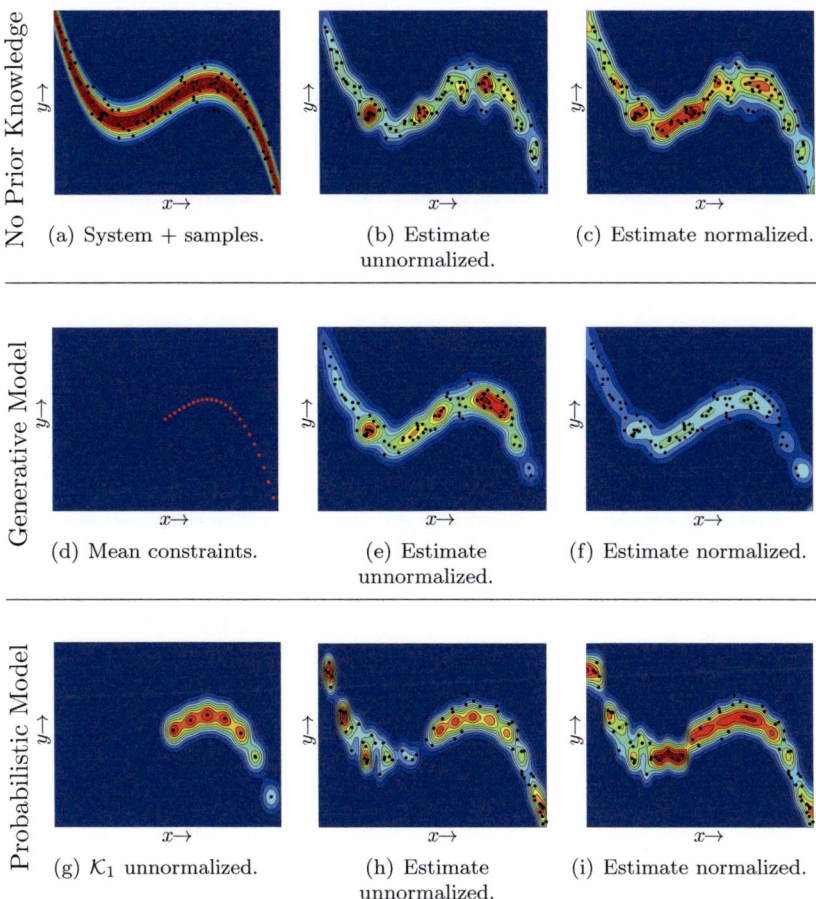

Figure 6.3: (a) True system with samples generated accordingly for $x \in [-3, 3]$, (b-c) conditional density estimate (un)normalized without prior knowledge, (d) prior knowledge in the form of mean function values, (e-f) conditional density estimate (un)normalized, (g) prior knowledge in the form of a PM, and (h-i) conditional density estimate (un)normalized. The depicted results were obtained by modification of the LCD-based optimization problem [105].

For the comparison, the results of conditional density estimation based on samples of (6.12) only are compared to the estimation results when these samples and prior knowledge in the form of additional mean constraints or a Gaussian mixture approximation of parts of the probabilistic model derived from (6.12) are given. For the experiments, 100 samples were generated by sampling (6.12) uniformly at random for $x \in [-3, 3]$. The mean function constraints were 25 uniformly distributed samples with $x \in [0, 3]$ with $y = g(x) = 2\,x - 0.5\,x^3$. The Gaussian mixture approximation was obtained by manually specifying the positions of the components' means. The components' covariances were axis-aligned and the main-diagonal elements were obtained by minimizing the MCvMD between the true probabilistic model of (6.12) and the Gaussian mixture approximation.

Evaluation Criteria   The use of the prior knowledge as modeled in this chapter is meant to reduce the deviation between the expected function values and the mean function or the conditional density function surfaces of the true and the estimated conditional density function surfaces. For comparing the deviation between the conditional expectations of the estimate and the true mean function g the l_1-distance is employed and calculated numerically for the considered interval. For comparing the true conditional density function $\tilde{f}$ with the estimate f, the total variation normalized to the considered interval in x-direction

$$\nu = \frac{1}{2(x_{\max} - x_{\min})} \int_{\mathcal{X}} \int_{\mathcal{Y}} |\tilde{f}(y'|x') - f(y'|x')| \; \mathrm{d}y' \; \mathrm{d}x', \qquad (6.13)$$

is calculated for the intervals $\mathcal{X} := [x_{\min}, x_{\max}]$ and $\mathcal{Y} := [y_{\min}, y_{\max}]$ numerically. The values of the total variation as defined in (6.13) are independent of the x-range considered.

Implementation Details   In order to show that the two proposed approaches of incorporating prior knowledge work for the class of conditional density estimators, which are implemented as standard constrained optimization problems, the proposed approaches are tested with two implementations. Both approaches are variants of the nonparametric conditional density estimators proposed in Sec. 3.4 producing Gaussian mixture model estimates. The first implementation is based on [107]. As it is closely related the conditional density estimator proposed in [190, Ch. 7] it will be denoted for the rest of this section as the SVM implementation. The main characteristics are that the distance term is calculated

Table 6.1: Average results for ten experiments: l_1-error $\pm\sigma$ of the mean, total variation $\nu \pm \sigma$, and the number of components for the normalized and unnormalized conditional densities obtained by the SVM and LCD approach without and with prior knowledge in the form of mean constraints (μ) and the Gaussian mixture approximation (GM). The errors are calculated w.r.t. the part of the state space with the prior knowledge, i.e., $x \in [0,3]$.

Estimator	Normalized Results		Unnormalized Results		Components
	$l_1(\mu)$	ν	$l_1(\mu)$	ν	
	No Prior Knowledge				
SVM	0.30 ± 0.08	0.24 ± 0.03	0.50 ± 0.21	0.26 ± 0.03	99.9
LCD	0.37 ± 0.04	0.24 ± 0.03	0.63 ± 0.14	0.27 ± 0.04	95.3
	Mean Constraints				
SVM-μ	0.23 ± 0.08	0.21 ± 0.03	0.27 ± 0.19	0.23 ± 0.03	71.2
LCD-μ	0.30 ± 0.09	0.22 ± 0.02	0.59 ± 0.16	0.25 ± 0.02	100
	Prob. Model				
SVM-GM	0.12 ± 0.02	0.11 ± 0.01	0.25 ± 0.08	0.13 ± 0.02	88.5
LCD-GM	0.14 ± 0.03	0.12 ± 0.01	0.36 ± 0.13	0.13 ± 0.01	57.9

based on the l_1-distance between the empirical and estimated conditional density function at the sample points [107], a regularization based on the norm of in the RKHS of the Gaussian kernel function (3.15), and "slice" mass constraints. The second implementation is based on [105] and uses the MCvMD of the LCD transforms of the empirical and estimated conditional density function (3.28), a regularization based on the negative Rényi-entropy (3.19), and "interval" mass constraints (3.26). Both implementations were written in Matlab [188] and use the CVX library [67] for the solution of the respective convex quadratic problems.

Results The results of the above described experiments are given in Fig. 6.3 and Tab. 6.1. The true system, the unnormalized, and normalized[2] estimate given only the samples are depicted in Fig. 6.3 (a)-(c). An exemplary effect of mean function constraints is shown in Fig. 6.2 (a)-(b), where the deviation between the conditional expectations and the mean function is reduced in the part of the state space influenced by the prior knowledge. Fig. 6.2 (c) shows an exemplary improvement in terms of the

---

[2] The normalization corresponds to a numeric normalization of the GM approximation of a conditional density function to a valid conditional density function.

l_1-distance. The results for SVM-μ and LCD-μ in Tab. 6.1 are average deviations for ten MC experiments and support the visual results. Besides the improvement in the mean function deviation, the introduction of mean function constraints also reduces the normalized total deviation between the true and the estimated conditional density function. Regarding the incorporation of prior knowledge in the form of a Gaussian mixture approximation of the prior knowledge Fig. 6.3 (g), Fig. 6.3 (h)-(i) depict some exemplary results. Especially the improvement w.r.t. the unnormalized results is drastic and can be observed in Tab. 6.1 too. In addition, the number of components in the estimates as listed in Tab. 6.1 is reduced. This shows, that even though the incorporation of prior knowledge into the conditional density estimation increases the training time, the testing time, i.e., the computational effort necessary for evaluating or further processing the estimate is reduced. The experiments and results presented in this chapter are reproduced from [108].

6.4 Properties and Restrictions

In this section, two approaches to introducing prior knowledge into conditional density estimation have been presented. These approaches are based on two specific approximations of the prior knowledge, which may be generalized to other approximations of the prior knowledge.

- The introduction of prior knowledge by definition increases the prescriptive validity and descriptive validity. This statement is of course bound to the fact that the prior knowledge is correct and the combination with the samples is non-trivial, i.e., the prior knowledge is not redundant.

- For prior knowledge in the form of a generative model, the approximation of the mean function dominates the information gain achievable. The approximation quality increases with the number of sample points, i.e., the constraints.

- The location-based mixture kernel approach may be extended to include more probabilistic models, i.e., a mixture of multiple kernels. In order to allow for more models, only (6.9) and (6.10) have to be extended to yield valid convex combinations of kernels so that the overall kernel satisfies the conditions in Appendix A.1.5. Additionally, as presented above the mixing proportions are fixed a priori, even though these may be optimized simultaneously with the other parameters.

- The size of the representation dominates the effort for using the estimate. The worst-case size of the representation is not increased for the mean function constraint approach, thus remains $|\mathcal{D}|$. When using the location-based kernel, the worst-case number of components is increased by the number of components in the Gaussian mixture kernel encoding the prior knowledge: Using the following abbreviations for the mixing function

$$p_{i,j} = \mathrm{P}\left(k = j \,\middle|\, \begin{bmatrix} u_i \\ v_i \end{bmatrix}\right),$$

and the default as well as the prior knowledge kernel

$$\mathcal{K}_{i,0} = \mathcal{K}\left(\begin{bmatrix} x \\ y \end{bmatrix}, \begin{bmatrix} u_i \\ v_i \end{bmatrix}\right), \quad \mathcal{K}_{i,1} = \sum_{j=1}^{L} \beta_j\, \mathcal{K}_1^j\left(\begin{bmatrix} x \\ y \end{bmatrix}, \begin{bmatrix} u_j \\ v_j \end{bmatrix}\right),$$

it is straightforward to obtain the following result by simple rearrangements

$$f(y|x) = \sum_{i=1}^{|\mathcal{D}|} \alpha_i \left[p_{i,0}\, \mathcal{K}_{i,0} + p_{i,1} \left(\sum_{j=1}^{L} \beta_j\, \mathcal{K}_1^j \right) \right]$$

$$= \sum_{i=1}^{|\mathcal{D}|} \alpha_i\, p_{i,0}\, \mathcal{K}_{i,0} + \sum_{j=1}^{L} \underbrace{\sum_{i=1}^{|\mathcal{D}|} \alpha_i\, p_{i,1}\, \beta_j\, \mathcal{K}_1^j}_{\beta_j'}$$

$$= \sum_{i=1}^{|\mathcal{D}|} \alpha_i'\, \mathcal{K}_{i,0} + \sum_{j=1}^{L} \beta_j'\, \mathcal{K}_1^j,$$

$$= \sum_{i=1}^{|\mathcal{D}|+L} \gamma_i\, \mathcal{K}_i',$$

where the kernels $\mathcal{K}_i'$ correspond to either the default kernel at different locations or the kernels encoding the prior knowledge, i.e., the Gaussian mixture kernels of $\mathcal{K}_1$.

- Regarding the computational complexity of Alg. 1, the addition of mean function constraints will increase the complexity by the number of constraints, cf. Appendix A.4.3 or [21, Ch. 1]. The location-based kernel will change all components in Alg. 1 involving the kernel function, i.e., the distance term D, the regularization term R, and the constraints. The effort for evaluating each component involving these terms will increase due to the additional number of mixture components encoding the prior knowledge. This means training time is drastically increased.

- The restriction to location-based mixture kernels based on a Gaussian mixture representation or approximation of the prior knowledge may be relaxed to other kernels in the sense of Appendix A.1.5. Note, that the favorable computational properties, e.g., that the product of two Gaussian densities is an unnormalized Gaussian density, will typically not be obtained. This is the main objection against a higher-order Bayesian approach to the introduction of prior knowledge, which would be theoretically optimal.

6.5   Main Contributions

In this chapter, the incorporation of prior knowledge into the conditional density estimation algorithms presented in Ch. 3 and Ch. 4 was demonstrated. The main contributions may be summarized as follows.

- The conditional density estimation based on samples and prior knowledge was demonstrated for two specific approximations of the prior knowledge. These approximations are generic as, e.g., the Gaussian mixture densities are universal approximators. The presented methods for incorporating prior knowledge is generically applicable for all conditional density estimators based on standard constrained optimization problems.

- The use of prior knowledge increases the prescriptive validity as shown in the experiments for both approximations and for two different estimators each.

- Even though the approach using mean function constraints increases training time less than the use of the proposed location-based mixture kernel, both approaches increase the training time necessary for obtaining the conditional density estimate.

It is a precarious undertaking
to say anything reliable about aims and intentions.
—ALBERT EINSTEIN

7 Intention Recognition

The second part of this thesis is concerned with intention recognition as a basis for the non-verbal communication between a human and a humanoid robot. Intention recognition is the process of estimating the intention of a human. The intention is not directly observable, i.e., hidden, and needs to be estimated from noisy and error-prone measurements of the human's behavior, e.g., from visual observations. In this thesis, a model-based approach is adopted, i.e., given the observations, the hidden intention is inferred using a model of the human rationale. Even though the recognized intention is typically only one input to a control of the humanoid robot, taking the information non-verbally conveyed by the human into account is decisive to enable close cooperation. This is especially important for humanoid robots.

Challenge The main problem addressed in this chapter is the scalability of the intention recognition under the constraints of uncertain asynchronous observations and real-time inference as required for interactive behavior by the robot. In most realistic scenarios, e.g., in a kitchen, many objects are present and may be used in conjunction with other objects in a large variety of workplaces for a lot of purposes. All of these object-action-place combinations need to be considered when inferring the intention of the human. For example in a kitchen, food may be processed by chopping, stomping, etc. in pots, pans, or on plates, which may in turn be located on the stove, table, or counter. Additionally, the available observations are uncertain, e.g., depend on specific lighting conditions, and are error-prone, i.e., sensors may fail or a person's object manipulations may be occluded. Furthermore, it may not be possible to obtain all measurements in each time step, but asynchronously and/or in batches. Fast inference in such a setting is challenging, but a *conditio sine qua non*. No human will tolerate a humanoid robot in his kitchen, which needs minutes to recognize that support in "washing the dishes" or "loading the dishwasher" is required.

Key Idea The key idea of the approach to efficient inference in large scale models given uncertain observations is to exploit that human behavior is bound to specific preconditions. For example, in order to "wash dishes", a human needs to be in the kitchen and will most likely perform this task only at certain times of the day. This definition of prerequisite conditions to human behavior matches the definition of a situation given in Def. 2.4. The key idea may be summarized as exploiting the situation-specific structure of the intention recognition problem. The advantage of conditioning the intention recognition on the prevailing situation is that the number of object-action-place combinations to be considered may be reduced drastically—allowing for faster inference. The remainder of this chapter is organized into sections considering the model of the human rationale and a computational model thereof, inference exploiting the situation-specific structure and using asynchronous measurements, learning the model parameters, and the experimental validation in a video-based and extended-range telepresence setups.

7.1 Model of the Human Rationale

The following exposition is based on [103, 169, 171] as summarized in [168] and shall be part of the control architecture for a humanoid robot as presented in [159, 160, 172]. The section is structured as follows. Initially, a causal model of the intentions is developed relating relevant objects with actions and places in the world. This type of modeling is intuitive but not sufficient if observations are uncertain as in the considered problem. For this reason, a computational model in the form of a Bayesian network is introduced, which extends the causal model by qualitative relations. Finally, a fragment-based model generation is proposed for the human-robot-cooperation problem with detailed, i.e., large models.

7.1.1 Causal Model

The causal model describes the causality between intentions and actions in the form of a graph $\mathcal{G}$ consisting of vertices $x_i \in \mathcal{V}$, $i \in \{1, \dots |\mathcal{V}|\}$ and directed edges $\mathcal{E}$ between vertices,

$$\mathcal{G} = (\mathcal{V}, \mathcal{E}), \qquad \mathcal{V} = \{x_i\}_{i=1,\dots|\mathcal{V}|}, \qquad \mathcal{E} = \{(x_i \rightarrow x_j)\}.$$

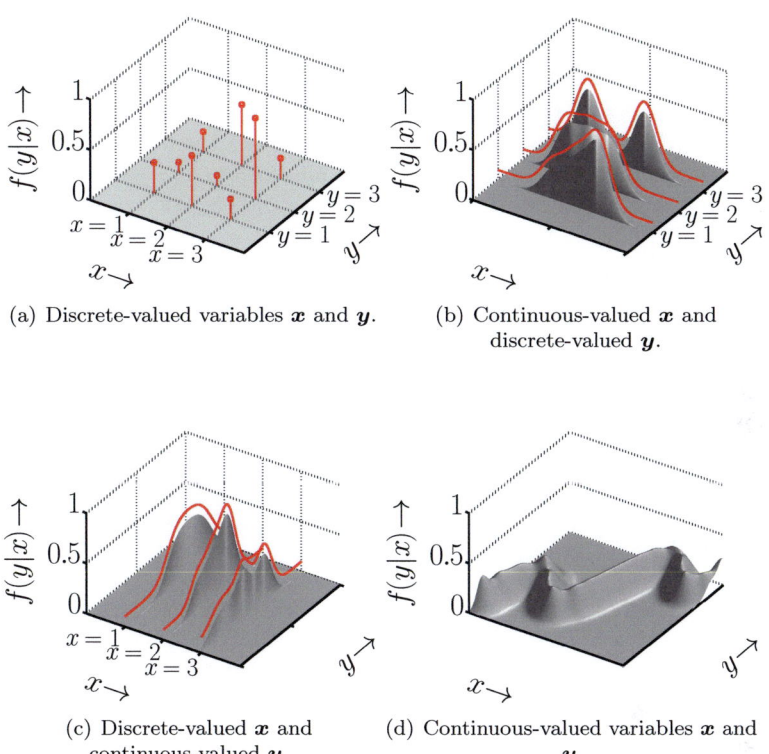

(a) Discrete-valued variables $\boldsymbol{x}$ and $\boldsymbol{y}$.

(b) Continuous-valued $\boldsymbol{x}$ and discrete-valued $\boldsymbol{y}$.

(c) Discrete-valued $\boldsymbol{x}$ and continuous-valued $\boldsymbol{y}$.

(d) Continuous-valued variables $\boldsymbol{x}$ and $\boldsymbol{y}$.

Figure 7.1: Four types of hybrid conditional density functions for scalar in- and output dimension $\boldsymbol{x}$ and $\boldsymbol{y}$.

The vertices correspond to causes and effects, i.e., the intention, action, objects, or places. The edges relate causes to effects. Due to this interpretation ($x_i \rightarrow x_j$), $i \neq j$ follows as neither may a cause be a cause nor an effect be an effect of itself. An example for a causal model [168, 170] is depicted in Fig. 7.2 (b). In this example, the cause "intention" may attain values in a set $\mathcal{A} = \{\, \mathrm{C}ook\,, \mathrm{Wash\ dishes}\,, \ldots \,\}$. The effect of the "action" caused by the "intention" may also attain values from an alphabet only. In contrast, the effect "distance" caused by the "action" is continuous-valued and may attain values, e.g., in $\mathbb{R}$. The shape of the nodes in the graphical models reflects this difference, i.e., rectangles for discrete-valued variables and ellipses for continuous-valued variables. Additionally, this example shows the dynamic dependencies of the intention, as the intention in each time step[1] depends on the intention in the previous time step. For example, if one did not prepare a meal one can not eat it. This model describes the causal dependencies governing the changes of the state of the world due to the human manipulation but does not account for any modeling or measurement uncertainty. For example the action Bring Object X to Place Y requires a change of location, but certainly no human will arrive at the precisely same location when repeating this action. From a practical point of view, observations are uncertain and ambiguous, i.e., disallowing for a mapping to one cause only. Therefore, a computational model capable of processing uncertain information is required.

7.1.2 Computational Model

In order to process uncertain information, the causal model is extended by mapping the vertices $\mathcal{V}$ of the directed graphical model to random variables and the edges $\mathcal{E}$ to conditional densities

$$x_i \mapsto \boldsymbol{x}_i, \quad \{ (x_i \rightarrow x_j), \ldots, (x_k \rightarrow x_j) \} \mapsto f(x_j \,|\, x_i, \ldots, x_k).$$

In contrast to the causal model, all dependencies with the same effect need to be converted into one conditional density function with all causes for the effect as arguments. The obtained probabilistic directed graphical model is a Bayesian network (BN) [142, 143][2] if only one time step is considered. Adding the dynamic dependencies, converts the model into a Dynamic Bayesian network (DBN) [39, 134]. As the set of random variables is mixed-valued, Hybrid Dynamic Bayesian network (HDBN) are considered [99, 116, 134, 168]. For the remainder of the thesis, HDBN of the type proposed in [168, 170, 173] and described below are considered.

Hybrid Dynamic Bayesian Network Many types of Hybrid BN (HBN) exist, cf. [99, 116, 134, 183] for an overview and [119] for theoretical limitations. All of these HBNs may be converted to HDBNs by appending temporal dependencies. Yet, none of these approaches allow for continuous

---

[1]In this thesis only discrete-time systems are considered. The interested reader is referred to [134] for more information about continuous time modeling.

[2]The interested reader is referred to [32, 101, 118] for concise introductions to BN and to [18, 99] for a more detailed treatment. A more generic review of BN in the context of undirected probabilistic graphical models may be found in [54, 111, 121, 18].

causes to discrete effects. Most approaches are limited to conditional linear Gaussian dependencies, which have the advantage of allowing for closed-form inference. Arbitrary nonlinear dependencies prohibit closed-form inference in general and typically require approximate inference. The representation proposed initially in [167, 170] and reformulated in [168, 173] is an exception. There are two key ideas underlying this type of HDBN: a mapping of discrete-valued variables into the continuous domain and a mixture density representation of both, the discrete- and continuous-valued random variables and dependencies. A discrete-valued random variable x_d is mapped to a continuous-valued random variable x_c as follows

$$
\begin{bmatrix} \text{Cook} \\ \text{Clean} \\ \vdots \end{bmatrix} \mapsto \begin{bmatrix} x_1 \\ x_2 \\ \vdots \end{bmatrix} , \quad \Rightarrow \quad \underline{\xi} = \begin{bmatrix} f(x = \text{Cook}) \\ f(x = \text{Clean}) \\ \vdots \end{bmatrix}
$$

$$
\approx f_c(x_c) = \sum_{i=1}^{|\mathcal{A}|} \alpha_i \, \delta \, (x_c - x_i) \, ,
$$

with $\text{Cook}, \text{Clean}, \ldots \in \mathcal{A}$, $x_i \in \mathbb{R}$, $i = 1, \ldots, |\mathcal{A}|$, $\delta(.)$ the Dirac delta distribution as defined in Appendix A.1.3, $f_c : \mathbb{R} \mapsto \mathbb{R}$, and α_i the probability values. Using this definition f_c returns non-zero values only at the locations x_i, which correspond to the events of the discrete valued random variable, cf. Fig. 7.1 (a). The above mapping allows for a unified modeling of discrete- and continuous-valued random variables as both density types may be described uniformly [168, 170, 173]. A hybrid conditional density function may be defined for the generic case of D discrete-valued and C continuous-valued parent variables where $N = D + C$ by

$$
f(y|x_1, \ldots, x_N) = \sum_{i=1}^{M} f^{(i)}(y) \prod_{d=1}^{D} f^{(i)}(x_d) \prod_{c=1}^{C} f^{(i)}(x_c) , \tag{7.1}
$$

and the scalar densities f are Dirac mixture densities in the case of discrete-valued and Gaussian densities in the case of a continuous-valued x or y. If only continuous-valued random variables are considered, Def. 7.1 corresponds to a Gaussian mixture representation of a conditional density with axis-aligned components. An extensive example and more explanation of this modeling can be found in [168, Ch. 3.6]. Note that a Gaussian mixture representation of a conditional density with axis-aligned components may be estimated with the approaches to conditional density estimation proposed in the first part of this thesis, cf. Ch. 3 and 4. If only discrete-valued random variables are given, the default matrix vector operations for discrete-valued BN [142, 143] are obtainable [168]. The modeling in 7.1 allows for continuous-valued random variables being parents of discrete-valued random variables. For scalar input and output values, the four different value-combinations of $f(y|x)$ are shown in Fig. 7.1.

7.1.3   Fragment-based Model Generation

In order to work with the proposed computational model, the causal structure and the respective conditional density functions need to be determined. Neither may such a model be hand-made exclusively due to its mere size, as, e.g., several hundreds of objects exist in a typical kitchen, nor may it be derived automatically exclusively, due to the large parameter space. Additionally, an automatically created model is not likely to be readable for a human, i.e., prohibiting error correction or adaption by the human. From a practical point of view model generation is most often performed by using expert knowledge and automatic model identification jointly. For example, the causal dependencies and the higher level conditional density functions may be easily determined by an expert, while the sensor models may be determined, e.g., by one of the estimation algorithms presented in the first part of this thesis. Additionally, the given problem may be simplified by reducing the number of parameters to be determined. One approach towards reducing the number of parameters to be estimated is the use of standardized model fragments, which share parameter [168, 169]. By using this parameter-tying, the number of parameters to be determined is drastically reduced. A typical fragment for the considered HRI problem might be, e.g., Take Object X, which models the process of holding an abstract object X [168]. Such a fragment is depicted in Fig. 7.2 (a, left) and may be used as a building block of a larger fragment Fig. 7.2 (a, right). which in turn is appended to an existing model as shown in Fig. 7.2 (b). Note that before combing the models, each fragment needs to be instantiated, i.e., the observable variables need to reference the variable of the world they model. For example, the observable variables distance and grasp of the fragment Take Object X, cf. Fig. 7.2 (a), need to reference the distance to the glas and the grasp of a glas. Appending the fragment then only requires adjusting the conditional density from the hidden node to each action, i.e., modeling the impact of an intention to Take Object(glas) w.r.t. all other actions.

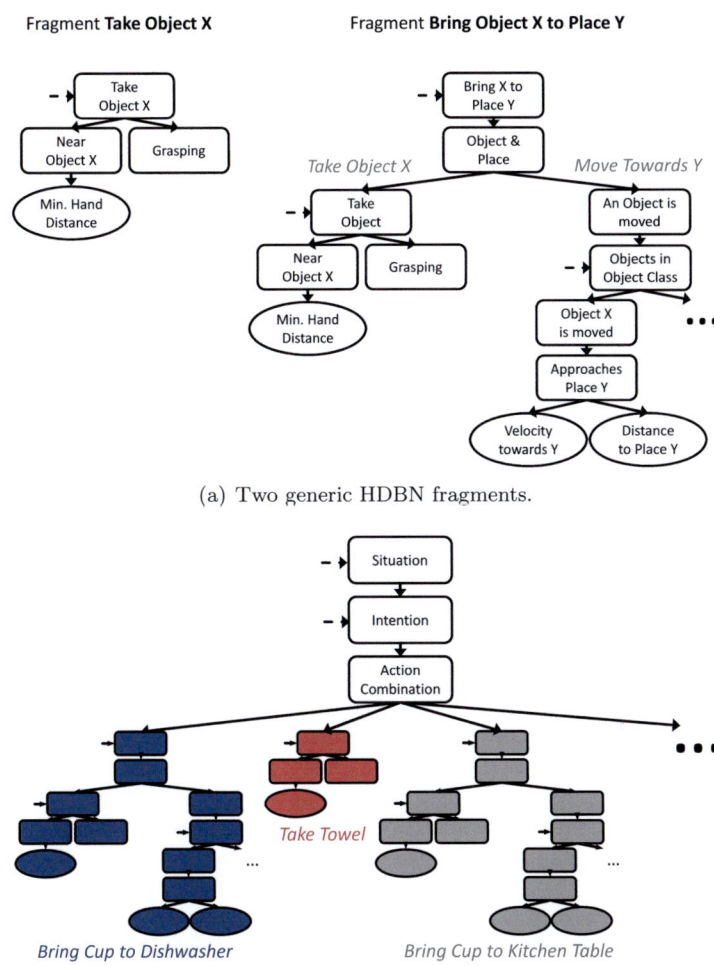

(a) Two generic HDBN fragments.

(b) Exemplary HDBN generated from a set fragments (a).

Figure 7.2: A HDBN may be constructed from generic fragments (a), which relate abstract objects X with abstract places Y. An exemplary HDBN for the intention recognition is shown in (b). It may be constructed using two stacked chains of dynamic dependencies for the situation and intention as well as a hidden node modeling action combinations. The actions are instantiated fragments (blue, red, gray). For example, object X corresponds to any cup, the place may be the dishwasher and the observable nodes, i.e., the leafs are the minimal hand distance to any cup as well as the hand distance and velocity of a specific cup towards the dishwasher.

Example 7.1: Exemplary HDBN Generation from Fragments
In this example, a rudimentary HDBN for estimating the intentions *Lay Table*, *Load Dishwasher*, and *Clear Table* will be created from the abstract fragments[3] shown in Fig. 7.2 (a). The HDBNs *Take Object X* and *Bring Object X to Place Y* correspond to the two abstract fragments shown in Fig. 7.2 (a). The fragment *Take Object X* consists of four random variables **Min. Hand distance** attaining values in $\mathbb{R}$ as well as **Near Object X**, **Grasping**, and **Take Object X** all using the alphabet { *Yes, No* }. The hybrid conditional density function between **Min. Hand distance** and **Near Object** assigns a high probability to *Yes* and low probability to *No* if a human is close to the Object X or vice versa. The conditional densities between **Near Object**, **Grasping** and **Take Object X** each model that the value *Yes* for **Take Object X** is assigned a high probability if the human is near the object or grasps it and a uniform distribution otherwise. During inference the probability for *Yes* will be very high if the human is close to the object and grasps. If only one event occurs *Yes* will be less likely but still will be more likely than *No*. The second abstract fragment *Bring Object X to Place Y* consists of two components: The first is the already described fragment *Take Object X*. The second is an HDBN modeling that a specific object is moved towards a specific location. The reasoning underlying the fragment for moving an object towards location Y resembles *Take Object X*. For more details, refer to [1, Ch. 5]. The remaining two random variables in this fragment are **Bring Object X to Place Y** with alphabet { Yes, No } and **Object & Place** with an alphabet consisting of the four combinations for binary-valued *Close to Place* × *Approaching Place*. Only the leaf nodes, e.g., distances to objects or velocities, of both fragments may be observed. In order to generate an HDBN for inferring the three intentions the abstract fragments need to be combined into one HDBN as shown in Fig. 7.2 (b). The basis of the HDBN in Fig. 7.2 (b) are three random variables **Situation**, **Intention**, and **Action combinations**. The alphabets are the set of situations, the set of intentions, and the number of relevant action combinations[4]. As the **situation** is prerequisite for a specific **intention**, which is causal for an **Action combination** consisting of actions, the fragments from Fig. 7.2 (a) are appended to the random variable **Action combination** in the HDBN in Fig. 7.2 (b). Note that each abstract fragment needs to be instantiated, e.g., a fragment **Take Object X** is instantiated as

---

[3]This example is based on the fragments as initially presented in [1] and further described in [168, Ch. 7] and [169]. The descriptions of all conditional density functions used in these fragments may be found in [1, 168].

[4]For an exact model, the number of actions combinations grows by $2^{\#\text{Actions}}$, cf. [169].

Take Object Towel by replacing the abstract object by the towel to which the distance is modeled. In order to improve efficiency, the distance may be calculated w.r.t. all objects satisfying the properties of a towel. Note that this extension of the graphical model is straightforward, but the conditional density functions relating the intentions with the combinations and the combinations with the actions, i.e., the fragments, need to be determined. The former should be learned from data. The latter may be an automatically generated conditional probability table (CPT), i.e., for each specific action combination the probability for a specific fragment is set. Details of the specific conditional density functions may be found in [169]. ∎

Properties and Restrictions The fundamental properties and restrictions of the proposed model as well as the fragment-based model generation are summarized in the following list.

- In this section, the derivation of an HDBN model extending the causal model to incorporate uncertainties has been discussed. An HDBN can handle uncertainty consistently, but is limited in its modeling capacity by having a fixed structure. Inference using an HDBN is therefore less powerful than, e.g., first-order logic.

- The size of a model constructed from fragments, may be approximated in terms of the variables/nodes. Let d be the depth of the tree corresponding to the average fragment, cf. Fig. 7.2 (a), and b be the branching factor of the tree composed from fragments, e.g., Fig. 7.2 (b). Then the size of the model is approximately in $\mathcal{O}\left(b^d\right)$. Note that this approximation assumes that with an increasing number of fragments, the number of nodes in the fragments increases simultaneously.

- The computational complexity of inference with an HDBN depends on the graph structure and the type of dependencies. Within each time-slice, the graph structure is a polytree [143, 156]. Additionally, the time, position, and distance measurements are continuous-valued, i.e., parts of the measurement system, and all other nodes are discrete-valued.

7.2 Inference

In the last section, a computational model of the human rationale in the form of a specific type of HDBN has been proposed. Intention recognition is performed by using the given observations of the human and performing inference from effect to cause with this model. The complexity of inference in a BN depends on the structure of the graphical model and the state spaces [141]. Intuitively, inference is harder if more quantities are interconnected and need to exchange information, e.g., calculating the posterior probability densities for a BN with a chain structure is easier than if a loop is present in the graph [18]. In general, inference in BNs with arbitrary graphs is NP-hard [18, 32, 99]. The computational complexity for purely discrete-valued BNs, with special types of graph structures, e.g., chains or polytrees grows polynomially with $|\mathcal{A}|$ and linearly with $|\mathcal{V}|$ [18, 32, 141]. In [119], it was shown, that there exist HBN (CLG) with polytree structure for which inference is NP-hard. Thus, inference in a HBN is at least as hard as for discrete-valued BN. Inference as such may be performed for a BN based on localized calculations of posterior densities, so-called "message passing" [32, 142, 143]. A generalization of this inference method w.r.t. Dynamic Bayesian network [39] is discussed in [99, 134] and a uniform framework for directed and undirected probabilistic graphical models is given, e.g., in [18, 99]. For the type of HDBN used in this thesis, a generalization of the "message passing" algorithm [32, 142, 143] has been proposed in [167, 168, 170]. This HDBN inference algorithm calculates the posterior densities of all random variables in the HDBN in closed form. For the remainder of this thesis, this algorithm will be used. The model this algorithm is applied to will be a polytree, where inference in the continuous-valued parts is limited to the leaf nodes and standard filtering, cf. Fig. 7.2 (b). The number of dynamic dependencies in this model is bounded and therefore negligible. Since the measurement system within each time slice corresponds to a polytree with discrete-valued variables—except for the leafs – inference in this model has a time complexity linear in the number of variables in the model, i.e., the number of nodes $|\mathcal{V}|$ in the graphical model.

Challenge The challenge to intention recognition arises from the combination of the size of the computational model proposed in Sec. 7.1.2 and the complexity of the inference. Informally, this means combining the linear complexity of the inference method, w.r.t. $|\mathcal{V}|$ in the graphical model—given a fixed $|\mathcal{A}|$—with the size of the computational model. The time complexity of inference with such a model, e.g., the model derived in Ex. 7.1, is in

$$\mathcal{O}\left(c\,b^d\right),\tag{7.2}$$

with the expected depth of the measurement tree d, branching factor b, and constant term c from the complexity of inference. Due to the combinatorial explosion of the model size, the overall computational complexity (7.2) will drastically increase too. There are basically two approaches towards addressing this problem: approximate inference and approximate modeling. There is a large variety of approximate inference methods for BNs [134]. Due to their conceptual simplicity and easy implementation, the most popular approximate inference methods are based on non-deterministic sampling [6], e.g., the particle filter (PF) [46], marginalized PF [166], or rao-blackwellized PF [134]. We refer the interested reader to [37] for an overview. According to [134] for discrete-valued DBN and BN "[...] the [...] disadvantage of sampling algorithms is speed: they are often significantly slower than deterministic methods, often making them unsuitable for large models and/or large data sets. [...]" [134, Ch. 5 and B.7.4]. Additionally to the best of our knowledge, no approximate method of inference, especially no PF has been developed for the considered HDBN type. Even though deterministic sampling approaches [48, 155] or combinations of sampling with analytical calculations [82, 94] seem promising for inference for the considered HDBN type. Approximate modeling methods may be categorized as exploiting contextual independence in BNs [134, B.6] and approximate modeling of dynamic dependencies [134, Ch. 6]. As described in [134, B.6], the key idea of exploiting the contextual independence corresponds to making independence implicit in the conditional density functions explicit by adding logical nodes to the BN in order to perform evaluations more efficiently. For the considered application, this would correspond to enlarging an even larger model. Approximate modeling of dynamic dependencies corresponds basically to making the time update in inference tractable. In summary, neither the approximate inference methods nor the approximate modeling methods address the key challenge of the given application, i.e., the complexity of the measurement system.

Key Idea The key idea behind efficient inference in large computational models of the type presented in Sec. 7.1.2 is to exploit the situation-specific structure of the problem in order to reduce the model size. The proposed approach may be understood as a combination of approximate modeling with approximate inference. The approximate modeling corresponds to the construction of a set of smaller models, e.g., constructed from less fragments. The approximate inference corresponds to inference with a selected smaller model and the selection of the smaller model to consider in the next time step. Even though the approach will not change the complexity class of the problem—unless the smaller models are of constant size and the selection algorithms requires constant time—a drastic speed up may be obtained, as

$$b > a \implies \mathcal{O}\left(c\,b^d\right) \gg \mathcal{O}\left(c\,a^d\right),$$

which will be shown to correspond to significant reductions in computation time. There are two challenges associated with this approach. First, the approximate modeling corresponds to the determination of a set of smaller models. Even though these models are smaller, there are more of them and the determination may not be trivial. Second, the approximate inference corresponds to the default state estimation w.r.t. a small model, but additionally requires the selection of a model from the set of smaller models. In order to solve this model selection problem, an appropriate measure for the approximation quality and speed up has to be developed and the model selection problem has to be performed online, cf. Fig. 7.3. In contrast to Bayesian multinets [15], the proposed approach changes the entire network structure and the selection approach is not modeled by an additional dynamic model. The proposed approach resembles other structured generation algorithms for BN, e.g., object-oriented BNs (OOBNs) [100] or situation-specific BNs [114, 126], which are constructed w.r.t. a specific query of the BN. An extension of OOBNs to dynamic queries is described in [64], where first-order logic is employed to infer the network structure. In contrast, the proposed approach does not infer a BN's structure by means of rules or logic, but selects one model out of a set of smaller models. The key advantage of the approach proposed in the following section is the selection process being probabilistic and model-predictive. This means, that it accounts for uncertain state information and the future development of the state as predicted by the dynamic dependencies in the HDBN, cf. Fig. 7.4.

7.2.1 Efficient Inference by Online Model Selection

The structure of this section is as follows. The components of the proposed approach will be discussed: the definition of the situation-specific smaller

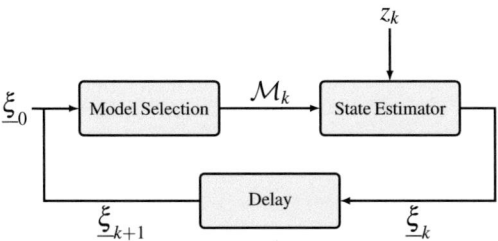

Figure 7.3: The current state estimate $\underline{\xi}_k$ is inferred based on the model $\mathcal{M}_k$ selected w.r.t. the prior state estimate $\underline{\xi}_0$ or last state estimate $\underline{\xi}_{k-1}$ and the current measurement $\hat{\underline{z}}_k$. The estimate $\underline{\xi}_k$ is then used to determine $\mathcal{M}_{k+1}$.

models, the model-predictive online model-selection, the selection criteria, and the properties as well as restrictions of the approach.

Definition of Submodels

In the remainder of this section, an efficient inference method based on selecting a smaller model, i.e., a submodel, is proposed. Given the exact, large model $\mathcal{U}$

$$\mathcal{U} = \{\, \mathcal{V}, \mathcal{C} \,\}\,,$$

a set of smaller submodels $\tilde{\mathcal{M}}$ is compiled. The large model $\mathcal{U}$ is defined by the set of all random variables $\mathcal{V}$ and conditional as well as prior density functions $\mathcal{C}$. Every random variable $v \in \mathcal{V}$ has its associated alphabet or domain $\mathcal{X}_v$. A submodel $\mathcal{M} \in \tilde{\mathcal{M}}$ is defined[5] by a set

$$\mathcal{M} = \{\, \mathcal{V}', \mathcal{C}' \,\}\,,$$

with $\mathcal{V}' \subset \mathcal{V}$ and conditional as well as prior density functions $\mathcal{C}' \subset \mathcal{C}$. Typically, it holds for two random variables $v \in \mathcal{V}$ and $v' \in \mathcal{V}'$ that $\mathcal{X}_{v'} \subset \mathcal{X}_v$ and for $\mathcal{M}, \mathcal{N} \in \tilde{\mathcal{M}}$ that $\mathcal{M} \cap \mathcal{N} \neq \emptyset$. The former is trivially achieved by means of zero-padding. For the investigated intention recognition problem, the challenge is to find a set of submodels $\tilde{\mathcal{M}}$, which describes the typical situations in the household scenario best.

---

[5]Note that the definition in terms of subsets is an abuse of notation as two discrete random variables with differing state spaces, e.g., $\mathcal{X}_v = \mathcal{X}_{v'} \cup \mathcal{A}$, with $\mathcal{A} \neq \emptyset$, are not identical. The same applies for the prior and conditional density functions.

Model-Predictive Approach

The model-predictive approach to inference in large HDBN may be under-stood as an online solution to the model selection problem, i.e., a sequential decision problem, cf. [10, 11] or [156, Ch. 17], taking the future develop-ment of the state into account. In each time step k, the model $\mathcal{M} \in \tilde{\mathcal{M}}$ to be used for the next time step $k + 1$ needs to be chosen. This is done w.r.t. an objective function $J(.)$ measuring the quality over a lookahead horizon defined by a maximum number of predicted future states K. In Fig. 7.4, the tree of model sequences for $K = 2$ is shown for the set of sub-models $\tilde{\mathcal{M}} = \{\, \mathcal{M}, \mathcal{N}, \mathcal{O}, \mathcal{P}\,\}$. Because the model selection is performed per time step and shall minimize the approximation error, it is proposed to minimize the distance between state estimates using the large model and submodel as a scalar-valued recursive cumulative objective function, cf. Appendix A.2.2. This recursive cumulative objective function[6] is defined for a finite time horizon $k \leq K$ by

$$ J(\underline{\xi}_k) = \min_{\mathcal{M}_k \in \tilde{\mathcal{M}}} \{\, g(\underline{\xi}_k, \mathcal{M}_k) + J(\underline{\xi}_{k+1})|_{\underline{\xi}_k, \mathcal{M}_k} \,\}, \qquad (7.3)$$

and the solution, i.e., the submodel to be used for inference in time step $k + 1$, is the minimizer

$$ \mathcal{M}_k^* = \arg \min_{\mathcal{M}_k \in \tilde{\mathcal{M}}} \{\, g(\underline{\xi}_k, \mathcal{M}_k) + J(\underline{\xi}_{k+1})|_{\underline{\xi}_k, \mathcal{M}_k} \,\}. \qquad (7.4)$$

In (7.3) and (7.4), the function $g(.)$ measures the quality of the selected model stepwise, e.g., in terms of approximation error or switching fre-quency. Note, for the sake of brevity the dependency on the sequence of predictions with the full model $\tilde{\underline{\xi}}_{k:k+K}$ and the previous submodel $\mathcal{M}_{k-1}$ was omitted. As the future state development is considered up to time step K only, the recursion in (7.3) ends with the following value

$$ J(\underline{\xi}_K) = \min_{\mathcal{M}_K \in \tilde{\mathcal{M}}} \{\, g(\underline{\xi}_K, \mathcal{M}_K) \,\}. \qquad (7.5)$$

Note that this definition of a sequential decision problem differs from the optimal control problem [10, 11] or the sensor selection problem [81]. The reason is that the expectation of future rewards w.r.t. future observations has been neglected. For the remainder of the section only discrete-valued

---

[6]For an overview of cumulative objective functions as used in sensor scheduling or selection, the interested reader is referred to [10, 11] in general, [81, 198] for continuous-valued (non)linear filter methods, and [203] for discrete-valued BN.

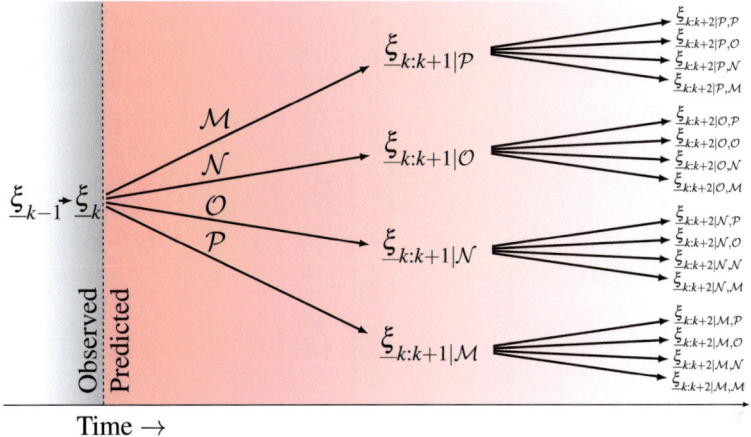

Figure 7.4: In the model-predictive approach, the possible state evolution is predicted given the current state estimate based on the observations made. The state evolution is predicted for the possible submodels, e.g., $\{\mathcal{M}, \mathcal{N}, \mathcal{O}, \mathcal{P}\}$, given the current estimate $\underline{\xi}_k$ until the desired prediction horizon is reached.

random variables and state-space models are considered. In the following two sections, applicable recursive cumulative objective functions for the model selection problem will be presented.

Recursive Cumulative Objective Function   There are basically two quantities, which the selection criteria needs to measure in each step:

$$\text{Deviation}(\tilde{\underline{\xi}}_k, \underline{\xi}_k), \qquad\qquad \# \text{ Model changes},$$

i.e., the deviation between the estimate produced by the large model $\tilde{\underline{\xi}}_k$ and its approximation $\underline{\xi}_k$ by using the selected submodel $\mathcal{M}_k$ as well as the number of model changes. In many cases, these measures are conflicting, i.e., choosing the model, which produces the least estimation error may mean switching the model in each and every step, e.g., flip-flopping between two models. In this thesis, two selection criteria will be investigated: mutual information and a distance between HMMs. The number of model changes may be modeled by a stepwise penalty.

(a) Mutual Information Mutual information I [18, 35, 123] is an information-theoretic criterion measuring the stochastic dependency between two random variables. Informally, the value of I may be understood as quantifying the mutual reduction in uncertainty by gaining information about one random variable. Mutual information is a measure commonly used in the sensor scheduling or selection problem both for scalar continuous-valued states [81, 83, 84, 198] and discrete-valued states [106, 203]. The mutual information between two continuous-valued random variables x and y is defined by

$$\mathrm{I}(\,x\,,\,y\,) = \int_{\mathcal{X}} \int_{\mathcal{Y}} f(x,y) \ln\left(\frac{f(x)\,f(y)}{f(x,y)}\right) \, dy \, dy, \qquad (7.6)$$

and for two discrete-valued random variables defined by

$$\mathrm{I}(\,x\,,\,y\,) = \sum_{x=1}^{\mathcal{X}} \sum_{y=1}^{\mathcal{Y}} f(x,y) \ln\left(\frac{f(x)\,f(y)}{f(x,y)}\right). \qquad (7.7)$$

From both (7.6) and (7.7), it can be seen that I is zero if x and y are independent and I attains higher values, the stronger the dependency is. For the given application I may quantify the strength of the stochastic dependency between $\widetilde{\xi}_k$ and its approximation $\underline{\xi}_k$. The submodel is a good approximation if the dependency between both variables is strong. For practical reasons this strength will be measured in the following sections relative to the entropy H.

(b) Distance Measure for HMM As shown in Sec. 7.1.3, the coarse dependencies in the HDBN are modeled by the relations between the intentions over time and the action combinations. If only a coarse estimate of the future state development is sought, it is sufficient to consider only the preceding and current intention as well as the action combination. These three nodes—as depicted in Fig. 7.2—constitute an HMM with discrete-valued state and observations, cf. [150]. A recent result from the literature about discrete-valued HMM compression [44] and decomposition [197] is a distance between two HMMs [201].

The key idea is to measure the distance in terms of total variation of the state estimate and all observations up to a given time step k produced, i.e., $\underline{\xi}_k$ and $\widetilde{\xi}_k$. As this distance calculation involves each and every observation combination, an approximate upper bound of the distance w.r.t. all observations has been proposed in [201], i.e.,

$$
\mathrm{D}\left(\underline{\xi}_k, \tilde{\underline{\xi}}_k\right) = \left\|\underline{\xi}_k - \tilde{\underline{\xi}}_k\right\|_{\mathrm{V}} \leq \left\|\underline{\xi}_{k-1} - \tilde{\underline{\xi}}_{k-1}\right\|_{\mathrm{V}} + \underbrace{a(\,\mathbf{F}, M_k\,)}_{\perp\,\underline{\xi}_{k-1},\tilde{\underline{\xi}}_{k-1}} . \qquad (7.8)
$$

This upper bound may be used as a substitute for the distance. Additionally, it avoids the determination of predicted future measurements as all measurements are considered. The generalized measurement update function $a(.)$ is independent of the predicted state estimates as well as the full model's estimate and may be calculated in advance. This distance measure may then be used straightforwardly in the optimization problem.

Probabilistic Branch- and Bound Algorithm   The aim of the optimization problem (7.3) is the determination of the submodel $\mathcal{M}_k$ to be used in the next inference step. In order to obtain the solution, the space of possible submodel sequences has to be searched for the minimizer of (7.3). As the size of the search tree grows exponentially with the prediction horizon K, branch-and-bound (BB) algorithms [156, Ch. 4] may be used to reduce the computational cost. A similar approach has been proposed for the sensor scheduling and selection problems [81, 195, 196]. The key idea of employing a BB algorithm is that the quality of some branches or nodes is dominated in the submodel sequence tree, cf. Fig. 7.4, and may be pruned during the incremental creation of the search tree [81, 156]. As the expansion of a node is based on a predicted state estimate, the proposed algorithm is denoted as a probabilistic BB (PBB) and summarized in Alg. 4. Starting with the given state estimate and the current model as the initial node in Alg. 4, the consecutive nodes are expanded w.r.t. the corresponding submodels, e.g., $\{\mathcal{M}, \mathcal{N}, \mathcal{O}, \mathcal{P}\}$ in Fig. 7.4. After this expansion, the respective child's $node.J$ value is calculated. The parent nodes' J values are recursively updated, i.e., the tree is traversed in backward direction. The $node.J$ value is calculated using a stepwise switching penalty $s(.)$ as well as (7.7) or (7.8), w.r.t. the prediction using the full model $\tilde{\underline{\xi}}_k$ and submodel $\mathcal{M}_k$, i.e., $\underline{\xi}_{k|\mathcal{M}_k}$

$$
g(\underline{\xi}_k, M_k) = s(\,M_k\,, M_{k-1}) + \begin{cases} 2\,\mathrm{H}\left(\tilde{\underline{\xi}}_k\right) - \mathrm{I}\left(\tilde{\underline{\xi}}_k, \underline{\xi}_{k|\mathcal{M}_k}\right), & \text{if } (7.7), \\ \mathrm{D}\left(\tilde{\underline{\xi}}_k, \underline{\xi}_{k|\mathcal{M}_k}\right), & \text{if } (7.8). \end{cases}
$$

Algorithm 4 Probabilistic Branch-and-Bound based on [195].

1: Initialize parameters
2: **while** not $\mathcal{N}$.exhausted **do**   ▷ Recurse until solution found
3:     **while** ($\mathcal{N}$.visited) **do**   ▷ Expand leaf nodes
4:         Calculate $\mathcal{N}.J$ for each child
5:         $\mathcal{C} \leftarrow$ Non-leaf child of $\mathcal{N}$ with $best..J$
6:         Recurse with $\mathcal{N} \leftarrow \mathcal{C}$
7:     **end while**
8:     **if** not ($\mathcal{N}$.visited) **then**
9:         **if** recursion level < horizon **then** ▷ Expand best search path
10:            $\mathcal{C} \leftarrow$ Instantiate child nodes of $\mathcal{N}$
11:            **for all** Children of $\mathcal{C}$ of $\mathcal{N}$ **do**
12:                $\mathcal{C}.J \leftarrow g(\mathcal{C}) + \text{Parent}(\mathcal{C}).J + \text{Switching Penalty}$
13:                $\mathcal{C}$.exhausted $\leftarrow$ FALSE
14:            **end for**
15:            Update $\mathcal{N}.J$ ▷ Update subtree value
16:        **else**
17:            $\mathcal{C}$.exhausted $\leftarrow$ TRUE
18:            Update parent J
19:        **end if**
20:        $\mathcal{N}$.visited $\leftarrow$ TRUE   ▷ Bookkeeping
21:    **end if**
22: **end while**
23: **Output:** Return $\mathcal{M} \leftarrow$ child with $best..J$

---

whereas, in contrast to [106], the mutual information score (7.7) is relative to the entropy H of the state estimate in order to obtain a minimization problem for both functions. The node with best *node.J* value is expanded. Alg. 4 terminates if there are no more nodes that may be expanded or all other nodes are dominated by an already expanded sequence.

7.2.2 Inference at Different Frame Rates

Inference in realistic scenarios is not only governed by a realistic number of objects and associated actions, but by realistic measurement setups. For example, there are potential delays induced by the network, which passes the sensor readings, the feature computation cannot deliver measurements in each time step, or the estimates are based on batches/windows of measurements. In Fig. 7.5 (a), an exemplary model is depicted for estimating the intention i_k from action estimates m_k and activity estimates a_k, which in turn are estimated from features v_k and v'_k. The assumption underlying the model shown in Fig. 7.5 (a) is, that all measurements are delivered in each time step. In realistic scenarios, measurements or updates arrive asynchronously and estimates from subsystems are based on batches of measurements, rather than a single measurement. This may be summarized as attributing an independent but constant update frequency for each subsystem and that the estimates correspond to batches of measurements. A realistic model based on these assumptions is given in Fig. 7.5 (b). In order to perform inference with a realistic model, one needs to adopt a "measure or predict" scheme as shown in [56] similar to the processing of out-of-sequence measurements [98]. For simplicity, consider m_k only and assume the measurements $\hat{\underline{v}}_{a:0}$, $a < k$ to be given. The intention estimate may be obtained from the following calculations, where $i_k \in \mathcal{I}_k$ and $m_k \in \mathcal{M}_k$

$$
f(i_k|\hat{\underline{v}}_{b:0}) \approx \int_{\mathcal{I}_{k:a}} \int_{\mathcal{M}_b} c \cdot \overbrace{f(i_{k:b+1}|i_b)}^{\text{Prediction}}
$$
$$
\cdot \underbrace{[f(\hat{\underline{v}}_{b:a}|m_b)f(m_b, i_{b:a+1}|i_a)]}_{\text{Measurement Update}} \underbrace{\cdot f(i_a|\hat{\underline{v}}_{a:0})}_{\text{Previous Filtering}} \mathrm{d}m_b \, \mathrm{d}i_{k:a} , \quad (7.9)
$$

if an estimate $f(\hat{\underline{v}}_{b:a}|m_b)$ for a batch of measurements $\hat{\underline{v}}_{b:a}$, $a < b < k$ is obtained. In (7.9), the state predictions for the time steps without measurements are calculated by

$$
f(i_{k:b+1}|i_b) = \prod_{l=b+1}^{k} f(i_l|i_{l-1}) ,
$$

$$
f(m_b, i_{b:a+1}|i_a) = f(m_b|i_b) \prod_{l=a+1}^{b} f(i_l|i_{l-1}) ,
$$

and the normalization constant in (7.9) is given by $c = 1/f(\hat{\underline{v}}_{b:a}|\hat{\underline{v}}_{a:0})$.

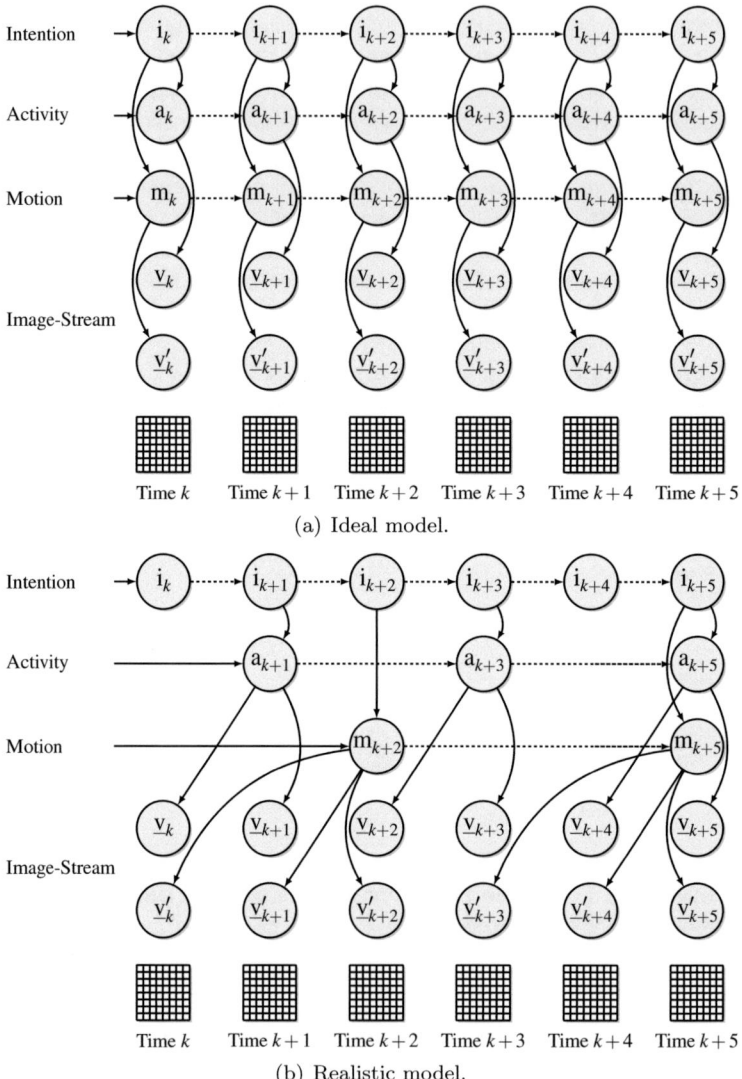

Figure 7.5: Ideal model assuming the availability of all measurements at all times (a) and a more realistic model assuming asynchronous, but constant measurement frequencies (b) for the video-based experiment of Sec. 7.4.1.

7.2.3 Properties and Restrictions

The properties and restrictions of the model-predictive approach for efficient inference and the inference with asynchronous measurements are discussed below.

- The proposed model-predictive approach is not optimal in the sense of an optimal solution to a control problem [10, 11, 81] as the expectation of the future objective function value w.r.t. future measurements has been omitted. The future measurements were either neglected or approximated. A further discussion of the optimality of the proposed approach remains future work.

- Regarding the inference at different frame rates, as discussed in Sec. 7.2.2, the proposed method is only approximate, as dependencies in the HDBN, e.g., the subsystems' dynamics, are neglected. Employing the prediction for the time steps, where no measurement is performed corresponds to assuming quasi-stationarity.

7.3 Learning

Learning the proposed HDBN is challenging for realistic scenarios. For example in the case of nine intentions manifesting in 60 actions, at least 531 conditional probability values need to be calculated. This number does not include the parameters involved in learning the continuous-valued measurement models. Learning may also involve not only fully observable, but also partially observable data. Data may be missing at random or not [99]. Approaches to learning HDBN may be categorized into approaches for learning single conditional density functions and entire networks, consisting of sets of conditional density functions and uncertain intermediary estimates. The first part of this thesis was concerned with learning conditional density functions relating only pairs of continuous random variables. The proposed approaches may be integrated into the approaches for learning entire networks. The interested reader is referred to [134] for an overview over learning entire networks. Note that learning DBNs may be subsumed by learning BNs with parameter-tying. In general two approaches for learning BN have been investigated: learning by maximizing the data log-likelihood by, e.g., a gradient ascent [9, 16] or by EM [75, 117]. A Bayesian approach towards learning discrete-valued BN has been proposed in [74]. Learning in the closely related mixture-of-experts framework

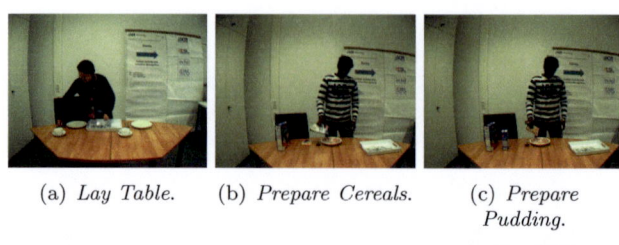

(a) *Lay Table.*   (b) *Prepare Cereals.*   (c) *Prepare Pudding.*

(d) *Eat with Spoon.*   (e) *Eat with Fork.*   (f) *Clear Table.*   (g) *Wipe Table.*

Figure 7.6: Snapshots of the seven different kitchen tasks considered in the video-based experiment in Sec. 7.4.1.

is discussed in [17, 90]. For learning hybrid BN, the interested reader is referred to [16, 132].

Properties and Restrictions

The properties and restrictions of learning HDBN are discussed below.

- Learning HDBN is challenging as it may involve a model selection problem for every conditional density function in the network. For a given network structure it may be impossible to learn certain relations as discussed in the context of blind source separation [186]. In general, no statement about the learning success is possible, e.g., about the convergence properties of EM [202]. Except for some special cases, e.g., fully-observable data in the limit, no descriptive or prescriptive validity may be proven.

- The computational complexity depends on the network structure as inference is used as a subroutine in learning. Inference has been shown to be NP-hard for hybrid networks even with polytree structure [119], i.e., at least as complex than in purely discrete networks.

7.4 Experimental Validation

The experiments in this section are part of the scenario used within the Collaborative Research Center 588 "Humanoid Robots - Learning and Co-operating Multimodal Robots"[7]. In the experiments, the properties and restrictions of inference with asynchronous measurements and the model-predictive approach for inference in large models are investigated. Video-based and extended range telepresence experiments are presented in this section. The former demonstrates inference with asynchronous measurements and may be understood as a proof of concept that the developed algorithms are applicable in a real-world setting. The latter allows for a discussion of the properties of the proposed inference methods for large models by varying the number of objects, places, and actions given a reproducible experimental setup.

7.4.1 Video-Based Experiments

The video-based experiments[8] are concerned with the actions, activities, and intentions of complex daily tasks in the kitchen setting as investigated in CRC 588. In the remainder of this section, the specific scenario, the specific underlying model, i.e., the considered actions, activities, and intentions, the experimental setup, as well as the results are presented.

Scenario In the considered scenario, a person enters a room, performs a task, e.g., laying the table, and then leaves the room again. The tasks may be understood as the visually observable manipulations of the world. Each of the considered tasks consists of different manipulations of objects as described in Tab. 7.1 and shown in Fig. 7.6 for seven different kitchen tasks. In this scenario, the considered set of intentions is the set of tasks further distinguished by knowledge of the current time, i.e., Eat with spoon is further discerned into Eat breakfast with spoon or Eat lunch with spoon depending on the time of day, cf. Tab. 7.1. An activity–as defined in Def. 2.6–is a distinct coarse movement in a part of the state space, i.e.,

---

[7]The German name is "Sonderforschungsbereich 588 Humanoide Roboter - Lernende und kooperierende multimodale Roboter" [182, 45] sponsored by the Deutsche Forschungsgemeinschaft (DFG).

[8]The results presented in this subsection are reproduced or extended versions of the joint work with Dirk Gehrig, Lukas Rybok et al. cf. [56] as part of the Collaborative Research Center 588 "Humanoid Robots - Learning and Cooperating Multimodal Robots"[9].

Table 7.1: Typical kitchen tasks and the corresponding intentions, activities, and actions as considered in the video-based experiment in Sec. 7.4.1. The seven different kitchen tasks listed below are depicted in Fig. 7.6.

Tasks	*Lay Table, Prepare Cereals, Prepare Pudding, Eat with Spoon, Eat with Fork, Clear Table, Wipe Table.*
⇓	
Intentions	*Lay Table, Prepare Cereals, Prepare Pudding, Spoon Breakfast, Spoon Lunch, Cut Breakfast, Cut Lunch, Clear Table, Wipe Table.*
Activities	*Lay Table, Prepare Meal, Eat with spoon, Eat with fork, Clear Table, Wipe Table.*
Actions	60 actions were defined, cf. [56], e.g., *Walk left, Pour, Stir, Place Object on Table*, etc.

manipulations by the human, but no objects are discernible [136, 157, 199]. This means that object and activity recognition are separated and their recognition results may be used complementarily. This alleviates the problem that some manipulations are ambiguous, but distinguishable by object knowledge. The set of activities is therefore a subset of the set of tasks. In this scenario, the tasks Prepare cereals and Prepare pudding correspond to the activity prepare meal, cf. Tab. 7.1. A fine-grained modeling of the human behavior into more than 60 actions[10]—in the sense of Def. 2.5— has been performed semi-automatically. Exemplary actions are Walk left, Pour, Stir, or Place Object on Table. These actions serve as an alphabet for a motion grammar [55], which describes the human behavior without knowledge about the present object or the time of day. The interested reader is referred to [56] for more information.

Specific Model   The considered model comprises five components: the intentions, actions, and activities, the object and time knowledge. As the computational model is an HDBN as described in Sec. 7.1.2, all of the five components are modeled as random variables with their respective

---

[10]In this thesis the term "action" is used synonymous with motion or motion primitive, cf. [55, 59, 56].

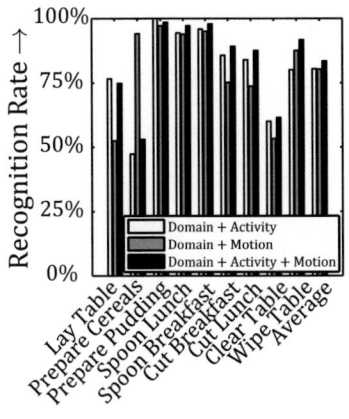
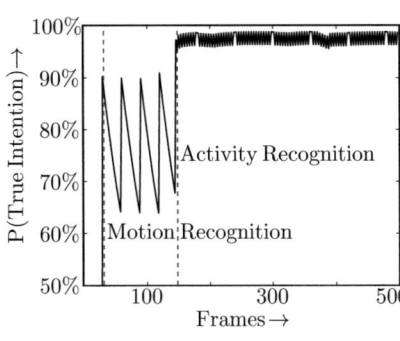

(a) Average recognition rates.

(b) Probability of the true intention over time.

Figure 7.7: The average recognition rates in terms of misclassifications of the ML estimate for each frame per intention is given in (a) for a model with uncertain object and time knowledge but with and without either the activity or the action recognition. The impact of the asynchronous measurement updates on the intention estimate for the video-based experiment of Sec. 7.4.1 is shown in (b). The results are based on [56].

relations. Such a model without object and time knowledge is given in Fig. 7.5 (a). The causal dependencies encoded in this model are as follows. The intention i_k as the force driving the human behavior causes both actions m_k and activities a_k. Neither actions m_k nor activities a_k are observable, but only specific features of the movements by the human are observable, which are caused by the actions and activities respectively, i.e., $\underline{\nu}_k$ and $\underline{\nu}'_k$. These features are directly calculated from each video frame, cf. [56]. Dynamic dependencies exist as the intentions, activities, and actions depend on their respective preceding values. The features as such are calculated for each image in the recorded video or incoming videostream. The models of the activities and actions, e.g. the action grammar, are described in [56].

Learning In order to obtain a realistic model, most of the parameters in the model shown in Fig. 7.5 (b) are learned automatically. From the five components the dependencies between the intention and activity as well

Ground Truth	Lay Table	Prepare Cereals	Prepare Pudding	Spoon Breakfast	Spoon Lunch	Cut Breakfast	Cut Lunch	Clear Table	Wipe Table	
Lay Table	5668 / 5.6%	57 / 0.1%	0 / 0.0%	0 / 0.0%	0 / 0.0%	0 / 0.0%	0 / 0.0%	1752 / 1.7%	92 / 0.1%	74.9% / 25.1%
Prepare Cereals	4015 / 4.0%	10890 / 10.8%	9970 / 9.9%	455 / 0.5%	440 / 0.4%	92 / 0.1%	98 / 0.1%	4538 / 4.5%	305 / 0.3%	35.4% / 64.6%
Prepare Pudding	44 / 0.0%	2 / 0.0%	0 / 0.0%	0 / 0.0%	0 / 0.0%	8 / 0.0%	8 / 0.0%	53 / 0.1%	6 / 0.0%	0.0% / 100%
Spoon Breakfast	0 / 0.0%	0 / 0.0%	12 / 0.0%	10527 / 10.5%	210 / 0.2%	119 / 0.1%	0 / 0.0%	0 / 0.0%	24 / 0.0%	96.6% / 3.4%
Spoon Lunch	0 / 0.0%	0 / 0.0%	0 / 0.0%	0 / 0.0%	10365 / 10.3%	114 / 0.1%	119 / 0.1%	0 / 0.0%	4 / 0.0%	97.8% / 2.2%
Cut Breakfast	90 / 0.1%	80 / 0.1%	80 / 0.1%	745 / 0.7%	80 / 0.1%	12433 / 12.4%	278 / 0.3%	93 / 0.1%	80 / 0.1%	89.1% / 10.9%
Cut Lunch	120 / 0.1%	120 / 0.1%	120 / 0.1%	120 / 0.1%	748 / 0.7%	124 / 0.1%	12387 / 12.3%	237 / 0.2%	120 / 0.1%	87.9% / 12.1%
Clear Table	1448 / 1.4%	100 / 0.1%	100 / 0.1%	100 / 0.1%	100 / 0.1%	100 / 0.1%	100 / 0.1%	3549 / 3.5%	175 / 0.2%	61.5% / 38.5%
Wipe Table	255 / 0.3%	181 / 0.2%	68 / 0.1%	8 / 0.0%	12 / 0.0%	0 / 0.0%	0 / 0.0%	203 / 0.2%	6079 / 6.0%	89.3% / 10.7%
	48.7% / 51.3%	95.3% / 4.7%	0.0% / 100%	88.1% / 11.9%	86.7% / 13.3%	95.7% / 4.3%	95.4% / 4.6%	34.0% / 66.0%	88.3% / 11.7%	71.5% / 28.5%

Estimate

(a) $\lambda = 0.00$.

Ground Truth	Lay Table	Prepare Cereals	Prepare Pudding	Spoon Breakfast	Spoon Lunch	Cut Breakfast	Cut Lunch	Clear Table	Wipe Table	
Lay Table	5668 / 5.6%	57 / 0.1%	0 / 0.0%	0 / 0.0%	0 / 0.0%	0 / 0.0%	0 / 0.0%	1752 / 1.7%	92 / 0.1%	74.9% / 25.1%
Prepare Cereals	4015 / 4.0%	11001 / 10.9%	304 / 0.3%	369 / 0.4%	376 / 0.4%	88 / 0.1%	92 / 0.1%	4538 / 4.5%	305 / 0.3%	52.2% / 47.8%
Prepare Pudding	44 / 0.0%	0 / 0.0%	9706 / 9.6%	30 / 0.0%	0 / 0.0%	8 / 0.0%	8 / 0.0%	53 / 0.1%	6 / 0.0%	98.5% / 1.5%
Spoon Breakfast	0 / 0.0%	0 / 0.0%	0 / 0.0%	10567 / 10.5%	180 / 0.2%	117 / 0.1%	0 / 0.0%	0 / 0.0%	24 / 0.0%	97.1% / 2.9%
Spoon Lunch	0 / 0.0%	0 / 0.0%	12 / 0.0%	0 / 0.0%	10430 / 10.4%	114 / 0.1%	117 / 0.1%	0 / 0.0%	4 / 0.0%	97.7% / 2.3%
Cut Breakfast	90 / 0.1%	80 / 0.1%	80 / 0.1%	769 / 0.8%	80 / 0.1%	12441 / 12.4%	250 / 0.2%	93 / 0.1%	80 / 0.1%	89.1% / 10.9%
Cut Lunch	120 / 0.1%	120 / 0.1%	120 / 0.1%	120 / 0.1%	789 / 0.8%	122 / 0.1%	12423 / 12.3%	237 / 0.2%	120 / 0.1%	87.7% / 12.3%
Clear Table	1448 / 1.4%	100 / 0.1%	100 / 0.1%	100 / 0.1%	100 / 0.1%	100 / 0.1%	100 / 0.1%	3549 / 3.5%	175 / 0.2%	61.5% / 38.5%
Wipe Table	255 / 0.3%	72 / 0.1%	28 / 0.0%	0 / 0.0%	0 / 0.0%	0 / 0.0%	0 / 0.0%	203 / 0.2%	6079 / 6.0%	91.6% / 8.4%
	48.7% / 51.3%	96.2% / 3.8%	93.8% / 6.2%	88.4% / 11.6%	87.2% / 12.8%	95.8% / 4.2%	95.6% / 4.4%	34.0% / 66.0%	88.3% / 11.7%	81.4% / 18.6%

Estimate

(b) $\lambda = 0.50$.

Ground Truth \ Estimate	Lay Table	Prepare Cereals	Prepare Pudding	Spoon Breakfast	Spoon Lunch	Cut Breakfast	Cut Lunch	Clear Table	Wipe Table	
Lay Table	5668 / 5.6%	51 / 0.1%	0 / 0.0%	0 / 0.0%	0 / 0.0%	0 / 0.0%	0 / 0.0%	1752 / 1.7%	92 / 0.1%	74.9% / 25.1%
Prepare Cereals	4015 / 4.0%	11028 / 11.0%	192 / 0.2%	140 / 0.1%	140 / 0.1%	28 / 0.0%	28 / 0.0%	4538 / 4.5%	305 / 0.3%	54.0% / 46.0%
Prepare Pudding	44 / 0.0%	0 / 0.0%	9828 / 9.8%	30 / 0.0%	0 / 0.0%	0 / 0.0%	0 / 0.0%	53 / 0.1%	6 / 0.0%	98.7% / 1.3%
Spoon Breakfast	0 / 0.0%	0 / 0.0%	10 / 0.0%	10705 / 10.6%	132 / 0.1%	117 / 0.1%	0 / 0.0%	0 / 0.0%	24 / 0.0%	97.4% / 2.6%
Spoon Lunch	0 / 0.0%	0 / 0.0%	0 / 0.0%	0 / 0.0%	10620 / 10.6%	110 / 0.1%	117 / 0.1%	0 / 0.0%	4 / 0.0%	97.9% / 2.1%
Cut Breakfast	90 / 0.1%	80 / 0.1%	80 / 0.1%	860 / 0.9%	80 / 0.1%	12515 / 12.4%	202 / 0.2%	93 / 0.1%	80 / 0.1%	88.9% / 11.1%
Cut Lunch	120 / 0.1%	120 / 0.1%	120 / 0.1%	120 / 0.1%	883 / 0.9%	120 / 0.1%	12543 / 12.5%	237 / 0.2%	120 / 0.1%	87.2% / 12.8%
Clear Table	1448 / 1.4%	100 / 0.1%	100 / 0.1%	100 / 0.1%	100 / 0.1%	100 / 0.1%	100 / 0.1%	3549 / 3.5%	175 / 0.2%	61.5% / 38.5%
Wipe Table	255 / 0.3%	51 / 0.1%	20 / 0.0%	0 / 0.0%	0 / 0.0%	0 / 0.0%	0 / 0.0%	203 / 0.2%	6079 / 6.0%	92.0% / 8.0%
	48.7% / 51.3%	96.5% / 3.5%	95.0% / 5.0%	89.5% / 10.5%	88.8% / 11.2%	96.3% / 3.7%	96.6% / 3.4%	34.0% / 66.0%	88.3% / 11.7%	82.0% / 18.0%

(c) $\lambda = 0.75$.

Ground Truth \ Estimate	Lay Table	Prepare Cereals	Prepare Pudding	Spoon Breakfast	Spoon Lunch	Cut Breakfast	Cut Lunch	Clear Table	Wipe Table	
Lay Table	5668 / 5.6%	51 / 0.1%	0 / 0.0%	0 / 0.0%	0 / 0.0%	0 / 0.0%	0 / 0.0%	1752 / 1.7%	92 / 0.1%	74.9% / 25.1%
Prepare Cereals	4015 / 4.0%	11032 / 11.0%	178 / 0.2%	16 / 0.0%	16 / 0.0%	0 / 0.0%	0 / 0.0%	4538 / 4.5%	305 / 0.3%	54.9% / 45.1%
Prepare Pudding	44 / 0.0%	0 / 0.0%	9852 / 9.8%	38 / 0.0%	8 / 0.0%	0 / 0.0%	0 / 0.0%	53 / 0.1%	6 / 0.0%	98.5% / 1.5%
Spoon Breakfast	0 / 0.0%	0 / 0.0%	8 / 0.0%	10775 / 10.7%	130 / 0.1%	117 / 0.1%	0 / 0.0%	0 / 0.0%	24 / 0.0%	97.5% / 2.5%
Spoon Lunch	0 / 0.0%	0 / 0.0%	0 / 0.0%	0 / 0.0%	10692 / 10.6%	110 / 0.1%	117 / 0.1%	0 / 0.0%	4 / 0.0%	97.9% / 2.1%
Cut Breakfast	90 / 0.1%	80 / 0.1%	80 / 0.1%	906 / 0.9%	80 / 0.1%	12543 / 12.5%	202 / 0.2%	93 / 0.1%	80 / 0.1%	88.6% / 11.4%
Cut Lunch	120 / 0.1%	120 / 0.1%	120 / 0.1%	120 / 0.1%	929 / 0.9%	120 / 0.1%	12571 / 12.5%	237 / 0.2%	120 / 0.1%	87.0% / 13.0%
Clear Table	1448 / 1.4%	100 / 0.1%	100 / 0.1%	100 / 0.1%	100 / 0.1%	100 / 0.1%	100 / 0.1%	3549 / 3.5%	175 / 0.2%	61.5% / 38.5%
Wipe Table	255 / 0.3%	47 / 0.0%	12 / 0.0%	0 / 0.0%	0 / 0.0%	0 / 0.0%	0 / 0.0%	203 / 0.2%	6079 / 6.0%	92.2% / 7.8%
	48.7% / 51.3%	96.5% / 3.5%	95.2% / 4.8%	90.1% / 9.9%	89.4% / 10.6%	96.6% / 3.4%	96.8% / 3.2%	34.0% / 66.0%	88.3% / 11.7%	82.3% / 17.7%

(d) $\lambda = 1.00$.

Figure 7.8: Impact of the uncertainty of the object knowledge on the recognition results. The confusion matrices give the classification rates in terms of the ML estimates matching the ground truth. The object knowledge varies from a uniform distribution ($\lambda = 0$) to 70% probability of the ground truth ($\lambda = 1$) for the experiments in Sec. 7.4.1.

as action, the dependencies between the actions and activities and their respective measurements are learned automatically. The dependencies between intention, object knowledge as well as the dynamic dependency of the intention are not learned but obtained from expert knowledge. For learning, a training data set in the form of videos of the seven tasks was recorded, cf. Tab. 7.1 and Fig. 7.6. This data set was split into an evaluation and a training set. The dependencies described above were learned separately, e.g., the dependency between action and features was optimized to yield the best recognition rates for this subsystem. Note that for learning the dependencies between the intention and activities or actions the estimated activities and actions were used. Learning the dependencies from features to activities and actions exceeds the scope of this thesis and the interested reader is referred to [56]. Regarding the dependencies between the intention and activities or actions the given estimates were assumed to be fully-observable data and learning then corresponds to calculating sample statistics [99]. The dynamic dependency of the intention is not learned, but set to a damping system, i.e., for continued predictions without measurements the intention estimate will converge towards a uniform distribution. All dependencies were learned using eight-fold LOO-CV, cf. Ch. 5.

Experimental Setup   The experimental setup for the recordings consisted of a fixed view-point camera on top of a tripod with the height of ca. 1.8 m. The camera was a Point Grey Dragon-Fly used with a frame rate of 30 fps and an image resolution of 640×480 pixel. The setup consisted of a table on which all manipulations were performed. The background is both plain and textured. Exemplary images of the setup are depicted in Fig. 7.6. As the experiments were recorded between 9 AM and 8 PM the lighting in the data varied from artificial to day light. The data corpus consists of recordings of all seven tasks for ten test persons. As each person performed each task ten times, a total of 700 videos were recorded. The recordings of the first two persons (140 videos) were used as evaluation and the other recordings (560 videos) as training set. The data set is publicly available from `http://www.sfb588.uni-karlsruhe.de/minta/`.

Results   As the focus of this thesis is on the intention recognition, the performance of the activity and action recognition system is not reported. The interested reader is referred to [56, Ch. VII] for more information. The presented results are either reproduced or extended versions of the results

(a) Head-mounted display for stereo display of the virtual household. (b) Bluetooh cyberglobe with wired acoustic hand tracking device. (c) Mobile computer used for visualization and tracking the head and hand.

Figure 7.9: Equipment for extended range telepresence experiments in Sec. 7.4.2: a head mounted display for a stereo visualization of the virtual household (a), a cyberglove with attached acoustic tracking system for measuring the finger angles (b), i.e., grasping activity, and a mobile computer (c) producing the visualization as well as the head and hand tracking calculations. A test person wearing all equipment is shown in Fig. 7.10.

presented in [56]. The recognition rate $R(.)$ of the estimator is calculated w.r.t. the number of frames $|\mathcal{F}|$ of the evaluation set $\mathcal{F}$, the true intention $\tilde{i}_k$ and the maximum likelihood estimate $\mathrm{ML}(\underline{i}_k)$ of the intention estimate $\underline{i}_k$ for each frame k.

$$R(\mathcal{F}) = \frac{1}{|\mathcal{F}|} \sum_{k=1}^{|\mathcal{F}|} |\mathrm{ML}(\underline{i}_k) \odot \tilde{i}| \qquad (7.10)$$

with the element-wise vector multiplication $\odot$. In Fig. 7.7 (a), the intention recognition results using either the activity or the action recognition, and both recognition systems are given as average ML recognition rates over all frames. The object and time knowledge was always supplied. The average intention recognition results (7.10) improve the more information is used, e.g., the complementarity of the activity and action recognition can be seen especially for two intentions lay table and wipe table. In Fig. 7.7 (b), the benefit of using a model for the coarse activities and fine-grained actions is shown over time. Additionally, the benefit of the object knowledge may be seen in the estimation results when using only object and time knowledge as well as the activity recognition. Only due to the object knowledge may Prepare Cereals and Prepare Pudding be distinguished. The impact of the time knowledge can be seen in the recognition results for the breakfast and lunch tasks. The impact of the object knowledge w.r.t. the level of uncertainty λ with which it was used is shown for four values of λ in Fig. 7.8. The results show that the object knowledge improves the results, but the estimation results without object knowledge would still be high for $\lambda = 0$. The intention is estimated every second frame. The estimates of the activity recognition start after ca. 120 frames and is updated every fourth frame. The action recognition results are available every 30th frame. The effect of the different update rates is shown in Fig. 7.7 (b). The impact of the damping system used for the prediction in the sense of Sec. 7.2 can be seen by a zig-zagging curve.

7.4.2   Extended-Range Telepresence Experiments

In order to determine the properties and restrictions of the model-predictive approach to inference in large models experiments using extended-range telepresence (ERT) were performed. In contrast to the video-based experiments, experiments in the ERT may be very easily extended to scale the number of objects. The experimental environment used for the experiments was initially developed in a student research project [1, German] as part of the CRC 588. An overview over the entire system is given in [168, Ch. 7.2]. The key idea of the ERT as an experimental environment for the intention recognition is that a test person is telepresent in a virtual 1:1 scale version of the CRC 588 household scenario. The test person wears a head mounted display on which a view of the household scenario relative to his pose in the virtual household is rendered, cf. Fig. 7.9 (a). The position of the test person's head and left hand in the real-world is tracked by an acoustic tracking system [13, 14], cf. Fig. 7.9 (b) and (c). The relative motions in the real world are mapped into motions in the virtual world, thus giving the test person the impression of moving in the virtual household, cf. Fig. 7.10. The advantage of this specific extended range telepresence system [14, 68, 154] is that the motion is compressed [137] mapping the test person's motions in the limited area, which is tracked, to a much larger virtual household and a potentially infinitely large environment. Besides the test person's head and hand positions his grasping activity is measured by a cyberglove device[11]. Using the grasping and position information, the object manipulations, i.e., the change in pose or stacking relations, are rendered in the virtual house. The object knowledge is thus directly obtainable from the computer graphics model underlying

---

[11]This cyberglove was produced by the Forschungszentrum Karlsruhe (FZK) within the CRC 588.

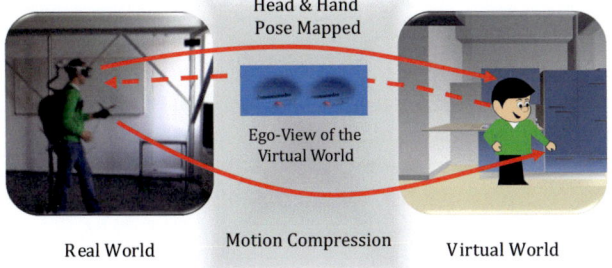

Figure 7.10: Setup for the ERT experiments: the user wearing a head-mounted display, a bluetooth cyberglove and tracking devices on the hand as well as the head (left). The tracked poses and grasp are mapped into the virtual household, e.g., into the kitchen (right), cf. Sec. 7.4.2.

the virtual house. In summary, the ERT experimental setup allows a test person to move naturally in a virtual model of the household scenario. The tracked grasping activity as well as the head and hand positions serve as input to the intention recognition. Note, that these measurements are subject to measurement noise. The ERT setup has two advantages in comparison with the video-based setup: scalability and reproducibility. The scalability refers to the virtual household size and the number of considered objects contained in the household. The size and number of objects of the virtual household may be as easy increased as a designer may create and add virtual objects. Additionally, the experimental setup may be reproduced exactly, i.e., a restart of the virtual household resets the state of all objects in the virtual household. Due to these two advantages, the ERT setup is especially advantageous for investigating the properties and restrictions of the proposed inference method for large models. The experiments and results are extended versions of the experiments presented in [104, 106].

Scenario In this scenario a test person performs a fixed task sequence in the household. The high-level description of this sequence is that the test person at first eats a meal, which consists of laying the table, cooking, and clearing the table. The more detailed task description[12], which was read to the test persons is given below.

Task description The person starts at the center of the virtual kitchen. He sets the table by putting a plate and a cup onto the table inside the kitchen. Thereafter the person performs a symbolic cooking procedure, consisting of approaching the stove, putting a pot onto the stove, and bringing the pot to the table. After waiting a couple of seconds in front of the table–which corresponds to symbolic eating the prepared meal– the person opens the dishwasher, puts an object from the table into the dishwasher, and closes the dishwasher again. This partial clearing of the table is meant as a decision point, where the humanoid robot may start helping the human by finishing the started task. After having closed the dishwasher the test person leaves the kitchen, walks down the hall-way into the living room.

This task has been performed ten times with six different test persons. Note that the test person were left with the choice in which order, the objects for laying the table were carried to the table and which object was put into the dishwasher for symbolically clearing the table.

Specific Model Two experiments in the ERT with different model sizes were performed to test the scalability of the approach, cf. Tab. 7.2. The full model used in Ex. 1 estimated ten intentions with a HDBN of 305 nodes. In Ex. 2, 15 intentions were estimated using 611 nodes in the full model. The set of submodels consists of four models, i.e., $\mathcal{M}, \mathcal{N}, \mathcal{O}$, and $\mathcal{P}$, with different numbers of nodes, cf. Tab. 7.2. These models are composed of all fragments associated with a given situation. For example all fragments for Lay Table and Clear Table were combined in one model. This may be understood as removing all nodes from the full model except for the fragments related to Lay Table and Clear Table.

Experimental Setup In this subsection details about the performed experiments as well as the technical details for the ERT as motivated in the beginning of Sec. 7.4.2 will be given. The execution of each sequence took ca. 10-20 Min. to complete. From all recordings the first 12.5 Min. were used. As the parameters of the models are not learned, this is directly the

---

[12]The detailed task description was read to the test person in German. The description given is a translation.

Table 7.2: Number of nodes in the full model
and submodels used for the ERT Ex. 1 and 2.

#Nodes	Full model	$\mathcal{M}$	$\mathcal{N}$	$\mathcal{O}$	$\mathcal{P}$
Ex. 1	305	243	229	179	49
Ex. 2	611	299	229	275	497

evaluation set for recognition rates presented in the following section. The
area covered by the tracking system of the ERT was ca. 3×4 m. The
setup of the tracking system follows [13, 14]. As all of the information
regarding the object poses, the head and hand position of the human as
well as the grasping activity were recorded by accessing the object model
underlying the visualization a uniform update rate of 750 ms was used.
Quantitatively, the noise is roughly normal in x- and y-direction and has
variances of $\sigma \approx 5$ cm as well as $\sigma \approx 10$ cm in z-direction. Regarding
the model-predictive approach the parameters are set as follows if not otherwise specified. The number of look-ahead steps is set to 2 and model
selection is performed in every fifth update step. Switching the model is
penalized by a $1/($number of intentions$)$. The complexity costs for each
model in the switching approach are set to the normalized sum of number
of nodes in each model, cf. Tab. 7.2, and [100 100 200 400], to equalize
the differnt model sizes. For the selection criteria, the switching penalty
and the complexity costs are weighted against the similarity score by factors of 0.2 and 2, i.e., switching is less penalized than complexity costs in
order to show the speed-up achievable if only a small estimation error is
accepted. A tiny value was used for the mutual information criterion and
set to $1e^{-04}$.

Results For assessing the quality two criteria are used: approximation
quality and speed-up. Regarding the approximation quality, the deviation
between the posterior densities of the intention D_f as estimated for time
step k using the standard approach $\tilde{\underline{\xi}}_k$ and the model-predictive approaches
$\underline{\xi}_k$ is measured according to

$$D_f(\tilde{\underline{\xi}}_k, \underline{\xi}_k) = \left\| \tilde{\underline{\xi}}_k - \underline{\xi}_k \right\|_1 ,$$

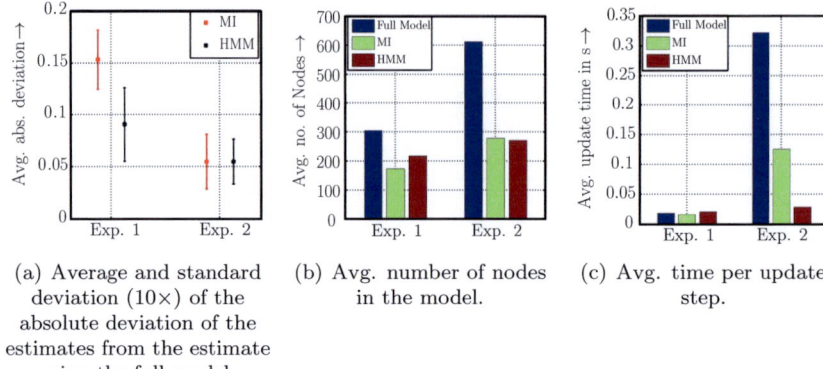

(a) Average and standard deviation (10×) of the absolute deviation of the estimates from the estimate using the full model.

(b) Avg. number of nodes in the model.

(c) Avg. time per update step.

Figure 7.11: Average difference between the intention estimates $\underline{i}_k$ using the full and the reduced model as well as the respective standard deviation for both experiments and both objective functions (a). The used average number of nodes and computation time per step for both objective functions are given in (b) and (c).

and the results are then given as average absolute deviations over all frames

$$D(\mathcal{F}) = \frac{1}{|\mathcal{F}|} \sum_{k=1}^{|\mathcal{F}|} D(\tilde{\underline{\xi}}_k, \underline{\xi}_k) \,. \tag{7.11}$$

The speed-up is defined as the decrease in processing time without input-/output operations per frame. The results of the experiments are given for the two model decompositions shown in Tab. 7.2. For a good decomposition scheme, a very low approximation error can be obtained, cf. Fig. 7.11 (a), allowing for the use of smaller models, cf. Fig. 7.11 (b), and thus resulting in a speed-up of up to one order of magnitude as shown in Fig. 7.11 (c). In contrast for a less favorable set of smaller models a worse approximation quality is inevitable and in some situations too many model changes may be observed.

7.5 Main Contributions

The main contributions of this chapter regarding the intention recognition for human-robot-cooperation are summarized in the following list w.r.t. descriptive and prescriptive validity as well as computational efficiency.

- In this chapter, a model-predictive approach for efficient inference in large-scale models based on online model selection was proposed. The presented approach reduces the descriptive and prescriptive validity as it approximates an already existing model, in order to allow for more efficient inference in the large model.

- Even though the proposed model-predictive approach does not change the computational complexity class, it improves the computational efficiency by a large factor and allows for real-time inference with larger and more realistic models. Two different objective functions aimed at an online model selection have been presented and discussed for this purpose. The proposed method enables non-verbal communications for more scenarios.

- A method for processing asynchronous measurements was proposed in this chapter. This method is of importance for the practitioner as in realistic scenarios, sensor information of mid-level fusion results are typically not instantaneously available to the estimator, but arrive in batches or aggregates of batches of measurements. The applicability of the method was demonstrated in video-based experiments.

- The practicability of the proposed approaches towards efficient inference with large models has been demonstrated using an extended range telepresence scenario with differing numbers of object-action-place combinations in the virtual household.

I enjoyed your seminar.
Before I was confused,
now I am still confused,
but on a higher level.
—Louis Pasteur

8 Conclusions and Future Work

In this thesis, methods for enhancing the intention recognition capabilities of technical devices, such as humanoid robots, were developed. The problem of inferring the intention of a human by a technical device was understood as a problem of modeling, inference with, and learning probabilistic graphical models. In detail, the proposed methods may be employed but are not restricted to Hybrid Dynamic Bayesian networks. In the following, the main contributions of this thesis and possible future work are summarized. In analogy to the structure of the thesis, these are categorized by the main challenges, which were addressed: model identification and intention recognition.

8.1 Model Identification

As described above, a probabilistic graphical model is used for the intention recognition. These probabilistic models not only describe the existence of dependencies between random variables, but also their quality in terms of density and conditional density functions, i.e., prior densities and state transitions. In this thesis, model identification by estimating density and conditional density functions given the graphical model structure is considered. More specifically, the problem of determining continuous-valued density and conditional density functions from samples is discussed. In both cases, the estimation problem is further restricted to the estimation of functions in the form of Gaussian mixtures densities. The contributions presented in this thesis and possible future work are listed below.

Main Contributions

- A *sparse mixture density and conditional density estimation algorithm based on a weight optimization* has been proposed. This method restricts all components to be fixed to the sample points and the parameters for all component covariances to be identical. The method may be understood as an extension of kernel density estimation by a weight optimization. Whereas the optimization is performed w.r.t. a novel distance between localized cumulative distributions and a regularization term, e.g., a norm in an RKHS or a Rényi Entropy-based term. Due to the semi-definiteness of the elements of the target function it could be shown that the arising optimization problem is a constrained convex quadratic problem. The problem may therefore be solved in polynomial time w.r.t. the number of optimization variables and constraints.

- A full parameter identification algorithm, which lifts the restrictions of collocation of components' means with the data and parameter-tying of the components' covariances was introduced. For the purpose of an improved approximation and generalization quality, a superficial regularization term was derived, allowing for a simultaneous regularization of the surface of the conditional density function and a generative model potentially underlying the surface. In order to represent the model uncertainty in the presence of scarce or no data in parts of the state space, a method for calculating the component covariances w.r.t. the local data distribution was developed.

- A hyperparameter optimization algorithm determining the parameters not estimated by the non-parametric or full parameter identification algorithms, e.g., the trade-off between data fit and regularization or the kernel parameters, was presented. The proposed algorithm may be understood as a blend of a hyperparameter optimization used in SVMs and the ex-ante parameter estimation in classical kernel density estimation. The algorithm is the first approach towards a cross-validation–based hyperparameter optimization algorithm for the proposed non-parametric or full parameter density and conditional density estimation.

- A method for the incorporation of prior knowledge to allow for exploiting expert knowledge not given in the form of samples or previously compiled models was proposed and shown to improve the estimation quality. Prior knowledge given in the form of generative and probabilistic models is approximated by means of additional constraints and a mixture kernel respectively. These approximations are generic and simple to introduce into the presented and all other conditional density estimation algorithms, which may be phrased as a constrained weight optimization problem.

Future Work

- Efficiency may be improved by exploiting the locality inherent in the problem. Due to the availability of large data sets relevant for many applications, e.g., "A Mine of its own" [192], an improvement in training time will be necessary to address large data sets. A very promising approach in this direction is the truncation of mixture components of the density and conditional w.r.t. their distance based on existing error bounds. This allows for an efficient processing of the functions, e.g., by dual-tree schemes [78] and may additionally offer significant speed-ups for recursive state estimation.

- The learning problem may be reduced from high-dimensional spaces to manifolds. Many data sets and the respective full parameter identification require the solution of the density and conditional density estimation problem in a high-dimensional space. This challenge is inherent in the problem. If these estimation problems may be considered locally only, the estimation problem is likely to be intrinsically of lower dimension. Therefore, one potential solution to this problem is to determine the intrinsic manifold and perform the estimation only w.r.t. this lower-dimensional space [145].

- Models should be learned incrementally. This feature is crucial in order to develop adaptive nonlinear state estimators. The challenge lies not only in the unavailability of exact state values, but also in the dynamic regularization of the estimates. One possible direction for further work is a Bayesian adaption scheme based on the model uncertainty as obtained from the full parameter identification.

8.2   Intention Recognition

The capability to recognize the intention as the driving force behind the human behavior is of importance to many technical devices. One important challenge to intention recognition in general is the efficient inference in complicated scenes with many objects to take into account. This problem is especially important for the intention recognition by humanoid robots. These robots shall assist the human and therefore have to cooperate closely with the human. If the inference in non-trivial models is too slow, no useful reactive assistance by the humanoid robot will be possible. The contributions of this thesis towards alleviating this problem and possible future work is summarized in the following lists.

Main Contributions

- A model-predictive approach towards efficient inference in large scale models based on online model selection has been proposed. The method is based on the key idea that a human's intentions are bound to preconditions, i.e., situations, and these situations may be exploited to restrict inference to smaller models. In order to solve the model selection problem of finding the appropriate smaller model in a set of small models, selection criteria based on mutual information and a distance between HMM have been proposed. Using the model-predictive approach with online model selection allows for inference to be sped up by up to an order of magnitude at low approximation errors.

- Inference with asynchronous measurements has been proposed. One of the main challenges for the implementation of intention recognition systems involving multimodal sensors is the fusion of measurements or mid-level estimates at asynchronous update rates. Additionally, mid-level estimates may summarize batches of measurements. The proposed inference method compensates for these deficiencies and was shown to produce recognition rates of more than 80% in a video-based experiment.

Future Work

- Intention recognition will benefit from more domain knowledge and active sensing. As shown in the Sec. 7.2.2, the entire non-verbal communication may be modeled as one joint Bayesian network. This understanding motivates that in the sense of Pearl's message passing algorithms measurement systems, such as the activity and action recognition, may use domain knowledge or higher-level information to refine their respective estimates. It seems promising that the view of a camera system of a humanoid robot may be adjusted to allow for the most informative measurements.

- Automated situation decomposition will facilitate inference in large scenarios. The central prerequisite for the proposed model-predictive approach to efficient inference based on online model selection is the availability of a set of situation-specific smaller models. For large scenarios, a manual construction of this situation-specific models is not possible and thus automated model construction methods appear to be inevitable.

A Appendix

For the sake of self-containedness, in the remaining part of this chapter basic definitions are restated as well as abbreviated calculations and omitted proofs are given. Throughout the appendix, the definitions $x, \mu \in \mathbb{R}$, $\sigma \in \mathbb{R}_+$, $\underline{x}, \underline{\mu} \in \mathbb{R}^N$, and $\mathbf{C} \in \mathbb{R}^{N \times N}$, $\mathbf{C}$ p.s.d., will be used.

A.1 Density Representations

In this section, the definition of a density and relevant representations are described. These definitions were compiled from from [127, 139, 180] and [92, German]. A generic function

$$ f : \Omega \longmapsto [0, 1] , \tag{A.1} $$

mapping from a probability space Ω, e.g., $\mathbb{R}^N$, to the interval $[0, 1]$ is a valid probability density function (PDF), if and only if,

$$ \int_\Omega f(\underline{x}) \, \mathrm{d}\underline{x} = 1 . $$

Note, (A.1) particularly implies $f(\underline{x}) \geq 0$.

A.1.1 Normal Density

Due to its many advantageous properties, e.g., entropy maximization and minimization of the Kullback-Leibler divergence [72], the normal density, for the scalar case defined as

$$ \mathcal{N}(x - \mu, \sigma) := \tfrac{1}{\sqrt{2\pi}\sigma} \exp\left\{ -\tfrac{1}{2} \tfrac{(x-\mu)^2}{\sigma^2} \right\} , \tag{A.2} $$

and for the multivariate case defined as

$$ \mathcal{N}(\underline{x} - \underline{\mu}, \mathbf{C}) := \tfrac{1}{\sqrt{\det(2\pi\mathbf{C})}} \exp\left\{ -\tfrac{1}{2}(\underline{x} - \underline{\mu})^{\mathrm{T}} \mathbf{C}^{-1}(\underline{x} - \underline{\mu}) \right\} , \tag{A.3} $$

is a very common density function. The normal density is said to be *axis-aligned*, if

$$ \mathbf{C} = \mathrm{diag}(\underline{\sigma}) , \tag{A.4} $$

with $\underline{\sigma} = [\sigma_1^2 \ldots \sigma_N^2]^T \in \mathbb{R}^N$, which allows a decomposition according to

$$\mathcal{N}(\underline{x} - \underline{\mu}, \mathbf{C}) = \prod_{i=1}^{N} \mathcal{N}(x_i - \mu_i, \sigma_i). \qquad (A.5)$$

Even if (A.4) doesn't hold, it is often used an approximation to the non-aligned density. A heavily exploited property of the normal density, is that the product of two normal densities yields an (unnormalized) normal density again as

$$\mathcal{N}(x - \mu, \sigma) \cdot \mathcal{N}(x - \nu, \tau) = \mathcal{N}(\mu - \nu, \sqrt{\sigma^2 + \tau^2}) \cdot \mathcal{N}(x - \mu', \sigma'), \quad (A.6)$$

for the scalar case, with $\mu' = \frac{\mu\tau^2 + \nu\sigma^2}{\sigma^2 + \tau^2}$, $\sigma' = \frac{\tau^2\sigma^2}{\sigma^2 + \tau^2}$, and for the multivariate case

$$\mathcal{N}(\underline{x} - \underline{\mu}, \mathbf{C}) \cdot \mathcal{N}(\underline{x} - \underline{\nu}, \mathbf{D}) = \mathcal{N}(\underline{\mu} - \underline{\nu}, \mathbf{C} + \mathbf{D}) \cdot \mathcal{N}(\underline{x} - \underline{\mu}', \mathbf{C}'), \quad (A.7)$$

with $\underline{\mu}' = (C^{-1} + D^{-1})^{-1}(D^{-1}\mu + C^{-1}\nu)$ and $\mathbf{C}' = (C^{-1} + D^{-1})^{-1}$.

A.1.2 Gaussian Mixture Density

A Gaussian mixture density (GM)[1] is a weighted summation of normal densities, i.e.,

$$f(\underline{x}) = \sum_{i=1}^{L} \alpha_i \mathcal{N}(\underline{x}; \underline{\mu}_i, \mathbf{C}_i), \qquad (A.8)$$

with $L \in \mathbb{N}^+$, $\underline{\alpha} = [\alpha_1 \ldots \alpha_L]^T \in \mathbb{R}^L$, and $\underline{\alpha}^T \underline{1} = 1$. In contrast to normal densities, GM allow for the representation of multimodal densities. Additionally, with an infinite number of components, GM are universal approximators [72]. Because the only condition imposed on the mixture is $\underline{\alpha}^T \underline{1} = 1$, negative weights are possible. In order to facilitate the computations, the stricter condition $0 \leq \alpha_i \leq 1$ may be enforced too, as positivity of the GM is guaranteed, if all components are positive. Introducing $f_i(\underline{x}) := \mathcal{N}(\underline{x} - \underline{\mu}_i, \mathbf{C}_i)$ and $\underline{f}(\underline{x}) = [f_1(\underline{x}) \ldots f_L(\underline{x})]^T$, (A.8) may be rewritten into

$$f(\underline{x}) = \sum_{i=1}^{L} \alpha_i f_i(\underline{x}) = \underline{\alpha}^T \underline{f}(\underline{x}). \qquad (A.9)$$

---

[1]The terms Gaussian Mixture Model/Density (GMM) or Normal Mixture Model are used synonymously in this thesis.

A.1.3 Dirac Delta Distribution

The Dirac delta distribution δ may be derived as a special case of the normal density by

$$\delta(x, x') = \lim_{\sigma \to \infty} \mathcal{N}(x - x', \sigma).$$

The Dirac delta distribution has a function value of zero over the entire state space except for the point $x = x'$. This property is exploited in the definition of the empirical probability density function, where a Dirac delta distribution is located at each data point. The Dirac delta distribution fulfills the sifting property, which is, e.g., exploited for the unified treatment of discrete- and continuous-valued random variables [167].

A.1.4 Dirac Mixture Density

In analogy to the extension of one Gaussian density to a Gaussian mixture density, a Dirac mixture density is defined by

$$f(\underline{x}) = \sum_{i=1}^{L} \alpha_i \, \delta(\underline{x} - \underline{x}_i). \tag{A.10}$$

with $L \in \mathbb{N}^+$, $\underline{\alpha} = [\alpha_1 \dots \alpha_L]^{\mathrm{T}}$, $\alpha_i \geq 0$, and $\underline{\alpha}^{\mathrm{T}} \underline{1} = 1$. The empirical probability density function is then given by setting $\mathcal{D} = \{\underline{x}_i\}_{1 \leq i \leq |\mathcal{D}|}$ and all $\alpha_i = \frac{1}{|\mathcal{D}|}$. The function in (A.10) satisfies all properties of a valid density function, i.e., integration to one and non-negativity. Note that evaluations at singular points of a continuous density functions are not defined.

A.1.5 Kernel Functions

The term kernel (function) is widely used in the literature and defined differently depending on the context. For the sake of clarity, the definitions of a kernel in the relevant literature are discussed in the following, i.e., the kernel definitions for kernel density estimation [179], SVMs [164], and $\mathcal{GP}s$ [152]. In general, they are given or have outputs in the form of

$$f(\underline{x}) = \sum_{i=1}^{L} \alpha_i \, \mathcal{K}_i(\underline{x}, \underline{x}_i). \tag{A.11}$$

In order for (A.11) to be a valid density or conditional density function, the kernel function $\mathcal{K}$ is assumed to be a valid density satisfying the following constraints

$$\int_{\mathbb{R}^N} \mathcal{K}(\underline{x}, \underline{x}_i) \, d\underline{x} = 1 \,, \qquad \mathcal{K}(\underline{x}, \underline{x}_i) \geq 0 \,. \qquad (A.12)$$

The mass and positivity constraint enforce, that a convex combination of kernel functions yields a valid density function. These conditions may be relaxed to allow for $\mathcal{K}$ to be proportional to a density function, e.g., a positive constant normalization factor may be absorbed by the weights. In the remaining part of this section, the validity of the mass and positivity constraints for kernel functions used in kernel density estimation, SVMs, and $\mathcal{GP}$s are discussed.

As the form resulting from kernel density estimation (KDE) is a mixture density of the type shown in (A.11), the kernel functions need to fulfill the above conditions to yield valid density estimates. This condition is trivially met for kernel functions being valid probability density functions. Typically, radially-symmetric, unimodal probability density function kernels are used [179], e.g., the multivariate normal density or an Epanechnikov kernel, i.e.,

$$\mathcal{K}(\underline{x}, \underline{0}) = \begin{cases} \frac{1}{2} v_d^{-1} \, (d+2) \, \left(1 - \underline{x}^{\mathrm{T}} \underline{x}\right) & , \text{ if } \underline{x}^{\mathrm{T}} \underline{x} < 1 \\ 0 & , \text{ else} \end{cases} , \qquad (A.13)$$

with the v_d volume of the d-dimensional unit sphere [179, Ch. 4.2]. Other definitions of kernel functions, which are not valid probability density functions exist [87]. When these kernels are used, e.g., renormalization is needed, to satisfy (A.12). The difference between kernel functions in KDE and SVM is the interpretation and the conditions that a kernel function has to fulfill. In SVM, the kernel function measures the similarity between two points. The kernel functions correspond to scalar products in not-explicitly constructed feature spaces. Following [164, Ch. 2], a kernel for $\underline{x} \in \mathbb{R}^N$ is given by

$$\phi : \mathbb{R}^N \mapsto \mathcal{H} \,, \qquad \mathcal{K}(\underline{x}, \underline{x}') = \, < \phi(\underline{x}), \phi(\underline{x}') >_{\mathcal{H}} \,, \qquad (A.14)$$

where $\mathcal{H}$ may be a higher-dimensional space of which only the scalar product needs to be calculated. Since $\mathcal{K}$ is a scalar product, the function satisfies

$$\mathcal{K}(\underline{x}, \underline{x}') \geq 0 \,, \forall \underline{x} \in \mathbb{R}^N \,, \qquad \mathcal{K}(\underline{x}, \underline{x}') = 0 \iff \underline{x} = \underline{0} \,, \qquad (A.15)$$

i.e., the positivity constraint is fulfilled. Even though some kernels fulfill the mass constraint (up to a normalization constant), e.g., the radial basis function kernel, in general, the SVM kernel functions will not satisfy this condition. An example, where the mass constraint is violated is the popular polynomial kernel for degree d

$$\mathcal{K}(\underline{x}, \underline{x}') = < \phi(\underline{x}), \phi(\underline{x}') >^d .$$

This limitation needs to be taken into account, when combining kernels as discussed in [18, 36, 178] or [164, Ch. 13]. A kernel which can be used with both SVM and the algorithms is presented in [190, 191],

$$\mathcal{K}_\gamma(\underline{x}, \underline{x}') = c(\gamma) \, \mathcal{K}\left(\frac{\underline{x} - \underline{x}'}{\gamma}\right) , \qquad \mathcal{K}_\gamma(\underline{x}, \underline{x}) = 1 , \qquad (A.16)$$

where γ is a scaling parameter, $c(\gamma)$ a normalization factor, which is constant w.r.t. $\underline{x}$, and $\mathcal{K}$ non-negative. For an appropriate normalization factor, (A.16) satisfies the mass and positivity constraints. $\mathcal{GP}$ and SVM use kernel functions in a similar way. In $\mathcal{GP}$s, the kernel are also termed covariance functions measuring the dependency of two data points. The kernel functions are used in the definition of both, the mean and covariance function, cf. Sec. 2.1.3 and [152]. The kernel function needs to be p.s.d. in the sense of integral operator theory [152, Ch. 4]. In order to give valid covariance matrices, the kernel needs to be symmetric. Similar to the kernels used in SVM, the mass constraint is not enforced, i.e., only some kernels used in $\mathcal{GP}$s are applicable for the density and conditional density estimation.

Additionally, in this thesis kernel functions are employed in the definition of the localized cumulative distribution, Def. 3.1. These kernel functions are used for comparing local probability masses of multivariate random variables. The suitable kernels for this definition are symmetric and integrable [70], e.g., a rectangle functions [71] or a (axis-aligned) Gaussian function [70]. Again, some admissible kernels satisfy the positivity and mass constraint, but this is in general not the case.

A.2   Norms, Distances and Scores

In this thesis, norms, distances, and scores are used in manifold ways. In the following, the definition of a norm and distance will be given as well as distances for comparing densities and conditional densities will be presented.

A.2.1 Definition of Norm and Distance

In the following, a definition of a norm is given as well as the corresponding derivation of a distance based on this norm as compiled form [21] and [27, German].

Definition A.1 (Norm) *Let V be a vector space for the field $\mathbb{K}$, the function $f : V \mapsto \mathbb{R}_+$ is denoted as a norm if for arbitrary $x, y \in V$ and $\alpha \in \mathbb{K}$ the following conditions hold*

(Non-Negativity)	$f(x) \geq 0\,,$	(A.17)
(Definiteness)	$f(x) = 0 \Leftrightarrow x = 0\,,$	(A.18)
(Homogeneity)	$f(\alpha\,x) = \lvert\alpha\rvert\,f(x)\,,$	(A.19)
(Triangle Inequality)	$f(x+y) \leq f(x) + f(y)\,.$	(A.20)

A specific norm is typically denoted with $\lVert.\rVert_{\mathrm{Name}}$. Given a norm as defined above a distance between arbitrary elements of the vector space $x, y \in V$ may be defined by

$$D\left(x\,,\,y\right) = \lVert x - y \rVert \,. \tag{A.21}$$

A.2.2 Comparing Densities

In order to compare the results of the density and conditional density estimation algorithm appropriate measures are required. For comparing two densities $\tilde{f}$ and f of a scalar, continuous-valued random variable, the integral squared distance (ISD) can be used

$$D\left(\tilde{f},\,f\right) = \sqrt{\int_{\mathbb{R}} \left(\tilde{f}(x) - f(x)\right)^2 \mathrm{d}x}\,. \tag{A.22}$$

The normalized ISD [69] as defined below allows for more interpretation of the distance values

$$D\left(\tilde{f},\,f\right) = \sqrt{\frac{\int_{\mathbb{R}} \left(\tilde{f}(x) - f(x)\right)^2 \mathrm{d}x}{\int_{\mathbb{R}} \left(\tilde{f}(x)\right)^2 \mathrm{d}x + \int_{\mathbb{R}} \left(f(x)\right)^2 \mathrm{d}x}}\,, \tag{A.23}$$

with $D : \mathcal{F} \times \mathcal{F} \to [0, 1]$, i.e., a value of zero is returned for identical functions $\tilde{f}$ and f in (A.23). At maximum a value of one for differing functions is returned. For the comparison of two conditional densities $\tilde{f}$ and f, the ISD may be defined analogously

$$\mathrm{D}\left(\tilde{f}, f\right) = \frac{1}{\mathrm{vol}\left(\mathcal{X}\right)} \sqrt{\int_{\mathcal{X}} \int_{\mathbb{R}} \left(\tilde{f}(y|x) - f(y|x)\right)^2 \mathrm{d}y \,\mathrm{d}x}, \qquad (A.24)$$

where $\mathcal{X} \subset \mathbb{R}$ is the considered domain of x. If the difference in the "tails" of the conditional density functions shall be emphasized, the total variation (TV) can be employed

$$\mathrm{D}\left(\tilde{f}, f\right) = \frac{1}{\mathrm{vol}\left(\mathcal{X}\right)} \int_{\mathcal{X}} \int \left|\tilde{f}(y|x) - f(y|x)\right| \,\mathrm{d}y \,\mathrm{d}x. \qquad (A.25)$$

The TV may be calculated for discrete-valued random variables too, e.g., $x \in \mathbb{N}$

$$\underline{\zeta} = \left[\, f(x=1) \,\ldots\, f(x=N)\,\right]^{\mathrm{T}}, \quad \underline{\tilde{\xi}} = \left[\, \tilde{f}(x=1) \,\ldots\, \tilde{f}(x=N)\,\right]^{\mathrm{T}},$$

for which x attains values in the alphabet $\mathcal{A}$, $|A| = N$, and thus

$$\mathrm{D}\left(\underline{\xi}, \underline{\tilde{\xi}}\right) = \frac{1}{2} \sum_{i=1}^{N} |\underline{\xi}_i - \underline{\tilde{\xi}}_i|. \qquad (A.26)$$

The values of (A.26) range from 0, if $\underline{\xi} = \underline{\tilde{\xi}}$, and 1, if the densities differ most. It is instructive to understand the relation between the (negative) log-likelihood and the Kullback-Leibler (KL) divergence [112] as difference measure of probability density functions. In the following, it is shown that maximizing the log-likelihood is equivalent to minimizing the KL divergence. Given the true, underlying density function $\tilde{f}$ and its estimate f, the KL divergence is defined as

$$\mathrm{KL}\left(\tilde{f} \,\|\, f\right) = \int_{\mathbb{R}} \tilde{f}(x) \ln\left(\frac{f(x)}{\tilde{f}(x)}\right) \,\mathrm{d}x, \qquad (A.27)$$

which may be simplified to

$$\mathrm{KL}\left(\tilde{f} \,\|\, f\right) = \int_{\mathbb{R}} \tilde{f}(x) \ln\left(f(x)\right) \,\mathrm{d}x - \underbrace{\left(\int_{\mathbb{R}} \tilde{f}(x) \ln\left(\tilde{f}(x)\right) \,\mathrm{d}x\right)}_{\text{Entropy of } \tilde{f}}. \qquad (A.28)$$

As (A.28) shall be minimized w.r.t. parameters $\underline{\theta}$ of f, the entropy of $\tilde{f}$ in (A.28) may be neglected. If $\tilde{f}$ is approximated by samples $f_{\mathcal{D}}$ in the form of (2.1), $\underline{\theta}^*$ is obtained by solving

$$\underline{\theta}^* = \arg\min_{\underline{\theta}} \, \mathrm{KL}\left(f_{\mathcal{D}} \parallel f\right) = \arg\max_{\underline{\theta}} \, \frac{1}{|\mathcal{D}|} \sum_{i=1}^{|\mathcal{D}|} \ln\left(f(\underline{x}_i)\right) . \qquad (A.29)$$

The right-hand side of (A.29) is the log-likelihood, which shows that minimizing the KL divergence is identical to maximizing the log-likelihood. Note, that a different understanding of the log-likelihood w.r.t. the information theory and entropy exists, cf. [3, 18], and KL is not symmetric w.r.t. its arguments.

A.3 A Multivariate Parametric Minimum Distance Estimator

The simplest density estimator derivable on the basis of the mCvMD as discussed in Ch. 3 is an unregularized parametric minimum density estimator (MDE). In the following, an MDE for estimating an arbitrary Gaussian mixture density from data as presented in [102] is described. The MDE corresponds to a minimization of the mCvMD by means of a standard function minimization algorithm. This implies that in each step of the iterative function minimization, the LCDs of the empirical probability density function $f_{\mathcal{D}}$ and the target density f in Gaussian mixture form as well as the mCvMD need to be calculated, cf. Sec. 3.1. The parameters of (3.8), which are optimized in order to minimize the mCvMD are

$$\underline{\alpha} := \left[\alpha_1 \dots \alpha_L\right]^{\mathrm{T}} ,$$

$$\underline{\mu} := \left[\underline{\mu}_1^{(1)} \dots \underline{\mu}_1^{(N)} \dots \underline{\mu}_L^{(1)} \dots \underline{\mu}_L^{(N)}\right]^{\mathrm{T}} ,$$

$$\underline{\Sigma} := \left[\sigma_1^{(1)} \dots \sigma_1^{(N \cdot N)} \dots \sigma_L^{(1)} \dots \sigma_L^{(N \cdot N)}\right]^{\mathrm{T}} ,$$

w.r.t. an N-dimensional random variable, L components, weights $\alpha_i \in [0,1]$, $\underline{\alpha}^{\mathrm{T}} \underline{1} = 1$, means with $\underline{\mu}_i^{(j)} \in \mathbb{R}$ and covariance matrix entries $\sigma_i^{(j)} \in \mathbb{R}^+$. Collecting all parameters into one vector gives the vector of optimization variables

$$\underline{\theta} = \left[\underline{\alpha}^{\mathrm{T}} , \underline{\mu}^{\mathrm{T}} , \underline{\Sigma}^{\mathrm{T}}\right]^{\mathrm{T}} . \qquad (A.30)$$

The MDE estimate $\underline{\theta}^*$ may then be found by minimizing the mCvMD w.r.t. to F and $F_{\mathcal{D}}$, the LCDs of f and $f_{\mathcal{D}}$, i.e.,

$$\underline{\theta}^* = \arg\min_{\underline{\theta}} \int_{\mathbb{R}^+} w(b) \int_{\mathbb{R}^N} \left(F(\underline{m}, b) - F_{\mathcal{D}}(\underline{m}, b)\right)^2 \, \mathrm{d}\underline{m} \, \mathrm{d}b, \qquad (A.31)$$

by the application of a standard nonlinear function minimization algorithm. Similar to [71], the function $w(.)$ is selected to ensure the convergence of the integral over b

$$w(b) = \begin{cases} \frac{1}{b^{N-1}} & , b \in [0, b_{\max}] \\ 0 & , \text{elsewhere} \end{cases},$$

where $b_{\max}$ may be set to a multiple, e.g., $10\times$ the maximum distance between two samples.

Efficient Solution

For the MDE approach, the integrals about the kernel position $\underline{m}$ and width b in (A.31) have to be calculated in each minimization step. For the given density representations closed-form solutions to the integral over $\underline{m}$ exist [102] yielding

$$\underline{\theta}^* = \arg\min_{\underline{\theta}} = \int_{\mathbb{R}^+} w(b) \det\left(2\pi \Sigma_b\right) \left(P_1 - 2\,P_2 + P_3\right) \mathrm{d}b . \qquad (A.32)$$

In (A.32), P_1, P_2, and P_3 denote the results of integrating each summand of the resolved binomial term $\left(F(\underline{m}, b) - F_{\mathcal{D}}(\underline{m}, b)\right)^2$ in (A.31) over $\underline{m}$. The term P_3 in (A.32) may be neglected for the function minimization, as it is constant w.r.t. $\underline{\theta}$. It may be understood as describing the self-similarity of the LCD for $f_{\mathcal{D}}$. The integral over the kernel width b in (A.32) has to be solved by numerical integration, as no closed-form solution to these terms for arbitrary Gaussian mixture densities is known up to now. Additionally, any algorithm for solving (A.32) has to assert the positivity of $f(\underline{x})$ and validity of the covariance matrices. This may be achieved by standard methods, such as the method of Lagrange or the addition of penalty functions, a reformulation of the problem in terms of squared weights $\sqrt{\alpha_i}$ or $\sqrt{\Sigma}$, but also by an iterative resampling scheme, as proposed in [102]. For further information refer to [102].

Properties and Restrictions

The main properties and restrictions of this naive MDE approach may be summarized as follows.

- Regarding the descriptive validity, this naive approach fits an arbitrary Gaussian mixture to the data and minimizes the distance of the estimate to the data. Therefore, the approach produces estimates, which represent the data well. Up to now, no proof of (asymptotic) consistency of this approach exists.

- The approach only optimizes the data fit and lacks a robust mechanism to avoid overfitting, thus asserting for prescriptive validity.

- This approach is computationally inefficient. Let M and L be the number of components in f_D and the estimate f. Further, let e be the number of points used by the numerical integration, and s the number of steps until converging to the minimum solution. Based on (A.32), the computational complexity of the MDE approach is at least in $\mathcal{O}\left([L \cdot L + L \cdot M] \cdot e \cdot s\right)$ evaluations of an N-dimensional normal density.

- Note, that $\underline{\theta} \in \mathbb{R}^{L(1+\mathrm{N}+\mathrm{N}^2)}$ implies that the function minimization needs to be performed w.r.t. a large space. No analytic expression for the gradient of the mCvMD is available up to this point in time, requiring a numerical calculation of the gradient.

- The algorithm for solving this minimization problem needs to assert the positivity of the resulting density estimate and that the integral of the density estimate over the state space equals one. Without proof, it has been noted in [102] that these constraints are practically asserted by the mass comparison performed by the minimization of mCvMD.

A.4   Miscellanea

In this section various mathematical background material for all chapters of this thesis has been collected. The relevant sources are given in the respective sections.

A.4.1 Matrix Properties & Operations

This section is based on [21, 79, 151] as well as [27, 77, both in German]. For an efficient implementation of the the matrix operations the interested reader is referred to [66, 146].

Definition A.2 (Positive [Semi-]Definiteness of a Matrix) A given symmetric matrix $\mathbf{A} \in \mathbb{R}^{N \times N}$ is positive [semi-]definite (p.[s.]d.), if for all $\underline{\alpha} \in \mathbb{R}^N, \underline{\alpha} \neq \underline{0}$

$$\underline{\alpha}^{\mathrm{T}} \mathbf{A} \, \underline{\alpha} \underset{[\geq]}{>} 0 \,. \tag{A.33}$$

As the addition of matrices is considered, the following properties are required.

Corollary A.1 (Addition of Positive Semi-Definite Matrices) If two matrices $\mathbf{A}, \mathbf{B} \in \mathbb{R}^{N \times N}$ are positive semi-definite according to (A.33), the following inequality holds [79]

$$\underline{\alpha}^{\mathrm{T}} \left(\mathbf{A} + \mathbf{B} \right) \underline{\alpha} = \underline{\alpha}^{\mathrm{T}} \mathbf{A} \, \underline{\alpha} + \underline{\alpha}^{\mathrm{T}} \mathbf{B} \, \underline{\alpha} \overset{(A.33)}{\geq} 0 \,, \tag{A.34}$$

stating that an addition of p.s.d. matrices is still p.s.d.

The above lemma allows for determining the definiteness of a sum of matrices based on the definiteness of the added matrices. Matrices resulting from dyadic products have the following property, which is relevant for Ch. 3 and Ch. 4.

Lemma A.1 (Symmetry of Dyadic Product Matrix) Let $\underline{w} \in \mathbb{R}^N$ be given, the matrix $\mathbf{W} \in \mathbb{R}^{N \times N}$ resulting from the dyadic product of $\underline{w}$

$$\mathbf{W} = \underline{w} \, \underline{w}^{\mathrm{T}} \,, \tag{A.35}$$

is symmetric.

Proof. Let $\underline{w} = [w_1 \ \ldots \ w_N]^{\mathrm{T}}$, $w_i \in \mathbb{R}$, the elements of the matrix $\mathbf{W} = \underline{w} \, \underline{w}^{\mathrm{T}}$ be given, then

$$\mathbf{W}_{ij} = w_i \cdot w_j \,,$$

and Lemma A.1 follows from

$$\mathbf{W}_{ij} = \mathbf{W}_{ji} \,.$$

$\square$

Using Lemma A.1, the following property can be shown.

Lemma A.2 (Positive Semi-Definiteness of Dyadic Product Matrix) Any matrix $\mathbf{W} \in \mathbb{R}^{N \times N}$ resulting from a dyadic product of a vector $\underline{w} \in \mathbb{R}^{N}$, i.e., $\mathbf{W} = \underline{w}\,\underline{w}^{\mathrm{T}}$, is p.s.d.

Proof. In order for $\mathbf{W}$ to be p.s.d., $\mathbf{W}$ has to be symmetric and needs to fulfill (A.33). Due to Lemma A.1, $\mathbf{W}$ is symmetric. The positivity follows from

$$\underline{\alpha}^{\mathrm{T}}\,\mathbf{W}\,\underline{\alpha} = \underline{\alpha}^{\mathrm{T}}\,\left(\underline{w}\,\underline{w}^{\mathrm{T}}\right)\,\underline{\alpha} = \left(\underline{\alpha}^{\mathrm{T}}\,\underline{w}\right)^{2} \geq 0\,,$$

for all $\underline{\alpha} \in \mathbb{R}^{N}$ and thus $\mathbf{W}$ is p.s.d. according to Def. A.2. $\qquad\square$

Corollary A.2 (Positive Semi-Definiteness of the Superficial Regularizer) According to [151], given a density representation with a kernel function $k(\underline{x})$

$$f(\underline{x}) = \sum_{i=1}^{L} \alpha_{i}\,k_{i}(\underline{x}) = \underline{\alpha}^{\mathrm{T}}\,\underline{k}(\underline{x})\,, \tag{A.36}$$

and $D^{m}\underline{x}$ a differential operator w.r.t. m, using commutativity and linearity, one may obtain

$$\int_{\mathbb{R}^{N}} \left(D^{m}f(\underline{x})\right)^{2}\,\mathrm{d}\underline{x} = \int_{\mathbb{R}^{N}} D^{m}\underline{\alpha}^{\mathrm{T}}\underline{k}(\underline{x}) \cdot D^{m}\underline{\alpha}^{\mathrm{T}}\underline{k}(\underline{x})\,\mathrm{d}\underline{x}$$

$$= \int_{\mathbb{R}^{N}} \underline{\alpha}^{\mathrm{T}}\left(D^{m}\underline{k}(\underline{x}) \cdot D^{m}\underline{k}(\underline{x})^{\mathrm{T}}\right)\underline{\alpha}\,\mathrm{d}\underline{x}$$

$$= \underline{\alpha}^{\mathrm{T}}\left(\int_{\mathbb{R}^{N}} D^{m}\underline{k}(\underline{x})D^{m}\underline{k}(\underline{x})^{\mathrm{T}}\,\mathrm{d}\underline{x}\right)\underline{\alpha}$$

$$= \underline{\alpha}^{\mathrm{T}}\,\mathbf{D}\,\underline{\alpha}\,,$$

with

$$\mathbf{D}_{ij} = \int_{\mathbb{R}^{N}} \left(D^{m}k_{i}(\underline{x})\right)\left(D^{m}k_{j}(\underline{x})^{\mathrm{T}}\right)\,\mathrm{d}\underline{x}\,. \tag{A.37}$$

The p.s.d. property follows.

A detailed derivation of Corollary A.2 can be found in [151].

A.4.2 Proof of Theorem 4.1 - Properties of the scalar Superficial Regularizer

Proof. In the following, the proofs are given for each property. The derivation is adapted from [109]. For the sake of brevity, the following abbreviation will be used in the further calculations

$$\underline{k}(x,y) = \left[\begin{array}{c} \mathcal{N}(x; \mu_{x,1}, \sigma_{x,1})\, \mathcal{N}(y; \mu_{y,1}, \sigma_{y,1}) \\ \vdots \\ \mathcal{N}(x; \mu_{x,L}, \sigma_{x,L})\, \mathcal{N}(y; \mu_{y,L}, \sigma_{y,L}) \end{array} \right] =: \underline{k},$$

with $(x,y) = p \in \mathbb{R}^2$ is used. The first property is derived by successively approximating the definition of the squared curvature of the entire surface of the scalar density function f.

Property 1: The square of the surface's curvature of f is simplified by using (A.8), the linearity of the integral, and the commutativity of the inner product, giving rise to

$$\begin{aligned} K(f) &= \int_{\mathbb{R}^2} \left[f_{xx}(\underline{p})\, f_{yy}(\underline{p}) \right]^2 \, d\underline{p} \\ &= \int_{\mathbb{R}^2} \left[\underline{\alpha}^{\mathrm{T}} \underline{k}_{xx}\, \underline{k}_{yy} \underline{\alpha}^{\mathrm{T}} \right]^2 \, d\underline{p} \\ &= \int_{\mathbb{R}^2} [\underline{\alpha}^{\mathrm{T}} \underbrace{\left(\underline{k}_{xx}\, \underline{k}_{yy}^{\mathrm{T}} \right)}_{\mathbf{M}} \underline{\alpha}]^2 \, d\underline{p} \;. \end{aligned} \qquad (A.38)$$

with $\mathbf{M} \in \mathbb{R}^{N \times N}$. The above transformations use the separability of the mixture density, the linearity of the integral, and the commutativity of the inner product. Further simplification of (A.38) gives the approximate upper bound

$$\int_{\mathbb{R}^2} [\underline{\alpha}^{\mathrm{T}} \mathbf{M} \underline{\alpha}]^2 \, d\underline{p} = \int_{\mathbb{R}^2} \underline{\alpha}^{\mathrm{T}} \mathbf{M} \underline{\alpha}\, \underline{\alpha}^{\mathrm{T}} \mathbf{M} \underline{\alpha} \, d\underline{p} \approx c_{\mathbf{M}}\, \underline{\alpha}^{\mathrm{T}} \mathbf{R} \underline{\alpha} \;,$$

the desired result with $c_{\mathbf{M}}$ a constant independent of $\underline{\alpha}$

$$\mathbf{R}_{ij} = \sum_{k=1}^{L} \int_{\mathbb{R}^2} k_{xx}^{(i,k)}(\underline{p})\, k_{yy}^{(i,k)}(\underline{p}) \cdot k_{xx}^{(k,j)}(\underline{p})\, k_{yy}^{(k,j)}(\underline{p}) \, d\underline{p}. \qquad (A.39)$$

In order to proof the second property, the regularization expression is derived for one point and shown to be an upper bound on the curvature of the generative model. The upper bound is then extended to the entire surface.

Property 2: The integral squared curvature of $y = g(x)$, i.e., a curve in the xy-plane at x, may be upper bounded according to the following inequality

$$\int_{\mathbb{R}} \frac{\left[\frac{\partial}{\partial x \partial x} g(x)\right]^2}{\left[1 + \left(\frac{\partial}{\partial x} g(x)\right)^2\right]^3} \leq \int_{\mathbb{R}} \left[\frac{\partial}{\partial x \partial x} g(x)\right]^2 dx . \qquad (A.40)$$

This upper bound of the curvature of g is related to an upper bound of the squared curvature of the conditional density function's surface f according to

$$f_{xx}(\underline{p}) \, f_{yy}(\underline{p}) - f_{xy}^2(\underline{p}) = c_1 \cdot f^2(y - g(x)) \, h(y - g(x)) \, \frac{\partial^2}{\partial x \partial x} g(x) . \quad (A.41)$$

For Gaussian additive noise, integrating (A.41) over the in- and output dimension yields

$$\begin{aligned} K(g) &= \int_{\mathbb{R}} \int_{\mathbb{R}} \left(f_{xx}(x,y) \, f_{yy}(x,y) - f_{xy}^2(x,y)\right)^2 dy \, dx \\ &= \int_{\mathbb{R}} c_2 \cdot \left(\frac{\partial^2}{\partial x \partial x} g(x)\right)^2 dx , \end{aligned}$$

with $c_2 \in \mathbb{R}^+$ and c_2 independent of g. The result then follows from $K(g) \leq K(f)$. $\qquad \square$

A.4.3 Nonlinear Optimization

A special type of nonlinear optimization is convex optimization, which entails as an important special case convex quadratic optimization. This section gives a brief review of the most important properties of this sort of optimization problems based on [21, 27]. In nonlinear optimization, one seeks to minimize an objective function[2] $f : \mathbb{R}^N \to \mathbb{R}$ for the optimization variables $\underline{\alpha} \in \mathbb{R}^N$ w.r.t. a set of P inequality constraints $g_i : \mathbb{R}^N \to \mathbb{R}$ and Q equality constraints $h_j : \mathbb{R}^N \to \mathbb{R}$, i.e.,

$$\begin{aligned} \text{minimize} \quad & f(\underline{\alpha}) && (A.42) \\ \text{subject to} \quad & g_i(\underline{\alpha}) \leq 0, && i = 1, \ldots, P, \\ & h_j(\underline{\alpha}) = 0, && j = 1, \ldots, Q. \end{aligned}$$

---

[2]The objective function is also denoted as the target function.

The set of constraints defines the feasible set of solutions. Depending on the properties of f, g_i, and h_j, the nonlinear problem in (A.42) may be further qualified, potentially allowing for a more efficient solution of the problem. If the objective function in (A.42) is quadratic and the constraint functions are affine, the nonlinear optimization problem is called a quadratic optimization problem [21]. The problem (A.42) may then be written in the following form

$$\text{minimize} \quad \frac{1}{2} \underline{\alpha}^{\mathrm{T}} \mathbf{C} \, \underline{\alpha} + \underline{c}^{\mathrm{T}} \underline{\alpha} + r \tag{A.43}$$
$$\text{subject to} \quad \mathbf{A} \underline{\alpha} \preceq \underline{b},$$
$$\mathbf{D} \underline{\alpha} = \underline{e},$$

where $\mathbf{C} \in \mathbb{R}^{N \times N}$, $\underline{c} \in \mathbb{R}^{N}$, $r \in \mathbb{R}$, $\mathbf{A} \in \mathbb{R}^{P \times N}$, $\underline{b} \in \mathbb{R}^{P}$, $\mathbf{D} \in \mathbb{R}^{Q \times N}$, $\underline{e} \in \mathbb{R}^{Q}$, and $\preceq$ denotes the component-wise inequality. The objective function in (A.43) is (strictly) convex, if $\mathbf{C}$ is p.(s.)d. Due to the convexity, the optimality properties are inherited from convex optimization problems. In detail, any local minimum is a global minimum, i.e., optimum, w.r.t., the feasible region. Further information about other theoretical properties, such as existence and uniqueness of the solution, can be found in [21]. Detailed implementation advice and applications, e.g., w.r.t. learning problems can be found in [164]. For the experiments in this thesis, the problems were converted to the standard form and solved with the implementation [67] or [188]. For a practitioner, the time complexity of the algorithm solving (A.43) is an important property. From a theoretical perspective, it was shown, that for convex problems, i.e., $\mathbf{C}$ p.s.d., (A.43) may be solved in a time depending polynomially on the number of optimization variables N and constraints $P+Q$. The complexity of a naive implementation involves $\mathcal{O}\left(N^{3}\right)$ operations [21, Ch. 1] per iteration. Note that specialized solvers, e.g., for SVM, exist and may be computationally more efficient than the default solvers at the cost of optimality [164].

Lists of Figures, Tables, Algorithms, and Examples

List of Figures

List of Tables

List of Algorithms

List of Examples

Bibliography

[1] D. Albrecht. Aufbau einer virtuellen Simulationsumgebung für die Mensch–Roboter Kooperation zur Erkennung von Benutzeraktionen. Student Research Project (Diplomarbeit), Lehrstuhl für Intelligente Sensor-Aktor-Systeme, Universität Karlsruhe (TH), 2007.

[2] D. Albrecht, I. Zukerman, and A. Nicholson. Bayesian Models for Keyhole Plan Recognition in an Adventure Game. User Modeling and User-Adapted Interaction, 8(1-2):5–47, 1998.

[3] J. Aldrich. R. A. Fisher and the Making of Maximum Likelihood 1912-1922. Statistical Science, 12(3):162–176, Aug. 1997. ISSN 0883-4237.

[4] D. L. Alspach and H. W. Sorenson. Nonlinear Bayesian Estimation using Gaussian Sum Approximation. IEEE Transactions on Automatic Control, 17(4):439–448, Aug. 1972.

[5] G. E. M. Anscombe. Intention. Harvard University Press, 1957. ISBN 9780674003996.

[6] M. S. Arulampalam, S. Maskell, N. Gordon, and T. Clapp. A Tutorial on Particle Filters for On-line Non-linear/Non-Gaussian Bayesian Tracking. IEEE Transactions on Signal Processing, 50(2): 174–188, 2002.

[7] D. Avrahami-Zilberbrand, G. A. Kaminka, and H. Zarosim. Fast and Complete Plan Recognition: Allowing for Duration, Interleaved Execution, and Lossy Observations. In International Joint Conference on Artificial Intelligence (IJCAI-05) Workshop on Modeling Others from Observations, Aug. 2005.

[8] F. R. Bach, G. R. G. Lanckriet, and M. I. Jordan. Multiple Kernel Learning, Conic Duality, and the SMO Algorithm. In Proceedings of the Twenty-first International Machine Learning Conference (ICML 2004). Banff, Canada, July 2004.

[9] E. Bauer, D. Koller, and Y. Singer. Update Rules for Parameter Estimation in Bayesian Networks. In Proceedings of the Thirteenth Annual Conference on Uncertainty in AI (UAI), pages 3–13. Providence, Rhode Island, Aug. 1997.

[10] D. P. Bertsekas. Dynamic Programming and Optimal Control, volume 1. Athena Scientific, Belmont, Massachusetts, U.S.A., 2nd edition, 2000.

[11] D. P. Bertsekas. Dynamic Programming and Optimal Control, volume 2. Athena Scientific, Belmont, Massachusetts, U.S.A., 2nd edition, 2000.

[12] D. P. Bertsekas. Nonlinear Programming. Athena Scientific Optimization and Computation Series ; 4. Athena Scientific, Belmont, Massachusetts, 2nd print. edition, 2008. ISBN 1-886529-00-0 ; 978-1-886529-00-7.

[13] F. Beutler. Probabilistische Modellbasierte Signalverarbeitung zur Instantanen Lageschätzung. Dissertation, Karlsruhe Institute of Technology, ISAS - Intelligent Sensor-Actuator-Systems Laboratory, Karlsruhe Series on Intelligent Sensor-Actuator-Systems 8, 2009. ISBN 978-3-86644-442-3.

[14] F. Beutler and U. D. Hanebeck. Closed-Form Range-Based Posture Estimation Based on Decoupling Translation and Orientation. In Proceedings of the 2005 IEEE International Conference on Acoustics, Speech, and Signal Processing (ICASSP 2005), volume 4, pages 989–992. Philadelphia, Pennsylvania, Mar. 2005.

[15] J. Bilmes. Dynamic Bayesian Multinets. In Proceedings of the 16th Conf. on Uncertainty in Artificial Intelligence, pages 38–45. Morgan Kaufmann Publishers, INC., San Francisco, California, 2000.

[16] J. Binder, D. Koller, S. Russell, and P. Smyth. Adaptive Probabilistic Networks with Hidden Variables. Machine Learning, 29:213–244, 1997.

[17] C. M. Bishop. Mixture Density Networks. Neural Computing Research Group Report NCRG/94/004, Aug. 1994.

[18] C. M. Bishop. Pattern Recognition and Machine Learning. Springer Science+Business Media, LLC, 2006.

[19] N. Blaylock and J. F. Allen. Fast Hierarchical Goal Schema Recognition. In Proceedings of National Conference on Artificial Intelligence (AAAI 06), volume 21, pages 796–801. AAAI Press, Boston, Massachusetts, July 2006.

[20] A. F. Bobick and J. W. Davis. The Recognition of Human Movement Using Temporal Templates. IEEE Transactions on Pattern Analysis and Machine Intelligence, 23(3):257–267, 2001.

[21] S. P. Boyd and L. Vandenberghe. Convex Optimization. Cambridge University Press, Cambridge, United Kingdom, 2004. ISBN 978-0-521-83378-3.

[22] M. Bratman. Intention, Plans, and Practical Reason. Harvard University Press, 1987. ISBN 9780674458185.

[23] C. Breazeal. Robots in Society: Friend or Appliance? In Proceedings of the 1999 Autonomous Agents Workshop on Emotion-Based Agent Architectures (EBAA99), pages 18–26. Seattle, Washington, May 1999.

[24] C. Breazeal, B. Scassellati, C. Breazeal, and B. Scassellati. How to Build Robots That Make Friends and Influence People. In Proceedings of the 1999 IEEE/RSJ International Conference on Intelligent Robots and Systems (IROS 1999), volume 2, pages 858–863, 1999.

[25] L. Breiman, W. Meisel, and E. Purcell. Variable Kernel Estimates of Multivariate Densities. Technometrics, 19(2):135–144, May 1977.

[26] F. Brockhaus Mannheim (Firm). Brockhaus Enzyklopädie: In zwanzig Bänden. Brockhaus Enzyklopädie: In zwanzig Bänden, Siebzehnte Neubarbeitete Auflage des Großen Brockhaus. F. A. Brockhaus, 1966.

[27] I. Bronstein and K. Semendjajew. Taschenbuch der Mathematik, 25. 1991. ISBN 978-3-8171-2006-2.

[28] T. Brox, B. Rosenhahn, D. Cremers, and H.-P. Seidel. Nonparametric Density Estimation with Adaptive, Anisotropic Kernels for Human Motion Tracking. In Proceedings of the 2nd Conference on Human Motion: Understanding, Modeling, Capture and Animation, pages 152–165. Springer-Verlag, Berlin, Heidelberg, 2007. ISBN 3-540-75702-3, 978-3-540-75702-3.

[29] H. H. Bui. A General Model for Online Probabilistic Plan Recognition. In Proceedings. of the International Joint Conference on Artificial Intelligence (IJCAI), pages 1309–1315, Aug. 2003.

[30] S. Carberry. Techniques for Plan Recognition. User Modeling and User-Adapted Interaction, 11:31–48, 2001.

[31] M. D. Carmo. Differential Geometry of Curves and Surfaces. Prentice-Hall, Englewood Cliffs, NJ, 1976. ISBN 0-13-212589-7.

[32] E. Charniak. Bayesian Networks without Tears. AI Magazine, pages 50–63, 1991.

[33] E. Charniak and R. P. Goldman. A Bayesian Model of Plan Recognition. Artificial Intelligence, 64:53–79, 1993.

[34] P. R. Cohen, J. L. Morgan, and M. E. Pollack. Intentions in Communication. Bradford Books. MIT Press, 1990. ISBN 978-0-26203150-9.

[35] T. M. Cover and J. A. Thomas. Elements of Information Theory. John Wiley & Sons, Inc., 1991.

[36] N. Cristianini and J. Shawe-Taylor. An Introduction to Support Vector Machines and other Kernel-Based Learning Methods. Cambridge Univ. Press, Cambridge, 10th pr. edition, 2006. ISBN 0-521-78019-5.

[37] F. Daum. Nonlinear filters: Beyond the Kalman filter. Aerospace and Electronic Systems Magazine, IEEE, 20(8):57–69, Aug. 2005.

[38] K. Dautenhahn. Robots as Social Actors: AURORA and The Case of Autism. In Proceedings of the Third International Cognitive Technology Conference (CT99), San Francisco, Aug. 1999.

[39] T. Dean and K. Kanazawa. A Model for Reasoning about Persistence and Causation. Computational Intelligence Journal, 5(3):142–150, 1989.

[40] D. Decoste and B. Schölkopf. Training Invariant Support Vector Machines. Machine Learning, 46:161–190, 2002. ISSN 0885-6125. URL http://dx.doi.org/10.1023/A:1012454411458.

[41] M. P. Deisenroth. Efficient Reinforcement Learning using Gaussian Processes. Dissertation, Karlsruhe Institute of Technology, ISAS - Intelligent Sensor-Actuator-Systems Laboratory, Karlsruhe Series on Intelligent Sensor-Actuator-Systems 9, 2009. ISBN 978-3-86644-569-7.

[42] M. P. Deisenroth, M. F. Huber, and U. D. Hanebeck. Analytic Moment-based Gaussian Process Filtering. In 26th International Conference on Machine Learning (ICML 2009) in Montreal, Canada, June 2009.

[43] A. P. Dempster, N. M. Laird, and D. B. Rubin. Maximum Likelihood from Incomplete Data via the *EM* Algorithm. Journal of the Royal Statistical Society. Series B (Methodological), 39(1):1–38, 1977. ISSN 0035-9246.

[44] S. Dey. Reduced-Complexity Filtering for Partially Observed Nearly Completely Decomposable Markov Chains. IEEE Transactions on Signal Processing, 48(12):3334–3344, 2000.

[45] R. Dillmann and T. Asfour. Collaborative Research Center on Humanoid Robots (SFB 588). KI - Zeitschrift Künstliche Intelligenz, 4: 26–28, 2008.

[46] A. Doucet, N. de Freitas, and N. Gordon. Sequential Monte Carlo Methods in Practice. Statistics for Engineering and Information Science. Springer Verlag, 2000.

[47] R. O. Duda, P. E. Hart, and D. G. Stork. Pattern Classification. Wiley & Sons, 2nd edition, 2000.

[48] H. Eberhardt, V. Klumpp, and U. D. Hanebeck. Optimal Dirac Approximation by Exploiting Independencies. In Proceedings of the 2010 American Control Conference (ACC 2010). Baltimore, Maryland, July 2010.

[49] P. B. Eggermont and V. N. LaRiccia. Maximum Penalized Likelihood Estimation, volume 1: Density Estimation. Springer, New York, 2001. ISBN 0-387-95268-3.

[50] Eric Driver and Darryl Morrell. Implementation of Continuous Bayesian Networks Using Sums of Weighted Gaussians. In Proceedings of the Eleventh Annual Conference on Uncertainty in Artificial Intelligence (UAI), pages 134–140. Montreal, Canada, Aug. 1995.

[51] T. Evgeniou, M. Pontil, and T. Poggio. Regularization Networks and Support Vector Machines. Advances in Computational Mathematics, 13:1–50, 2000. ISSN 1019–7168. URL http://dx.doi.org/10.1023/A:1018946025316.

[52] M. Fagan and P. Cunningham. Case-Based Plan Recognition in Computer Games. volume 2689 of Lecture Notes in Computer Science, pages 161–170. Springer, 2003. ISBN 3-540-40433-3.

[53] M. Figueiredo and A. Jain. Unsupervised Learning of Finite Mixture Models. IEEE Transactions on Pattern Analysis and Machine Intelligence, pages 381–396, 2002.

[54] B. J. Frey and F. R. Kschischang. Probability Propagation and Iterative Decoding. In Proceeings of the 34th Annual Allerton Conf. Commun., Control, and Computing. Monticello, Illinois, Oct. 1996.

[55] D. Gehrig, A. Fischer, H. Kuehne, T. Stein, A. Woerner, H. Schwameder, and T. Schultz. Online Recognition of Daily-Life Movements. In IEEE-RAS International Conference on Humanoid Robots (Humanoids 2008). Workshop Imitation and Coaching in Humanoid Robots. Daejeon, Korea, Dec. 2008.

[56] D. Gehrig, P. Krauthausen, L. Rybok, H. Kühne, T. Schultz, U. D. Hanebeck, and R. Stiefelhagen. Combined Multi-Level Intention, Actitvity, and Motion Recognition for a Humanoid Household Robot. In Proceedings of the 2011 IEEE/RSJ International Conference on Intelligent Robots and Systems (IROS 2011). San Francisco, California, Sept. 2011.

[57] D. Gehrig, H. Kühne, and T. Schultz. Erkennung von menschlichen Bewegungen mit Hidden Markov Modellen. In Sportinformatik trifft Sporttechnologie, Tagung der dvs-Sektion Sportinformatik in Kooperation mit der deutschen interdisziplin (DVS 2010). Darmstadt, Germany, Sept. 2010.

[58] D. Gehrig, H. Kühne, A. Woerner, and T. Schultz. HMM-based Human Motion Recognition with Optical Flow Data. In IEEE International Conference on Humanoid Robots (Humanoids 2009). Paris, France, Dec. 2009.

[59] D. Gehrig, T. Stein, A. Fischer, H. Schwameder, and T. Schultz. Towards Semantic Segmentation of Human Motion Sequences. In R. Dillmann, J. Beyerer, U. Hanebeck, and T. Schultz, editors, KI 2010: Advances in Artificial Intelligence, volume 6359 of Lecture Notes in Computer Science, pages 436–443. Springer Berlin / Heidelberg, 2010. ISBN 978-3-642-16110-0.

[60] C. W. Geib and R. P. Goldman. Partial Observability and Probabilistic Plan/Goal Recognition. In International Joint Conference on Artificial Intelligence (IJCAI-05) Workshop on Modeling Others from Observations. Aug. 2005.

[61] C. W. Geib, R. P. Goldman, C. Geib, and R. Goldman. Recognizing Plan/Goal Abandonment. In International Joint Conference on Artificial Intelligence, volume 18, pages 1515–1517. Morgan Kaufmann, INC., San Francisco, California, Aug. 2003.

[62] M. Girolami. Orthogonal Series Density Estimation and the Kernel Eigenvalue Problem. Neural Computation., 14(3):669–688, 2002.

[63] M. Girolami and C. He. Probability Density Estimation from Optimally Condensed Data Samples. IEEE Transactions on Pattern Analysis and Machine Intelligence, 25:1253–1264, 2003. ISSN 0162-8828.

[64] S. Glesner and D. Koller. Constructing Flexible Dynamic Belief Networks from First-Order Probabilistic Knowledge Bases. In Proceedings of the European Conference on Symbolic and Quantitative Approaches to Reasoning and Uncertainty (ECSQARU '95), pages 217–226, July 1995.

[65] R. P. Goldman, C. W. Geib, and C. A. Miller. A New Model of Plan Recognition. In Proceedings of the 1999 Conference on Uncertainty Artificial Intelligence, pages 245–254. Morgan Kaufmann, INC., July 1999.

[66] G. H. Golub and C. F. V. Loan. Matrix Computations – Third Edition. The Johns Hopkins University Press, 1996. ISBN 978-0-80185414-9.

[67] M. Grant and S. Boyd. CVX: Matlab Software for Disciplined Convex Programming, version 1.21. http://cvxr.com/cvx, Feb. 2011.

[68] H. Groenda, F. Nowak, P. Rößler, and U. D. Hanebeck. Telepresence Techniques for Controlling Avatar Motion in First Person Games. In Intelligent Technologies for Interactive Entertainment (INTETAIN 2005). Madonna di Campiglio, Italy, Nov. 2005.

[69] U. D. Hanebeck, K. Briechle, and A. Rauh. Progressive Bayes: A New Framework for Nonlinear State Estimation. In Proceedings

of SPIE, AeroSense Symposium, volume 5099, pages 256 – 267. Orlando, Florida, May 2003.

[70] U. D. Hanebeck, M. F. Huber, and V. Klumpp. Dirac Mixture Approximation of Multivariate Gaussian Densities. In Proceedings of the 2009 IEEE Conference on Decision and Control (CDC 2009), pages 3851–3858. Shanghai, China, Dec. 2009.

[71] U. D. Hanebeck and V. Klumpp. Localized Cumulative Distributions and a Multivariate Generalization of the Cramér-von Mises Distance. In Proceedings of the 2008 IEEE International Conference on Multisensor Fusion and Integration for Intelligent Systems (MFI 2008), pages 33–39. Seoul, Republic of Korea, Aug. 2008.

[72] U. D. Hanebeck and O. Schrempf. Text Book to the Lecture Stochastic Information Processing, Feb. 2011.

[73] T. Hastie, R. Tibshirani, and J. Friedman. The Elements of Statistical Learning: Data Mining, Inference, and Prediction. Springer series in statistics. Springer, New York, NY, 2nd edition, 2009. ISBN 978-0-387-84857-0.

[74] D. Heckerman. A Bayesian Approach to Learning Causal Networks. In Proceedings of the Eleventh Annual Conference on Uncertainty in Artificial Intelligence, pages 285–295. Montreal, Canada, 1995.

[75] D. Heckerman. A tutorial on Learning with Bayesian networks. MIT Press, Cambridge, MA, USA, 1999.

[76] C. Heinze. Modelling Intention Recognition for Intelligent Agent Systems. Phd, University of Melbourne, Australia, 2003.

[77] M. Hermann. Numerische Mathematik. Oldenbourg, Munich, 2001. ISBN 3-486-25558-4.

[78] M. P. Holmes, A. G. Gray, and C. L. Isbell. Fast Kernel Conditional Density Estimation: A dual-Tree Monte Carlo Approach. Computational Statistics and Data Analysis, 54, 2010.

[79] R. A. Horn and C. R. Johnson. Matrix Analysis. Cambridge University Press, Cambridge, United Kingdom, 1985. ISBN 0-521-38632-2.

[80] E. Horvitz, J. Breese, D. Heckerman, D. Hovel, and K. Rommelse. The Lumière Project: Bayesian User Modeling for Inferring the Goals and Needs of Software Users. In Proceedings of the Fourteenth Conference on Uncertainty in Artificial Intelligence, pages 256–265. Morgan Kaufmann, San Mateo, California, July 1998.

[81] M. Huber. Probabilistic Framework for Sensor Management. Dissertation, Universität Karlsruhe (TH), ISAS - Intelligent Sensor-Actuator-Systems Laboratory, Referent: U. D. Hanebeck, Korreferent: W. Koch, Karlsruhe Series on Intelligent Sensor-Actuator-Systems 7, 2009. ISBN 978-3-86644-405-8.

[82] M. F. Huber and U. D. Hanebeck. Hybrid Transition Density Approximation for Efficient Recursive Prediction of Nonlinear Dynamic Systems. In International Conference on Information Processing in Sensor Networks (IPSN 2007), pages 283–292. Cambridge, Massachusetts, Apr. 2007.

[83] M. F. Huber and U. D. Hanebeck. Priority List Sensor Scheduling using Optimal Pruning. In Proceedings of the 11th International Conference on Information Fusion (Fusion 2008), pages 1–8. Cologne, Germany, July 2008.

[84] M. F. Huber, E. Stiegeler, and U. D. Hanebeck. On Sensor Scheduling in Case of Unreliable Communication. In INFORMATIK 2007 - the 37th Annual Conference of the Gesellschaft für Informatik e.V. (GI), 3rd German Workshop Sensor Data Fusion: Trends, Solutions, Applications (SDF 2007), pages 90–94. Bremen, Germany, 2007.

[85] A. Ihler. Kernel Density Estimation Toolbox for Matlab, 2003. URL http://www.ics.uci.edu/~ihler/code/.

[86] J. Ijsselmuiden and R. Stiefelhagen. Towards High-Level Human Activity Recognition through Computer Vision and Temporal Logic, volume 6359 of Lecture Notes in Computer Science. Springer Berlin / Heidelberg, Berlin, Heidelberg, Sept. 2010. ISBN 978-3-642-16110-0.

[87] A. J. Izenman. Recent Developments in Nonparametric Density Estimation. Journal of the American Statistical Association, 86(413): 205–224, 1991. ISSN 01621459.

[88] T. Jebara, R. Kondor, and A. Howard. Probability Product Kernels. Journal of Machine Learning Research, 5:819–844, 2004.

[89] Joaquin Quiñonero-Candela and Carl Edward Rasmussen. A Unifying View of Sparse Approximate Gaussian Process Regression. Journal of Machine Learning Research, 6:1939–1959, 2005.

[90] M. Jordan and R. Jacobs. Hierarchical Mixtures of Experts and the EM algorithm. Neural Computation, 6(2):181–214, 1994.

[91] H. A. Kautz. A Formal Theory of Plan Recognition and its Implementation. In Reasoning About Plans, pages 69–125. Morgan Kaufmann Publishers, San Mateo, California, 1991.

[92] U. Kiencke. Signale und Systeme. Oldenburg, 1998. ISBN 3-486-25959-8.

[93] G. Kitagawa. Monte Carlo Filter and Smoother for Non-Gaussian Nonlinear State Space Models. Journal of Computational and Graphical Statistics, 5(1):1–25, 1996.

[94] V. Klumpp, F. Sawo, U. D. Hanebeck, and D. Fränken. The Sliced Gaussian Mixture Filter for Efficient Nonlinear Estimation. In Proceedings of the 11th International Conference on Information Fusion (Fusion 2008), pages 1–8. Cologne, Germany, July 2008.

[95] J. Ko and D. Fox. GP-BayesFilters: Bayesian Filtering Using Gaussian Process Prediction and Observation Models. In Proceedings of the 2008 IEEE/RSJ International Conference on Intelligent Robots and Systems (IROS), pages 3471–3476. Nice, France, Sept. 2008.

[96] J. Ko, D. Klein, D. Fox, and D. Haehnel. Gaussian Processes and Reinforcement Learning for Identification and Control of an Autonomous Blimp. In Proceedings of the International Conference on Robotics and Automation (ICRA), pages 742–747. Rome, Italy, Apr. 2007.

[97] J. Ko, D. Klein, D. Fox, and D. Haehnel. GP-UKF: Unscented Kalman Filters with Gaussian Process Prediction and Observation Models. In Proceedings of the 2007 IEEE/RSJ International Conference on Intelligent Robots and Systems (IROS), pages 1901–1907. San Diego, California, Oct. 2007.

[98] W. Koch. On Accumulated State Densities with Applications to Out-of-Sequence Measurement Processing. In Proceedings of the

12th International Conference on Information Fusion (Fusion 2009). Seattle, Washington, July 2009.

[99] D. Koller. Probabilistic Graphical Models: Principles and Techniques. MIT Press, Cambridge, Massachusetts, 2009. ISBN 978-0-262-01319-2 ; 0-262-01319-3.

[100] D. Koller and A. Pfeffer. Object-Oriented Bayesian Networks. In Proceedings of the 13th Annual Conference on Uncertainty in AI (UAI 1997), pages 302–313. Providence, Rhode Island, 1997.

[101] K. B. Korb and A. E. Nicholson. Bayesian Artificial Intelligence. Chapman & Hall/CRC, 2004. ISBN 1-58488-387-1.

[102] P. Krauthausen, H. Eberhardt, and U. D. Hanebeck. Multivariate Parametric Density Estimation Based On The Modified Cramér-von Mises Distance. In Proceedings of the 2010 IEEE International Conference on Multisensor Fusion and Integration for Intelligent Systems (MFI 2010). Salt Lake City, Utah, Sept. 2010.

[103] P. Krauthausen and U. D. Hanebeck. Intention Recognition for Partial-Order Plans Using Dynamic Bayesian Networks. In Proceedings of the 12th International Conference on Information Fusion (Fusion 2009). Seattle, Washington, July 2009.

[104] P. Krauthausen and U. D. Hanebeck. A Model-Predictive Switching Approach To Efficient Intention Recognition. In Proceedings of the 2010 IEEE/RSJ International Conference on Intelligent Robots and Systems (IROS 2010). Taipei, Taiwan, Oct. 2010.

[105] P. Krauthausen and U. D. Hanebeck. Regularized Non-Parametric Multivariate Density and Conditional Density Estimation. In Proceedings of the 2010 IEEE International Conference on Multisensor Fusion and Integration for Intelligent Systems (MFI 2010). Salt Lake City, Utah, Sept. 2010.

[106] P. Krauthausen and U. D. Hanebeck. Situation-Specific Intention Recognition for Human-Robot-Cooperation. In 33rd Annual German Conference on Artificial Intelligence (KI 2010). Gesellschaft für Informatik e.V., Karlsruhe, Germany, Sept. 2010.

[107] P. Krauthausen, M. F. Huber, and U. D. Hanebeck. Support-Vector Conditional Density Estimation for Nonlinear Filtering. In Proceedings of the 13th International Conference on Information Fusion (Fusion 2010). Edinburgh, United Kingdom, July 2010.

[108] P. Krauthausen, M. Roschani, and U. D. Hanebeck. Incorporating Prior Knowledge into Nonparametric Conditional Density Estimation. In Proceedings of the 2011 American Control Conference (ACC 2011). San Francisco, California, June 2011.

[109] P. Krauthausen, P. Ruoff, and U. D. Hanebeck. Sparse Conditional Mixture Density Estimation by Superficial Regularization. In Proceedings of the 14th International Conference on Information Fusion (Fusion 2011). Chicago, Illinois, July 2011.

[110] M. Kristan, D. Skocaj, and A. Leonardis. Online Kernel Density Estimation for Interactive Learning. Image and Vision Computing, 28(7):1106–1116, 2010. ISSN 0262-8856.

[111] F. R. Kschischang, B. J. Frey, and H.-A. Loeliger. Factor Graphs and the Sum-Product Algorithm. IEEE Transactions on Information Theory, 47(2):498–519, February 2001.

[112] S. Kullback and R. A. Leibler. On Information and Sufficiency. The Annals of Mathematical Statistics, 22(1):79–86, 1951. ISSN 00034851.

[113] V. N. LaRiccia and P. B. Eggermont. Maximum Penalized Likelihood Estimation, volume 2: Density Estimation. Springer, New York, 2001. ISBN 0-387-95268-3.

[114] K. Laskey and S. Mahoney. Network Fragments: Representing Knowledge for Constructing Probabilistic Models. In Proceedings of the 13th Annual Conference on Uncertainty in AI (UAI 1997), pages 334–341. Providence, Rhode Island, 1997.

[115] F. Lauer and G. Bloch. Incorporating Prior Knowledge in Support Vector Machines for Classification: A Review. Neurocomputing, 71 (7-9):1578–1594, 2008. ISSN 0925-2312.

[116] S. Lauritzen. Propagation of Probabilities, Means and Variances in Mixed Graphical Association Models. Journal of the American Statistical Association, 87:1098–1108, 1992.

[117] S. Lauritzen. The EM algorithm for Graphical Association Models with Missing Data. Compututational Statistics Data Analysis, 19 (2):191–201, 1995.

[118] S. Lauritzen. Graphical Models. Clarendon Press, 1998. ISBN 0-19-852219-3.

[119] U. Lerner. Hybrid Bayesian Networks for Reasoning About Complex Systems. PhD thesis, Stanford University, 2002.

[120] N. Lesh, C. Rich, and C. Sidner. Using Plan Recognition in Human-Computer Collaboration. In Proceedings of the Seventh International Conference on User Modeling, pages 23–32. Banff, Canada, June 1999.

[121] H.-A. Loeliger. An Introduction to Factor Graphs. Signal Processing Magazine, IEEE, 21(1):28–41, 2004. ISSN 1053-5888.

[122] D. O. Loftsgaarden and C. P. Quesenberry. A Nonparametric Estimate of a Multivariate Density Function. The Annals of Mathematical Statistics, 36(3):1049–1051, 1965. ISSN 00034851.

[123] D. MacKay. Information Theory, Inference, and Learning Algorithms. Cambridge University Press, 2003.

[124] R. Maclin, J. Shavlik, T. Walker, and L. Torrey. A Simple and Effective Method for Incorporating Advice into Kernel Methods. In Proceedings of the Twenty-First National Conference on Artificial Intelligence (AAAI 2006). Boston, MA., July 2006.

[125] P. C. Mahalanobis. On the Generalised Distance in Statistics. Proceedings of the National Institute of Sciences of India 2 (1), pages 49–55, 1936.

[126] S. Mahoney and K. Laskey. Constructing Situation Specific Belief Networks. In Proceedings of the 14th Annual Conference on Uncertainty in AI (UAI 1998), pages 370–378. Madison, Wisconsin, 1998.

[127] P. S. Maybeck. Stochastic Models, Estimation, and Control, Volume 2. Academic Press, 1982.

[128] V. Maz'ya and G. Schmidt. On Approximate Approximations using Gaussian Kernels. IMA Journal of Numerical Analysis, 16:13–29, 1996.

[129] G. McLachlan and D. Peel. Finite Mixture Models. Wiley-Inter., 978-0-47100626-8 2004.

[130] T. M. Mitchell. Machine Learning. McGraw-Hill Series in Computer Science. McGraw-Hill, New York, 2002. ISBN 0-07-042807-7 ; 0-07-115467-1.

[131] A. Mittal and N. Paragios. Motion-Based Background Subtraction using Adaptive Kernel Density Estimation. In Proceedings of the 2004 IEEE Computer Society Conference on Computer Vision and Pattern Recognition (CVPR), volume 2, June 2004. ISSN 1063-6919.

[132] S. Monti and G. F. Cooper. Learning Hybrid Bayesian Networks From Data. Learning in Graphical Models, pages 521–540, 1999.

[133] D. Moore and I. Essa. Recognizing Multitasked Activities Using Stochastic Context-Free Grammar. In Computer Vision and Pattern Recognition Workshop on Models vs. Exemplars in Computer Vision, 2001., 2001.

[134] K. Murphy. Dynamic Bayesian Network : Representation, Inference and Learning. PhD thesis, University of California, Berkeley, 2002.

[135] NA. Langenscheidts Schulwörterbuch - Latein. Langenscheidt KG, Berlin and Munich, 1999. ISBN 3-468-13200-X.

[136] K. Nickel and R. Stiefelhagen. Pointing Gesture Recognition based on 3D-Tracking of Face, Hands and Head Orientation. In Proceedings of the 5th International Conference on Multimodal Interfaces. Vancouver, Canada, Nov. 2003.

[137] N. Nitzsche, U. D. Hanebeck, and G. Schmidt. Motion Compression for Telepresent Walking in Large Target Environments. Presence: Teleoperators & Virtual Environments, 13(1):44–60, Feb. 2004.

[138] E. Osuna, R. Freund, and F. Girosi. An Improved Training Algorithm for Support Vector Machines. In Proceedings of the 1997 IEEE Workshop on Neural Networks for Signal Processing (IEEE-NNSP). Amelia Island, Florida, Sept. 1997.

[139] A. Papoulis and S. U. Pillai. Probability, Random Variables and Stochastic Processes. McGraw-Hill, 4th edition, 2002.

[140] E. Parzen. On Estimation of a Probability Density Function and Mode. Annals of Mathematical Statistics, 33(3):1065–1076, 1962.

[141] J. Pearl. Reverend Bayes on Inference Engines: A Distributed Hierarchical Approach. In Proceedings of the National Conference on Artificial Intelligence (AAAI 2006). Boston, MA., July 1982.

[142] J. Pearl. Fusion, Propagation, and Structuring in Belief Networks. Artificial Intelligence, 29:241–288, 1986.

[143] J. Pearl. Probabilistic Reasoning in Intelligent Systems: Networks of Plausible Inference. Morgan-Kaufmann Publishers, INC., 1988.

[144] K. Pearson. Contributions to the Theory of Mathematical Evolution. Philosophical Transactions of the Royal Society of London A, 186: 343–414, 1894.

[145] B. Pelletier. Kernel Density Estimation on Riemannian Manifolds. Statistics & Probability Letters, 73(3):297–304, 2005. ISSN 0167-7152.

[146] W. H. Press, S. A. Teukolsky, W. T. Vetterling, and B. P. Flannery. Numerical Recipes in C: The Art of Scientifc Computing. Cambridge University Press, 2nd edition, 1992. URL http://www.numerical-recipes.com/.

[147] D. V. Pynadath. Probabilistic Grammars for Plan Recognition. PhD thesis, University of Michigan, 1999.

[148] D. V. Pynadath and M. P. Wellman. Generalized Queries on Probabilistic Context-Free Grammars. IEEE Transactions on Pattern Analysis and Machine Intelligence, 20(1):65–77, 1998.

[149] D. V. Pynadath and M. P. Wellman. Probabilistic State-Dependent Grammars for Plan Recognition. In Proceedings of the 16th Conference on Uncertainty in Artificial Intelligence (UAI-00), pages 507–514. Morgan Kaufmann Publishers, INC., San Francisco, California, 2000.

[150] L. Rabiner. A Tutorial on Hidden Markov Models and Selected Applications in Speech Recognition. Proceedings of the IEEE, 77 (2), 1989.

[151] J. Ramsay and B. Silverman. Functional Data Analysis. Springer Series in Statistics. Springer, New York, Berlin, Heidelberg, 1997. ISBN 0-387-94956-9.

[152] C. Rasmussen and C. Williams. Gaussian Processes for Machine Learning. The MIT Press, Cambridge, Massachusetts, 2006. ISBN 978-0-262-18253-9.

[153] M. Rosenblatt. Remarks on Some Nonparametric Estimates of a Density Function. In The Annals of Mathematical Statistics, number 3. Institute of Mathematical Statistics.

[154] P. Rößler, F. Beutler, U. D. Hanebeck, and N. Nitzsche. Motion Compression Applied to Guidance of a Mobile Teleoperator. In Proceedings of the 2005 IEEE International Conference on Intelligent Robots and Systems (IROS 2005), pages 2495–2500. Edmonton, Canada, Aug. 2005.

[155] P. Ruoff, P. Krauthausen, and U. D. Hanebeck. Progressive Correction for Deterministic Dirac Mixture Approximations. In Proceedings of the 14th International Conference on Information Fusion (Fusion 2011). Chicago, Illinois, July 2011.

[156] S. J. Russell and P. Norvig. Artificial Intelligence : A Modern Approach. Prentice Hall Series in Artificial Intelligence. Prentice Hall, Upper Saddle River, NJ, 2nd internat. edition, 2003. ISBN 0-13-080302-2.

[157] L. Rybok, S. Friedberger, U. D. Hanebeck, and R. Stiefelhagen. The KIT Robo-Kitchen Data set for the Evaluation of View-based Activity Recognition Systems. In IEEE-RAS International Conference on Humanoid Robots. Bled, Slovenia, Oct. 2011.

[158] S. R. Sain. Multivariate Locally Adaptive Density Estimation. Computational Statistics & Data Analysis, 39:165–186, Apr. 2002. ISSN 0167-9473.

[159] A. Schmid. Intuitive Human-Robot Cooperation. PhD thesis, Karlsruhe Institute of Technology (KIT), 2008.

[160] A. J. Schmid, O. C. Schrempf, H. Wörn, and U. D. Hanebeck. Towards Intuitive Human-Robot Cooperation. In 2nd International Workshop on Human Centered Robotic Systems (HCRS 2006), pages 7–12. Munich, Germany, Oct. 2006.

[161] C. F. Schmidt, N. S. Sridharan, and J. L. Goodson. The Plan Recognition Problem: An Intersection of Psychology and Artificial Intelligence. Artificial Intelligence, 11(1–2):45–83, 1978.

[162] B. Schölkopf. Support Vector Learning. Phd, Technische Universität Berlin, 1997.

[163] B. Schölkopf, P. Simard, A. Smola, and V. Vapnik. Prior Knowledge in Support Vector Kernels. In Proceedings of the 1997 Conference on Advances in Neural Information Processing Systems 10, pages 640–646. MIT Press, Nov. 1998.

[164] B. Schölkopf and A. Smola. Learning with Kernels: Support Vector Machines, Regularization, Optimization, and Beyond. Adaptive Computation and Machine Learning series. MIT Press, Cambridge, Massachusetts, 2002. ISBN 0-262-19475-9 ; 978-0-262-19475-4.

[165] B. Schölkopf, A. Smola, R. Williamson, and P. Bartlett. New Support Vector Algorithms. Neural Computation, 12(5):1207–1245, 2000.

[166] T. Schön, F. Gustafsson, and P.-J. Nordlund. Marginalized Particle Filters for Nonlinear State-Space Models. Technical report, Division of Communication Systems, Department of Electrical Engineering, Linköpings University, Oct. 2003.

[167] O. Schrempf and U. D. Hanebeck. Evaluation of Hybrid Bayesian Networks using Analytical Density Representations. In Proceedings of the 16th IFAC World Congress (IFAC 2005). Czech Republic, 2005.

[168] O. C. Schrempf. Stochastische Behandlung von Unsicherheiten in Kaskadierten Dynamischen Systemen. Dissertation, Universität Karlsruhe (TH), ISAS - Intelligent Sensor-Actuator-Systems Laboratory, Referent: U. D. Hanebeck, Korreferent: J. Beyerer, Karlsruhe Series on Intelligent Sensor-Actuator-Systems 1, 2008. ISBN 978-3-86644-287-0.

[169] O. C. Schrempf, D. Albrecht, and U. D. Hanebeck. Tractable Probabilistic Models for Intention Recognition Based on Expert Knowledge. In Proceedings of the 2007 IEEE/RSJ International Conference on Intelligent Robots and Systems (IROS 2007), pages 1429–1434. San Diego, California, Nov. 2007.

[170] O. C. Schrempf and U. D. Hanebeck. A New Approach for Hybrid Bayesian Networks Using Full Densities. In Proceedings of the 6th International Workshop on Computer Science and Information Technologies (CSIT 2004), volume 1, pages 32–37. Budapest, Hungary, Oct. 2004.

[171] O. C. Schrempf and U. D. Hanebeck. A Generic Model for Estimating User Intentions in Human-Robot Cooperation. In Proceedings of the 2nd International Conference on Informatics in Control, Automation and Robotics (ICINCO 2005), volume 3, pages 251–256. Barcelona, Spain, Sept. 2005.

[172] O. C. Schrempf, U. D. Hanebeck, A. J. Schmid., and H. Wörn. A Novel Approach to Proactive Human-Robot Cooperation. In Proceedings of the 2005 IEEE International Workshop on Robot and Human Interactive Communication (ROMAN 2005), pages 555–560. Nashville, Tennessee, Aug. 2005.

[173] O. C. Schrempf, A. Hanselmann, and U. D. Hanebeck. Efficient Representation and Fusion of Hybrid Joint Densities for Clusters in Nonlinear Hybrid Bayesian Networks. In Proceedings of the 9th International Conference on Information Fusion (Fusion 2006). Florence, Italy, July 2006.

[174] D. W. Scott. Multivariate Density Estimation: Theory, Practice, and Visualization. Wiley Series in Probability and Mathematical Statistics - A Wiley Interscience Publication. Wiley, New York, 1992. ISBN 0-471-54770-0.

[175] D. W. Scott and W. F. Szewczyk. From Kernels to Mixtures. Technometrics, 43(3):323–335, 2001. ISSN 00401706.

[176] J. Searle. Collective Intentions and Actions. Intentions in Communication. MIT press/Bradford Books, P.Cohen, J. Morgan, and M.E. Pollack eds., Cambridge, Massachusetts, 1990.

[177] C. E. Shannon. A Mathematical Theory of Communication. ACM SIGMOBILE Mobile Computing and Communications Review, 5: 3–55, Jan. 2001. ISSN 1559-1662. URL http://doi.acm.org/10.1145/584091.584093.

[178] J. Shawe-Taylor and N. Cristianini. Kernel Methods for Pattern Analysis. Cambridge Univ. Press, Cambridge, 2004. ISBN 0-521-81397-2.

[179] B. W. Silverman. Density Estimation for Statistics and Data Analysis. Monographs on Statistics and Applied Probability ; 26. CRC Press, Boca Raton, 1998. ISBN 0-412-24620-1.

[180] D. Simon. Optimal State Estimation: Kalman, H-Infinity, and Nonlinear Approaches. John Wiley & Sons, 2006.

[181] E. Snelson and Z. Ghahramani. Sparse Gaussian Processes using Pseudo-Inputs. In Advances in Neural Information Processing Systems 18. Vancouver, Canada, 2005.

[182] P. Steinhaus, R. Becher, and R. Dillmann. Sonderforschungsbereich 588: Humanoide Roboter – Lernende und Kooperierende Multimodale Roboter. it – Information Technology, 46(2):94–100, April 2004.

[183] W. Sun, K.-C. Chang, and K. Laskey. Scalable Inference for Hybrid Bayesian Networks with Full Density Estimations . In Proceedings of the 13th International Conference on Information Fusion (Fusion 2010). Edinburgh, United Kingdom, July 2010.

[184] Z. Sun, Z. Zhang, and H. Wang. Incorporating Prior Knowledge into Kernel Based Regression. Acta Automatica Sinica, 34(12):1515–1521, 2008.

[185] K. A. Tahboub. Intelligent Human-Machine Interaction Based on Dynamic Bayesian Networks Probabilistic Intention Recognition. Journal of Intelligent Robotics Systems, 45(1):31–52, 2006. ISSN 0921-0296.

[186] A. Taleb. A Generic Framework for Blind Source Separation in Structured Nonlinear Models. IEEE Transactions on Signal Processing, 50:1819–1830, 2002.

[187] G. R. Terrell and D. W. Scott. Variable Kernel Density Estimation. The Annals of Statistics, 20(3):1236–1265, 1992.

[188] The MathWorks, Inc. MATLAB - The Language Of Technical Computing, Matlab2010b, 2011.

[189] D. Titterington, A. Smith, and U. Makov. Statistical Analysis of Finite Mixture Distributions. Wiley series in probability and mathematical statistics. Wiley Interscience, New York, 1985. ISBN 0-471-90763-4.

[190] V. Vapnik. The Nature of Statistical Learning Theory. Statistics for Engineering and Information Science. Springer, New York, 2nd edition, 2000. ISBN 0-387-98780-0.

[191] V. N. Vapnik. Statistical Learning Theory. Adaptive and Learning Systems for Signal Processing, Communications, and Control. Wiley, New York, 1998. ISBN 0-471-03003-1; 978-0-471-03003-4.

[192] S. Vasudevan, F. Ramos, E. Nettleton, and H. Durrant-Whyte. A Mine on Its Own. IEEE Robotics & Automation Magazine, 17:63–73, June 2010. ISSN 1070-9932.

[193] Vladimir Vapnik and Sayan Mukherjee. Support Vector Method for Multivariate Density Estimation. In Advances in Neural Information Processing Systems 12 (NIPS), pages 659–665, Nov. 1999.

[194] G. Wahba. Spline Models for Observational Data. In CBMS-NSF Regional Conference Series in Applied Mathematics, Vol. 59. SIAM, 1990.

[195] F. Weissel, M. F. Huber, and U. D. Hanebeck. A Nonlinear Model Predictive Control Framework Approximating Noise Corrupted Systems with Hybrid Transition Densities. In Proceedings of the 2007 IEEE Conference on Decision and Control (CDC 2007), pages 3661–3666. New Orleans, Louisiana, Dec. 2007.

[196] F. Weissel, T. Schreiter, M. F. Huber, and U. D. Hanebeck. Stochastic Model Predictive Control of Time-Variant Nonlinear Systems with Imperfect State Information. In Proceedings of the 2008 IEEE International Conference on Multisensor Fusion and Integration for Intelligent Systems (MFI 2008), pages 40–46. Seoul, Republic of Korea, Aug. 2008.

[197] L. White, R. Mahony, and G. Brushe. Lumpable Hidden Markov Models—Model Reduction and Reduced Complexity Filtering. IEEE Transactions on Automatic Control, 45(12):2297–2306, 2000.

[198] J. L. Williams. Information Theoretic Sensor Management. PhD thesis, Massachusetts Institute of Technology, 2007.

[199] C. Wojek, K. Nickel, and R. Stiefelhagen. Activity Recognition and Room Level Tracking in an Office Environment. In IEEE Int. Conference on Multisensor Fusion and Integration for Intelligent Systems. Heidelberg, Germany, September 2006.

[200] C. Wu. On the Convergence Properties of the EM Algorithm. The Annals of Statistics, 11(1):95–103, 1983.

[201] H. Wu and F. Noé. Probability Distance Based Compression of Hidden Markov Models. Multiscale Modeling and Simulation: A SIAM Interdisciplinary Journal., 2009. Available from http://compmolbio.biocomputing-berlin.de/index.php/publications.

[202] L. Xu and M. Jordan. On the Convergence Properties of the EM Algorithm for Gaussian Mixtures. Neural Computation, 8:129–151, 1983.

[203] Y. Zhang and Q. Ji. Efficient Sensor Selection for Active Information Fusion. IEEE Transactions on Systems, Man, and Cybernetics, Part B: Cybernetics, pp(99):1083–4419, 2009.

Own Publications

[204] D. Gehrig, P. Krauthausen, L. Rybok, H. Kühne, T. Schultz, U. D. Hanebeck, and R. Stiefelhagen. Combined Multi-Level Intention, Actitvity, and Motion Recognition for a Humanoid Household Robot. In Proceedings of the 2011 IEEE/RSJ International Conference on Intelligent Robots and Systems (IROS 2011). San Francisco, California, Sept. 2011.

[205] M. F. Huber, P. Krauthausen, and U. D. Hanebeck. Superficial Gaussian Mixture Reduction. In Proceedings of the IEEE ISIF Workshop on Sensor Data Fusion: Trends, Solutions, Applications (SDF 2011). Berlin, Germany, Oct. 2011.

[206] P. Krauthausen, H. P. Eberhardt, and U. D. Hanebeck. Multivariate Density Estimation using the Localized Cumulative Distribution. In Proceedings of the 2010 IEEE International Conference on Multisensor Fusion and Integration for Intelligent Systems (MFI 2010). Salt Lake City, Utah, Sept. 2010.

[207] P. Krauthausen and U. D. Hanebeck. Intention Recognition for Partial-Order Plans Using Dynamic Bayesian Networks. In Proceedings of the 12th International Conference on Information Fusion (Fusion 2009). Seattle, Washington, July 2009.

[208] P. Krauthausen and U. D. Hanebeck. A Model-Predictive Switching Approach To Efficient Intention Recognition. In Proceedings of the 2010 IEEE/RSJ International Conference on Intelligent Robots and Systems (IROS 2010). Taipei, Taiwan, Oct. 2010.

[209] P. Krauthausen and U. D. Hanebeck. Parameter Learning for Hybrid Bayesian Networks With Gaussian Mixture and Dirac Mixture Conditional Densities. In Proceedings of the 2010 American Control Conference (ACC 2010). Baltimore, Maryland, June 2010.

[210] P. Krauthausen and U. D. Hanebeck. Regularized Non-Parametric Multivariate Density and Conditional Density Estimation. In Proceedings of the 2010 IEEE International Conference on Multisensor Fusion and Integration for Intelligent Systems (MFI 2010). Salt Lake City, Utah, Sept. 2010.

[211] P. Krauthausen and U. D. Hanebeck. Situation-Specific Intention Recognition for Human-Robot-Cooperation. In 33rd Annual German Conference on Artificial Intelligence (KI 2010). Gesellschaft für Informatik e.V., Karlsruhe, Germany, Sept. 2010.

[212] P. Krauthausen, M. F. Huber, and U. D. Hanebeck. Support-Vector Conditional Density Estimation for Nonlinear Filtering. In Proceedings of the 13th International Conference on Information Fusion (Fusion 2010), 2010.

[213] P. Krauthausen, M. Roschani, and U. D. Hanebeck. Incorporating Prior Knowledge into Nonparametric Conditional Density Estimation. In Proceedings of the 2011 American Control Conference (ACC 2011). San Francisco, California, June 2011.

[214] P. Krauthausen, P. Ruoff, and U. D. Hanebeck. Sparse Conditional Mixture Density Estimation by Superficial Regularization. In Proceedings of the 14th International Conference on Information Fusion (Fusion 2011). Chicago, Illinois, July 2011.

[215] P. Ruoff, P. Krauthausen, and U. D. Hanebeck. Progressive Correction for Deterministic Dirac Mixture Approximations. In Proceedings of the 14th International Conference on Information Fusion (Fusion 2011). Chicago, Illinois, July 2011.

Own Student Publications

[216] F. Dellaert, A. Kipp, and P. Krauthausen. A Multifrontal QR Factorization Approach to Distributed Inference Applied to Multi-Robot Localization and Mapping. In Proceedings of the American Association for Artificial Intelligence (AAAI), pages 1261–1266. Pittsburgh, Pennsylvania, May 2005.

[217] P. Krauthausen, A. Kipp, and F. Dellaert. Exploiting Locality in SLAM by Nested Dissection. In Proceedings of Robotics: Science and Systems (RSS), pages 1–8. Philadelphia, Pennsylvania, Aug. 2006.

[218] P. Krauthausen and A. Laubenheimer. A Comparative Study of Decision Tree Approaches to Multi-Class SVM. In Proceedings of the 26th IASTED International Conference on Artificial Intelligence and Applications (AIA), pages 34–39. Innsbruck, Austria, Feb. 2008.

Supervised Student Theses

[219] D. Perpeet. Switching Multiple Hybrid Bayesian Networks. Student Research Project (Diplomarbeit), Intelligent Sensor-Actuator-Systems Laboratory, Karlsruhe Institute of Technology, 2009.

[220] M. Roschani. System-Identifikation durch Schätzung bedingter Dichten. Student Research Project (Diplomarbeit), Intelligent Sensor-Actuator-Systems Laboratory, Karlsruhe Institute of Technology, 2010.

[221] M. Ziebarth. Vergleich von Modellbewertungskriterien für das Lernen hybrider dynamischer Bayesnetze. Student Research Project (Studienarbeit), Intelligent Sensor-Actuator-Systems Laboratory, Karlsruhe Institute of Technology, 2010.

Index

Karlsruhe Series on Intelligent Sensor-Actuator-Systems

Edited by Prof. Dr.-Ing. Uwe D. Hanebeck // ISSN 1867-3813

Karlsruhe Series on
Intelligent Sensor-Actuator-Systems

Edited by Prof. Dr.-Ing. Uwe D. Hanebeck // ISSN 1867-3813

Die Bände sind unter www.ksp.kit.edu als PDF frei verfügbar oder als Druckausgabe bestellbar.